Mexicanos in Oregon

Mexicanos in Oregon
THEIR STORIES, THEIR LIVES

Erlinda Gonzales-Berry and Marcela Mendoza

Oregon State University Press
Corvallis

The paper in this book meets the guidelines for permanence and durability of the Committee on Production Guidelines for Book Longevity of the Council on Library Resources and the minimum requirements of the American National Standard for Permanence of Paper for Printed Library Materials Z39.48-1984.

Library of Congress Cataloging-in-Publication Data
Gonzales-Berry, Erlinda, 1942-
  Mexicanos in Oregon : their stories, their lives / Erlinda Gonzales-Berry and Marcela Mendoza.
    p. cm.
  Includes bibliographical references and index.
  ISBN 978-0-87071-584-6 (alk. paper)
  1. Mexican Americans--Oregon--History. 2. Mexican Americans--Oregon--Social conditions. 3. Mexican Americans--Cultural assimilation--Oregon. 4. Oregon--Emigration and immigration. 5. Oregon--Race relations. 6. Oregon--Politics and government. I. Mendoza, Marcela. II. Title.
  E184.M5G647 2010
  979.500468'72073--dc22
                                          2009054360

Oregon State University Press
121 The Valley Library
Corvallis OR 97331-4501
541-737-3166 • fax 541-737-3170
http://oregonstate.edu/dept/press

Contents

Illustrations

Acknowledgements

We are grateful to the many people who have contributed to this project. First on our list are the dozens of individuals who generously gave of their time to share their stories with us. Without their collaboration this book would not have been possible, and to them we say a humble *mil gracias*. Numerous students pitched in along the way, some interviewing and providing technical assistance, some transcribing, some chasing down sources, and some helping us make contacts: San Juana Acosta, José Luis Torres, Diego Mesa, Jennifer Bishop, Jessica Rojas, Ricardo Larios, José Otañez, Octavio Merecías, Marco Antonio Chávez, and Laura Cristal Magaña, our heartfelt thanks to all of you. To Evelyn Reynolds and Barbara Wegner, who scanned and copied, oversaw student assistants, taught us many technical tricks and on and on, our gratitude is great. To Dwaine Plaza, who shared his knowledge and bibliography with us, your voice lies between the lines of this book. To Mary Braun at the OSU Press, thank you for guiding us through this and for believing in us; without your nudging we might not be writing this. To our editor Jo Alexander, for her competence, and to Judy Radovsky who did the layout, for her sharp eye and patience, and great attitude, our deepest gratitude. We acknowledge also the generosity of the folks and institutions who gave us permission to use their photos (some at no cost—you know who you are!): Larry Landis at the Oregon State University Archives, Gwyn Fisher, Paulina Hermosillo, Justo Rodríguez, Javier Lara at OCIMO, San Juana Acosta, Carlos García, the Northern Lincoln County Historical Museum, Rocío Acosta-González, the UCLA Library, Scott Rook at the Oregon Historical Society, Drew Vattiat at *The Oregonian*. To the Oregon Council for the Humanities who gave E. Gonzales-Berry the opportunity to present her research to communities across Oregon, and to Oregon State University for a sabbatical that gave her the time she needed to dig into archives, to read, and to write, she is grateful. And of course we can never communicate to our *familias* how deeply we appreciate their support, their care, and their love even when we didn't have time for them because we were busy "working on our book."

Introduction

About the Authors

This book is the culmination of personal journeys for each of us. One of us is a sixth-generation U.S. citizen, whose ancestors did not migrate to this country, but who became citizens by virtue of the annexation of almost half of Mexico's territory to the United States in 1848; the other is a first-generation immigrant from Argentina. Below we tell our stories and how it is we came to be involved in a project that has fanned the flames of our intellectual curiosity and our personal passions.

I, *Erlinda Gonzales-Berry*, was raised in Northern New Mexico. A branch of my ancestors came from Spain and Mexico and, along the Rio Grande Valley, they mixed with local indigenous populations to form New Spain's northernmost colony in the Western Hemisphere in 1598. Almost sixteen generations later, Spanish was still spoken in our home, and Spanish monolingual grandparents steeped us in a rich oral tradition that was as much Mexican as it was Spanish and Native New Mexican. In grade school, I was exposed to another cultural tradition, one that was brought to our *patria chica* (petite homeland)—which is what New Mexico became to our people after it was truncated from "Old Mexico"—by *los americanos*, those intrepid interlopers who brought us a new language, new laws, new ways of being in the world. Memories of our former homeland were gradually excised from our ancestral memory, at least the English-speaking portion of that memory, as we were socialized into believing that at heart we were pure Spanish and that claims to a Mexican cultural identity were best avoided lest we bear the stigma of *Mexicannes*, a stigma borne by the dark-skinned people that for centuries crossed the Rio Grande and other more abstract dividing markers to reach El Dorado, the promised land of plenty. Fortunately for me, my family crossed the Rio Grande in the opposite direction in 1949, when my father took a job with the U.S. government, joining a corps of reverse *braceros*—a cadre of "U.S. guest workers"—among them Southwestern, Spanish-speaking ranchers who journeyed to Mexico to help eradicate the infamous Hoof and Mouth Disease before it made its way to infect herds in *el norte*. In Guadalajara, Mexico, I learned to read and write the language of my ancestors, and I became enamored of all things Mexican. I came to understand that, notwithstanding our dearest held myth of pure European provenance, I was indeed linked in a very profound way to Mexico. But my interest in and love of Mexico was, if not expunged, certainly laid aside as I became immersed in the foundational myths of the United States to which we returned in 1950. Among them, I recall the infamous story of the Alamo, which made me feel ashamed of being Mexican. I would have to wait until my stint in graduate school to reclaim the education that had begun in Guadalajara when I was eight years old. As a Ph.D. student at the University of New Mexico, I immersed myself in the study of Spanish grammar and syntax and of Mexican and Latin American histories and literatures and I felt as if I had recovered a piece of my annexed soul. The Chicano movement of the sixties and early seventies also played an important role in helping me recover the fractured pieces of my identity. As my academic career evolved, I made the study of the culture and literary texts of the Chicano people of Aztlán—that part of greater Northern Mexico that, through political machinations, was transformed into the Southwestern United States—central to my scholarly endeavors. In my teaching role, I made a deep commitment to helping the next generation of "Hispanic" New Mexicans explore its cultural roots and reclaim an identity embedded in historical realities rather than in facile nationalist mythologies. This included entering into an honest dialog about our ties to Mexico and her people.

In 1997 I left my homeland to take a job at Oregon State University. The two decades of scholarship I brought with me seemed out of place in the Great Northwest. Despite the abundance of water, I felt like a fish out of water—itself an inept metaphor for a desert dweller. During my first year at OSU, I team-taught a field course on cross-cultural issues in agricultural labor. I vividly recall a session with immigrant farmworkers; hearing their personal stories was a transformational experience for me in terms of both pedagogical practices and subject matter. I realized that the scholarship that was begging to be done in this, my new home, must involve these workers and the scores of young brown faces that graced my classes, and who in no uncertain terms informed me that they were not Chicanos, but rather Mexicans. Their question to me was, "What was you going to do to make our education relevant to our lives?" Thus, I embarked on a new intellectual trajectory, one not unrelated to my scholarship on Chicano culture and to my historical and emotional connections to Mexico. I began by reading everything I could get my hands on related to the experience of Mexicans in the Northwest. The OSU archival collection on *braceros* (World War II guest workers from Mexico) was as exciting a place as any in which to begin. In the scholarly arena, the work of Erasmo Gamboa was a beacon of light, but beyond that there were scant minor pieces of scholarship. So I dug into government and state agency reports, into newspapers and a handful of M.A. theses. Then I turned my attention to oral history. With Dwaine Plaza, an OSU professor whose area of expertise is Caribbean migration to Canada,

I trained students to collect oral histories. During my sabbatical in 2003-2004 I conducted dozens of interviews with early Mexican-origin settlers, and expanded my reading on Mexican migration to the United States, specifically to the Northwest. These early forays prompted me to design a course on Mexican Immigration to the United States and one on Life on the U.S./Mexico Border. As a significant number of students enrolled in these classes were themselves immigrants or the children of immigrants, I learned as much from them as they from me. They were, in fact, my human link to the Mexican immigrant community in Oregon. The following year, I submitted a proposal to the Oregon Council for the Humanities for a Chautauqua lectureship grant that would allow me to make public presentations on the experience of the Mexican-origin population in Oregon. During the past three years I have delivered more than thirty such lectures across Oregon.

In the fall of 2005, I was contacted by Marcela Mendoza, who had just moved to Oregon from Tennessee and was looking for a colleague interested in immigration studies; she wanted to continue developing her interest in the topic, something she had been working on in the American South. This was a partnership made in heaven. I say this because it was Marcela who encouraged me to work on this book project and who joined me as a most eager and skilled researcher and scholar. My involvement with the *mexicano* community does not end with this book. In 2008 I incorporated a non-profit organization, Casa Latinos Unidos de Benton County, dedicated to providing advocacy and educational services to *mexicanos* and other Latinos in my community.

I, *Marcela Mendoza*, am a fifth-generation Argentine of mixed European and indigenous descent, raised in the pampas of Buenos Aires province, in a small town at the core of a fertile agricultural region settled by Spanish, Italian, Basque, French, and Irish immigrants. I was trained as an ethnologist at the University of Buenos Aires during the late seventies, and developed a passion for the study of indigenous societies, which at the time was a subject far removed from the intellectual discussions of metropolitan scholars. I became part of a small team of local researchers that was developing an original line of inquiry on the social organization of hunter-gatherer societies, and the prehistoric peopling of the southern part of the continent. Like most of my peers at the time, I set off to pursue a doctoral degree overseas with the intention of bringing back new ideas to our academic community and hoping to learn from scholars who practiced an unrelated anthropology, different from the theoretical lines of inquiry we had in Argentina. I returned to the University of Buenos Aires after completing graduate course work at the University of Iowa, but this educational experience in the United States proved too enticing for me and my family. We decided to move to Memphis, Tennessee, in the late 1990s following a job offer for my husband at the University of Tennessee. The South had just become a true "new destination" for ambitious and entrepreneurial *mexicanos* displaced by economic instability and joblessness. When the results of the 2000 decennial census were released, I was a Spanish-speaking foreign-born anthropologist doing research and advocacy with Mexican immigrants in a place where the residents were eager to find this type of involvement. Memphians of all social and cultural backgrounds had noticed an increase in the number of Latinos around the city, and were fascinated by the statistical evidence that academic researchers were able to show. The pervasive presence of Mexican workers in the assembly lines of packing plants at industrial parks, in all-Mexican crews at construction sites, and in the manicured front yards of residential neighborhoods was exciting news to residents of a city whose population is majority African American. I was called to join the board of non-profit organizations, to give public lectures, to correspond with the local newspapers, and to talk on Spanish-language radio programs. In Memphis, I learned about the networks and the strategies for survival of the most disadvantaged *mexicanos* from a fellow-immigrant point of view. A shared sentiment of uprooting and displacement, similar challenges in raising bilingual and bicultural children, and membership in the same church made up for real and perceived differences in occupation or national origin between other immigrants and me. I felt that we understood one another. I brought this academic and experiential knowledge to my research in Oregon. Here I studied the process of migration in the Willamette Valley, interviewed Mexican farmworkers, and learned about their individual situations. I sought out the collaboration of Erlinda Gonzales-Berry, and our ongoing association opened new avenues to continue doing research and to advocate for the integration of immigrants and their children in this increasingly multicultural society. In 2009, I also expanded my involvement with the local *mexicano* community by assuming a position of leadership at Centro Latino Americano, a nonprofit organization in Eugene, Oregon, initiated in 1972 by activist Chicano students from the University of Oregon.

So it is that we have melded our individual intellectual practices and our personal passions to embark on an intellectual endeavor that has resulted in the book we here present to you.

Overview of Book

With the signing of the Treaty of Guadalupe Hidalgo on February 2, 1848, the United States acquired roughly half of Mexico's northern territory, and as a result approximately eighty thousand *mexicanos* inhabiting the states of California, Arizona, New Mexico, and Southern Colorado were granted automatic, albeit contested and second-class, citizenship in the United States (Acuña 2004). The treaty bonded the two countries in an asymmetrical relationship, the ramifications of which extend to the present moment. This history of imperialism and contiguity—the two countries share a two-thousand-mile border—cannot be ignored when studying the virtually uninterrupted northbound migrant flow that for over a century has cemented further the frequently troubled, sometimes felicitous, relationship between Mexico and the United States. An early account of America's attitude toward this colonized population divulges an unflattering portrayal based on a deeply embedded phenomenon we call racialization.[1] The product of densely intertwined social, cultural, and political texts that posit as their foundational ideological construct the notion of white supremacy, racialization alleges the inherent inferiority of groups and individuals excluded from the category "white" or "Caucasian." Fixating on the mixed-blood component of Mexican identity, this racialized discourse played no small role in justifying the war of the United States with Mexico in 1846 and it set the tone for perceptions about the conquered *mexicanos* who remained on this side of the border:

> As would naturally be the case, a people so various in their origin
> as the Mexicans, and in whose veins flows the blood of three distinct
> races, would present a corresponding diversity of character. They
> possess the cunning and deceit of the Indians, the politeness and
> spirit of revenge of the Spaniard, and the imaginative temperament
> and fiery impulses of the Moor ... They have inherited a portion of the
> cruelty, bigotry, and superstition that have marked the character of
> Spaniards from the earliest of times (Davis 1973, 217).

The relation established between the nation and its newly acquired population was based on a discourse that would brand the colonized Mexicans as inferior and deserving of condescension and discrimination. These colonized Mexicans and, subsequently, all future immigrants from Mexico to the area would be viewed as a people inassimilable by their "nature" (characterized by a constructed combination of biology and culture) and thus undeserving of fair and just treatment (Reisler 1996; Gonzales-Berry and Maciel 2000; Acuña 2004). In the Southwestern states and in California, the legacy of colonization would form the bedrock upon which *mexicano* identity would be constructed and would determine the treatment of this population as second-class citizens or immigrants aspiring to this brand of citizenship.

In removed areas such as Oregon, *mexicanos* would also bear the brunt of racialized thinking, but their experience would be somewhat different from that of *mexicanos* in the Southwest. Individuals and families who migrate to Oregon have not been seen as a population with an ancestral claim to a homeland in this country, but rather as immigrants, always already foreign, even if they were born in this country. In contrast, Texan and other Southwestern Mexicans who migrated to the region in the fifties and sixties, and who could, by virtue of being born in a region that once belonged to Mexico, lay claim to a homeland in what Acuña calls an "occupied territory" (2004). What would stand out about *mexicanos* here, in addition to their status as seasonal farmworkers, then as "illegal aliens," would be their position as non-white, as "people of color" (Silverstein 2005; Kretsedemas 2008; Maldonado 2009). *Mexicanos* would be included in a racialized hierarchy constructed in relation to African-American slaves rather than in relation to a conquered and colonized people. The formation of a *mexicano* identity in Oregon as a culturally distinct national/ethnic group would have other components as well, and it would be qualitatively different from the identity formation of their compatriots in California and the Southwest. In Border States there is always a sense among *mexicanos* of the contiguity of the mother country, of Mexican culture as a foundational substratum—the bounty of Spanish place names is but one of many reminders—and of the fact that Spanish is not a foreign language. In Oregon, *mexicanos* are more conscious of the distance that mediates between them and the homeland, of their outsider status, of the fact that their language and culture are indeed viewed as foreign. The border linking Mexico and the United States serves as a concrete iconic reminder of political separation but so too does it serve as powerful space of bilingual and bicultural linkage that nurtures a strong ethnic identity among both the colonized and immigrants along the border. That political border is too distant for *mexicanos* in Oregon to rally around it as a symbolic unifying idea. But that is not to say that a border does not exist in the distant localities they occupy in the Pacific Northwest. As Américo Paredes would remind us, a border is "not simply a line on a map but, more fundamentally, … a sensitized area where two cultures or two political systems come face to face" (cited in Rouse 1996, 255). The border for *mexicanos* in Oregon is a socio-spatial line that mediates between the reality of their lives at home and that of the public space of mainstream culture. Thus, it is more intensely personal and psychological and it functions as a reminder of their isolation and of their separation from the dominant society. Furthermore, the absence of a long-standing colonized population has meant the lack of a culturally constructed economic, social, and political infrastructure created by a people rooted in a space they could claim as their own, as is the case in the Border States. Consequently, early *mexicano* settlers in Oregon, unable to stake a claim upon a land previously belonging to their ancestors (as *tejano* [Texan Mexican] migrants had done for generations in their home state of Texas) had to begin from scratch. In this sense they were not able to rely on the protective psychological mechanism of belonging, but neither did they have to contend with the stigma borne by the colonized in Southwestern states.[2]

The notable growth in the Mexican-origin population in the last decade and a half has indeed created conditions that allow us to speak of Oregon as a "new destination," and we do so when exploring the spread of *mexicanos* within the state of Oregon. However, we maintain that Oregon has to some extent functioned as a traditional Southwestern target location. Mexican American (primarily from Texas but to a lesser extent from New Mexico and Colorado) and Mexican migrants who began to settle out in the early and mid-twentieth century carved out a space for themselves in Oregon cities and villages. Within their ethnic enclaves they created a social infrastructure sustained by dense social networks that gradually would anchor the third generation solidly as Oregonians. As in the Border States, new immigrants have thus been able to make use of many facets of that infrastructure as they struggle to anchor their own families and begin their lives anew.

These differences between the experiences of *mexicanos* in Oregon and the Southwest notwithstanding, there have been similarities in the sense that across time both groups have been viewed as a source of cheap labor, ready always to assume their position as low-wage earners, exploitable workers in a racially and ethnically stratified labor system. For those who have migrated from Mexico to Arizona, New Mexico, California, Texas, or Washington and Oregon, the policies of this nation have been arbitrary and ad hoc, assuming always that Mexicans are an expendable labor force, available in times of plenty and deportable in times of economic scarcity or of nativist displeasure. These then are the underlying tenets that underpin our exploration of the migration of *mexicanos*—both U.S.-born Mexican Americans and Mexican nationals—to Oregon, where for over a hundred years they have made their presence known.

Drawing from the disciplines of history, anthropology, sociology, gender and cultural studies, building on the work of earlier scholars, and providing new and original research, we present in this text a comprehensive view of the experiences of the Mexican-origin population in Oregon. We have plumbed the archival record, explored primary and secondary scholarly works, combed through demographic statistics, and collected the testimonies of dozens of Mexican-origin migrants and immigrants in an effort to shed light on the economic, political, social, and cultural conditions that have shaped their lives. We have blended scholarly research with individual stories in an effort to flesh out the complexity of the push-and-pull forces that produce migration in Oregon, and at the same time to focus on the human dimension of this phenomenon as it plays out in the state. We have been particularly interested in comprehending what motivates migrants to come to Oregon fields, construction sites, and warehouses, what their experiences have been when they live here, and how they adapt to life in the United States; in other words we are interested in understanding and appreciating their stories and their lives. Speaking with a broad cross section of people, including different generations, has been crucial in extending our work beyond the farmworker population—the most studied segment of Mexican migration to Oregon—and in putting into perspective the distinct facets (sojourning, settlement, and transnationalism) of the history of *mexicanos* in the state. Because integration is a relational process, as Mexican parents settle and their children develop a sense of belonging, we confidently anticipate that subsequent generations of *mexicanos* could be steadily included in the laudable immigrant epic most clearly articulated for Oregon's pioneers and settlers of northern European descent, thereby creating a public discourse that would view Mexicans as yet another immigrant population in the Pacific Northwest instead of a narrative fixated on the racialized prejudice and discrimination endured by these low-wage workers.

It is an accepted premise that *mexicanos* come here as laborers and this makes them, particularly those with little human capital, vulnerable to exploitation. The newsprint reviewed for this study amply documents exploitation and incidences of discrimination against the Mexican-origin population. Hence, throughout the study, we reference these phenomena. We argue that the effects of prejudice and stereotyping vary across individual dimensions such as education, occupation, English language proficiency, residential isolation, and the strength of a person's ethnic identity. Nonetheless, we propose that their effects on *mexicanos* in Oregon have been very real, particularly for those—maybe precisely for those—who because of persistent racialization and entrapment in low-wage occupations have not been able to overcome the social and educational achievement gap. However, we would be remiss if we did not demonstrate that these practices have not held *mexicanos* back in their quest for social adaptation, economic advancement, social justice, and integration. Hence, it has been our intent, throughout this book, to highlight the efforts and achievements of Oregon's *mexicanos* in this regard.

Paraphrasing the notion that the Pacific Northwest extends to "wherever the salmon can get to" (Harvey 1998)—even though large parts of the Columbia River watershed have been historically inaccessible to salmon— we propose that Oregon's *mexicano* communities extend to wherever women build domestic altars, which at this time is almost everywhere in the state. These diminutive memorials are meant to protect homes, restaurants, businesses, and other places where people come together; they are collections of religious images, of Virgins, saints, crucifixes, estampitas (illustrated religious cards with prayers), pedimentos (written requests), and photos of loved ones arranged on small tables or mantelpieces. Like shrines, these are expressions of spirituality deeply rooted in people's lives. They establish a spiritual lifeline between the country of origin and the adopted country, and are genuine examples of cultural mix or mezcla—a word that in this context stands for mestizo, católico, latinoamericano or mix-blood, Catholic, Latin American. Historian Gabriella Ricciardi (2006) interviewed altaristas (women who create home altars) in such diverse locations as Madras, John Day, Nyssa, Ontario, and Adrian in Eastern Oregon; Portland, Hillsboro, Forest Grove, Woodburn, and Salem in the Willamette Valley; and Medford in Southern Oregon. In each one of those places, *mexicanos* nurture their social, cultural, and religious traditions and contribute to the creation of tightly knit communities where families continue to speak their native languages at home—as we will note elsewhere, not all *mexicanos* are Spanish speakers.[3]

The first chapter is a historical overview of the myriad factors that for a century and a half have created the movement of peoples from Mexico to the United States. There exists a vast collection of literature pertinent to this topic, but we have chosen to synthesize the historical record in order to provide a background to readers who are interested in the immigration of Mexicans to Oregon, but who might not otherwise be familiar with the broader picture. This overview will allow the discerning reader to understand more fully the ambivalent nature and the ad hoc manner in which U.S. policies regarding Mexican immigration have been shaped and applied not once or twice, but repeatedly throughout the history of interdependent, albeit asymmetrical, relations between these two nations. We hope to provide a better understanding of how Mexican migrations to Oregon have not occurred in a vacuum, but are part of a long and complicated web of political and economic entanglements. The arrival of early sojourners, particularly the guest workers known as *braceros* who toiled the fields during World War II is discussed in this chapter. We contend that this cohort left a legacy that is still palpable today in the farming valleys of Oregon.

The second chapter explores the lives of Mexican-origin settlers—the majority of them U.S. citizens—during the mid-twentieth century. Drawing on personal narratives of members of this group, we highlight their experiences first as itinerant fieldworkers, then as early settlers in areas dominated by an agricultural economy that relied heavily on their presence and that benefited from their "settling out." Of special interest in this period is the involvement of Mexican-origin settlers in processes of community building and their engagement in self-determination endeavors.

Chapter 3 focuses on the economic and political conditions that altered the pattern of circular migration of male workers and encouraged family migrations and settlement. Here we look also at the impact of globalized markets and the North American Free Trade Agreement on the Mexican economy, and its connection to the subsequent out-migration that has brought several hundred thousand workers and their families to Oregon. Of special interest in this chapter are the themes of self-motivation, networks, individual and structural challenges, and cultural diversity within migrant streams, as well as the interactions of new immigrants with the *mexicanos* and *tejanos* living in older communities.

Chapter 4 provides an analysis of the most recent immigrant settlement patterns in metropolitan areas and in small towns. Documenting the employment of Mexicans in urban occupations, we note the emergence of a Spanish-surnamed middle class of Mexican descent in Oregon. We underscore the dependency of the local economy on the labor of these workers and seasonal agricultural laborers, many of whom are not authorized to be employed in the United States.

Chapter 5 turns the reader's attention to the gendered nature of migration and explores the experiences of women who have migrated both as members of families and as single individuals. We look at how migration is differentially experienced by males and females and how it contributes to changes in gender roles. This chapter also focuses on the impact of migration on family dynamics and on how families cope with the massive changes that result from the process—which affects parents and children in different ways—of becoming bilingual and bicultural.

In Chapter 6 we focus more narrowly on the experiences of the one-and-a-half generation, that is, the foreign-born children of immigrants, who were brought to this country during adolescence, and the unique nature of their experiences as they pursue social mobility and integration in Oregon. In this case study, we attempt to shed light on the challenges that the one-and-a-half generation faces in bridging two cultures as well as the generational conflicts that emerge as a result of their acculturation process.

The final chapter synthesizes the main social and cultural issues related to immigration that we found intertwined in the stories and lives of *mexicanos* in Oregon. We stress the repeated arrival of a "first generation" and the consequences of this pattern upon language and cultural preservation, and we draw attention to the formation of families whose members may have mixed immigration status. To understand the complexities related to the incorporation of Mexican families in Oregon we disentangle the individual legal status of family members from their generation-since-migration standing. We also refer in this chapter to the persistent low socio-economic status of many Oregonians of Mexican descent, and point to the downward assimilation that appears to affect some youth, particularly those living in the largest urban areas of the state. We underscore here the importance of providing economic and educational opportunities for Mexican American youth who currently represent the fastest-growing segment of Oregon's population.

Terminology and Testimonios

A word on our use of terms is in order.[4] We use Latino/Hispanic when referring to primary sources that employ these pan-ethnic categories to make sense of large sets of data. This is typically the case for demographic and economic statistics produced by state and federal agencies. Researchers who have conducted original investigations in the Pacific Northwest have also utilized these terms to refer to Spanish speakers in general, including indigenous peoples of Latin American origin who may, in fact, speak their own native languages. In all other cases, we use Mexican or *mexicano* to refer to foreign-born Mexicans, and Mexican American to designate Oregonians of Mexican descent (including *tejanos*). Because this population—regardless of place of nativity or generation—is most comfortable using the term *mexicano* to self-identify, we privilege this term throughout the text. We use the term in Spanish following the orthographic convention of this language that avoids the upper case for adjectives of nationality.

Historically, immigration defines a movement of people from one country to another with the purpose of settling. Migration refers to movement of people from one place to another, with or without settlement. It describes both internal movement of people (inside a country) and movement across national borders. Today's simple and comparatively more affordable transportation, coupled with the accumulative experience of previous transnational flows, create economic and social conditions that encourage people to live their lives in more than one place/nation. Thus the term international migration describes our present global reality. In analyzing the situation of their co-nationals in the United States, most Mexican scholars prefer the term migration to immigration. Our analysis examines the experiences of *mexicanos* from the point of view of migrants who initially may not have envisioned settling permanently in Oregon, but who nonetheless have been here for a number of years and have no actual plans to return to Mexico in the near future. These women and men are raising American-born children in Oregon. We call the children of these "settled" *mexicanos* the one-and-a-half or 1.5 generation (if they were born in Mexico and brought to Oregon after five and before sixteen years of age) and second-generation immigrants (if they were born in the U.S. or brought before the age of five). When we address the stories of the Mexican-origin population that engaged in internal (U.S.) migration during the mid-twentieth century, some of whom are *tejano*, we employ the term migration as it usually appears in the literature. Overall we refer to Oregonians of Mexican descent—who have already developed a sense of belonging in the Pacific Northwest—as immigrants, applying the same concept as is used in historical and sociological accounts of the integration of settlers of European descent in the state.

Many women and men who are either Oregonians of Mexican descent or foreign-born *mexicanos* have generously agreed to be interviewed for this project. The *tejanos* and a few Mexican nationals who shared their stories with us were resolute in wanting to insert themselves as subjects in the historical record and requested we use their names; most non-*tejanos*, however, requested anonymity. In the latter case, we used only first names in discussion and citations; in the former we included full names. We have cited these stories in the body of the text to elucidate our findings and we have also interspersed longer personal stories, or what we prefer to call *testimonios*, amidst the various chapters. Some of these testimonies (those of the 1.5 generation) are essays written by our students; others are synthesized excerpts from transcriptions—most of them translated by the authors from Spanish—of oral interviews. These *testimonios*, we believe, are crucial to revealing aspects of the actual lives of our subjects. For readers who have little or no contact with Mexican-origin individuals or families, these stories can provide intimate insights that hopefully will create understanding and empathy. Moreover, personal stories increasingly are being recognized by educators as powerful instructional tools, and we believe classroom instructors will welcome these narratives as useful tools for deepening the learning process.

In contextualizing their stories and their lives with what we have learned from published sources, we do not claim to have produced a definitive work on the subject of *mexicanos* in Oregon. We acknowledge that there are lacunae in this project. Also some of the topics have been explored by other authors. Certainly all of the themes developed in this book can be explored in greater depth. However, we believe we have added new materials to the existing resources on settler populations, and opened up new areas of exploration regarding the most recent migrations. A major contribution is the connection we have drawn between the various facets of Mexican stories and lives in Oregon, and our assertion that the state has functioned as both a traditional target location and a new destination where early settlers provided the economic and social foundation (so-called social capital) upon which new immigrant families have anchored and started new lives. We also highlight the fact that uninterrupted migratory flows throughout the twentieth century have lead to the settlement of repeated "first generations" both in rural and urban areas, which makes the Mexican case quite unlike the experience of Oregonians of European provenance. It is our hope that our analysis, which builds on a comprehensive updated bibliography and contains first-hand original accounts, will serve as an impetus, and perhaps a road map, for future scholars.

---

1. Silverstein (2005) describes racialization as the relational processes through which social markers such as class, ethnicity, generation from migration, and kinship are socially constructed as natural and/or embedded into a racial classification.

2. For a discussion of the effects of colonization on conquered *mexicanos* in the United States see Rudolfo Acuña 2004.

3. It is true that not all *mexicanos* are Catholic. However, throughout Oregon we find evidence of their strong adherence to Catholicism. We also find significant levels of membership in Christian and Pentecostal churches, and these, too, have played an important role in the creation of community.

4. For many decades, the Mexican American population—migrants or settled-out individuals—were referred to as "Spanish-American" in government reports and often in the media. This usage was common in New Mexico and to a lesser extent in Texas, where the preferred label was "Latin American." The racialized white/ color binary prevalent in the United States rendered the label Spanish-American a designator of white status, while the term Mexican connoted non-white status. This is complicated by the fact that individuals of Mexican origin (with the exception of 1930 decennial census, when the term Mexican appeared as a race designator) historically have been counted as whites in the U.S. census. In order to distance themselves from the conditions affecting African Americans in this country, many Mexican-American politicians and community leaders deployed strategies that ensured their always being categorized as whites (Foley 1997). The term Chicano came into usage during the period of grass roots social movements in the 1960s. Hispanic—a pan-ethnic label including all peoples from countries south of the U.S./Mexico border—was introduced as the official designator by the Nixon Administration, and Latino is used primarily by grass roots "Latino" organizations.

Chapter 1

South to North: An Overview of Early Mexican Migration to the United States and Oregon

The completion of a transcontinental railroad linked the two coasts of the United States and played a major role in integrating the Southwest into the nation's industrial economy. In the 1880s, the Southwestern United States entered an intensive phase of economic expansion. The creation of markets for western fruits and vegetables by the transcontinental railroad, the development of refrigeration, and the Newlands Reclamation Act, which provided federal funds for large-scale irrigation and reclamation projects, added agriculture as a gainful commercial venture (Taylor 1937; Gómez-Quiñones 1981). Given the scant population that inhabited the vast western landscapes of the U.S. that once were part of Northern Mexico, immigrant labor was crucial to the development of this emerging economic trio: railroads, commercial agriculture, and mining.

The curtailment of Chinese immigration in 1882 and the signing of the Gentleman's Agreement, which put an end to the immigration of Japanese laborers, created a demand for Mexican labor in the Southwestern United States. Anti-immigrant hysteria fueled by World War I and stoked by nativist rhetoric led to enactment of the Immigration Act of 1917, which restricted European immigration in several ways (Reisler 1976; Kiser and Kiser 1979; Scruggs 1988; Driscoll 1999). These measures coupled with World War I itself reduced considerably the European-origin labor force in steel mills and meat-packing and food-processing plants and opened the door to increasing numbers of Mexican workers who, given the tumultuous civil war conditions that prevailed in Mexico between 1910 and 1920, were only too happy to take advantage of the opportunity to find wage labor, not only in Western states, but in the Midwest as well.

U.S. private labor contractors turned south in pursuit of a new labor pool and "used a variety of coercive measures to recruit Mexican laborers and deliver them to jobs north of the border" (Massey et al. 2002, 27). As the Mexican government struggled to stabilize its political base and to consolidate an economy crippled by a decade of civil war, the United States sabotaged Mexico's efforts to keep its labor force (to which, despite its good intentions, Mexico could not afford to guarantee a living wage) at home by manipulating U.S. immigration law to encourage emigration from Mexico and guarantee a pool of cheap labor for the American Southwest and beyond. In fact, during World War I, the U.S. government itself became involved in recruitment programs (Massey et al. 2002). This pattern was, and is, typical of the ad hoc application of immigration law to the inevitable flow of migration from Mexico to the United States during the course of the twentieth century.

The Immigration Act of 1917 is a case in point. Immediately after its enactment, 1,771 illiterate Mexicans withdrew their applications and another 5,745 were turned away for not paying the eight dollar head tax mandated by the law (Reisler 1976). Faced with a labor shortage, agriculturalists in California and Texas mounted a campaign that convinced the federal government to enact the Ninth Proviso, which waived the Immigration Act literacy test and the head tax for Mexican immigrants. Depending on who is doing the counting, seventy-two thousand (Guerin-Gonzales 1994) or more than eighty thousand (Scruggs 1988) Mexican workers were imported under this emergency labor program to work in mining, construction, and railroads.

Ironically, as thousands of workers were brought in through waivers, the post-war recession of 1921 forced one hundred thousand jobless Mexican workers already in the United States—but who were not part of the emergency labor program—to return to Mexico. Reisler (1976) notes that during this period public sentiment against *mexicanos* escalated such that many acts of violence were committed against them, including the beating of hundreds of families in labor camps by "night riders."

No to Quotas, Yes to Borders

The Johnson Immigration Act of 1924, sponsored by the honorary president of the Eugenics Research Association (Pierpont 2004), likewise attests to the ambivalence of U.S. immigration law when it comes to Mexican labor. In that year, nativist propaganda aimed at further stemming the entry of Eastern and Southern Europeans led the Immigration Bureau to reduce the number of entries from all countries save those in the Western Hemisphere (quotas had been set in 1921 at 3 percent of the number of persons from that nation already present in the United States).

The U.S. Border Patrol was established the same year that the Johnson Immigration Act, sometimes called the National Origins Act, was passed. The enactment of this measure meant that the U.S. government, for the first time, set about defending the U.S.-Mexico border against illegal entry through the use of physical control, though this new approach served primarily a symbolic function (Massey et al. 2002). Designed to curb overland immigration, it only increased the activity of extralegal recruitment and smuggling of workers, an already well-entrenched method of bringing Mexican labor to the United States, giving rise to the "wetback industry" of the 1920s (Cardoso and Corwin 1979). While the establishment of a physical controlling force at the border and concomitant efforts by the border patrol to enforce its mission were manifestations of the country's ostensible determination to deal with illegal entry, the history of abject failure of the border patrol is likewise a sign of the arbitrary nature of the application of U.S. immigration law vis-à-vis its closest southern neighbor.

The Beat Goes On: 1925-1942

Despite the vulnerable position of undocumented *mexicanos* after the creation of the U.S. Border Patrol, so long as there were jobs on this side, these workers took their chances and continued to cross the border. Their resolve was strengthened by the fact that in the United States they were able to earn roughly six times the wages earned for the same work in Mexico (Gamio 1930). The common practice of using Mexican workers as scabs during labor strikes also added to the swelling ranks of *mexicano* workers at a time when labor militancy was particularly active in the United States. But not all went well in the Promised Land. Anti-immigrant sentiment was on the rise, with *mexicanos* a favorite target for nativist hostility and racialized rhetoric. These sentiments translated into a nationwide campaign that called for the inclusion of the Western Hemisphere in the National Origins Act. Congressman John Box from Texas led the charge in Washington. In 1929 he introduced the Box Bill, which called for quotas for Latin America and Mexico. In hearings on the bill, Mexicans were portrayed in the worst possible terms and, as in the case of the Chinese and Japanese before them, all their faults were attributed to their "inherent racial inferiority." While much of the nativist discourse, particularly that found in the public media, can be interpreted as a venting of frustrations by members of the exploited working class who felt threatened by foreign labor, much of it was the opinion of college professors, whose "scientific" proclamations regarding the inferiority of "non-white" races carried a good deal of clout in Washington.[1] Although *mexicano* migration to Oregon was scant in the early twentieth century, the restrictionist and quota debates of the 1920s did impact the state, as is evidenced by the fact that in 1929 the Oregon legislature drew up a memorial urging the United States Congress to establish quotas for Mexican migration.

Agriculturalists and other employers not surprisingly argued that it would be a mistake to ban Mexican labor. What made *mexicanos* an ideal reserve labor force for the United States was the fact that they were not a threat to white supremacy, quite simply because they did not "desire white women" and they did not settle (Reisler 1997, 37). Mexicans, argued employers, were like homing pigeons, always finding their way home (Reisler 1976; Guerin-Gonzales 1994).[2] And those who didn't? Well, those who didn't could always be deported when their services were no longer needed. Herein lays the basic tenet of the historical relationship of Mexican workers to U. S. labor (and to American society at large) and the practice of ad hoc application of immigration policy to Mexicans for almost a century.

Deportations and Repatriations during the Great Depression

By the end of the 1920s, approximately 1.5 million first- and second-generation *mexicanos* lived north of the border (Reisler 1976). This population had just been exposed to a virulent defamation campaign that had, in the minds of the American public, rendered it an inferior race of human beings—unclean, indolent, given to vice and crime—incapable of meeting standards that defined the ideal American citizen, and they were an easy target for the anger and frustration generated by the Great Depression.

One answer to this economic crisis seemed simple: rid the country of aliens who competed with legitimate Americans for jobs. Ordinary citizens, welfare agencies, patriotic groups like the American Veterans of Wars, the Lions Club, the American Legion, the America for Americans Club, and the press—most notably the *Chicago Tribune* and the *Saturday Evening Post*—urged local and federal governments to deport aliens (Kiser and Silverman 1979; Balderrama and Rodríguez 1995). Trains, cars, trucks, buses, ships, oil tankers, fruit boats, and empty cargo steamers were used to carry Mexicans to the border, forming what the journal *Living Age* called "A Caravan of Sorrow" (*Living Age* 332, cited in Balderrama and Rodríguez 1995). Just how many Mexicans returned to their homeland during the depression? Reisler (1976, 232) estimates the number "as high as four hundred thousand," while Balderrama and Rodríguez (1995) estimate one million. Whatever the exact numbers, one thing is certain: the massive use of force and police power turned out to be a most successful strategy, so successful that during the 1930s the size of the Mexican population of the United States was reduced by 41 percent (Massey et al. 2002), and the issue of Mexican immigration was to become a low-profile item on the national agenda until 1943.

Mexicanos *Come to Oregon*

The first person of Mexican origin listed in the Oregon Census (1850) is Guadalupe de la Cruz, a thirteen-year-old boy residing in Oregon City with

Spain in the Pacific Northwest

The Hispanic presence in Oregon antecedes by several centuries the arrival of immigrants from one nation/state (Mexico) to another (the United States). A cursory glance at a map of the Oregon coast alights on names such as Cape Blanco, Cape Heceta, Cape Sebastian, Cape Ferello, and Cape Falcon. These names attest to the many voyages of exploration carried out in the waters and along the coastline of the Pacific Northwest under the aegis of the Spanish Crown beginning in the sixteenth century, and it is worth keeping in mind that many of the sailors involved in these explorations were *mestizos* born in what today is known as Mexico. In 1543, Spanish navigator Bartolemé Ferrelo sailed north of California reaching waters near the Rogue River (Speck 1954). The names of Cape Blanco and Cape Sebastian are attributed to the 1602 expedition of Sebastián Vizcaína, though he did not touch land (Beals 1995). During the seventeenth and early eighteenth centuries, Spain concentrated its efforts on its lucrative trade in the Philippine Islands and ignored the Pacific Northwest, even though by virtue of the Treaty of Tordesillas it claimed all lands touching the eastern Pacific Ocean.[3]

By the middle of the eighteenth century, however, as British and Russian navigators in search of trade venues made their presence felt in the area, Spain resumed its expeditions along the Pacific Northwest coast, seeking to protect its territories. The navigators along the Pacific Northwest coast during this era include Juan Pérez, who made landfall in Alaska in 1774, then proceeded to explore the coast of British Columbia, Washington, and Oregon (Hitchman 1990). In 1775 the *Santiago* and the *Sonora* under the command of Bruno de Hezeta and Juan Francisco de la Bodega y Quadra sailed as far as Juneau and took possession of four points in the name of Spain. On their return journey, Hezeta sailed past the mouth of the Columbia River, making the first sighting by a European of that river (Weber 1998). Had he explored it, this mighty river would probably bear his name rather than that of James Cook's ship. Between 1788 and 1795 "over thirty voyages by vessels flying the red-and-yellow banner of Bourbon Spain plied Northwest waters" (Beals 1995, 28), but it is the Malaspina expedition of 1789-94 that stands out because of the wealth of botanical and ethnographic information that he and his crew gave to the world.

This fleeting overview unequivocally establishes an early Hispanic presence in Oregon, a presence that although recognized by Anglo-centric historians has only in recent years received significant attention.

lawyer E. Hamilton and his wife Catherine. The 1860 Census lists twenty individuals born in Mexico, among them five women—let us keep in mind that this number could include individuals born in California or other Southwestern states that belonged to Mexico until 1848. These individuals list the following as their occupations: miner, mule packer, washerwoman, seamstress, laborer; and they resided in Oregon City, The Dalles, Fairfield,

Salem, Rogue River, and Josephine County. A ten-month-old girl, Julia Billardo, born in Oregon to Mexican parents, may have been the first child of Mexican ancestry born in the state.

Gamboa, in his study of mule packers in Oregon, refers to thirty-seven Mexicans who served as support troops with the Second Regiment Oregon Mounted Volunteers in the Rogue River Wars of the mid-nineteenth century. He wrote that their services were valued because their "superiority stemmed from a centuries-long experience with mule packing throughout the Southwest and Mexico. When the mining frontier moved north from California into southern Oregon in 1851, Mexicans were the first to bring loaded pack trains across the Siskiyou Mountains and into the areas of the Rogue River" (1991, 45).

There is also documentation of the first Mexican cowboys to come to Oregon. They came from California where, under the flags of Spain and Mexico, there had developed a robust *vaquero* culture, the accouterments and practices of which form the foundation of contemporary U.S. cowboy culture. Boyd informs us that this culture was brought to Oregon in 1869 by John Devine, who brought with him "a herd of trail-worn cattle, a dozen California *vaqueros*, and the outfits' cook and chuck wagon" (1995, 31). Vicente and Juan Ortega, Francisco Chararateguey, Juan and Jesus Charris, Primo Ortega, and Joaquín Chino were among those who taught the art of taming horses and herding cattle to Anglo American farmhands who worked the P. Ranch in the High Desert of Oregon (Boyd 1995). In 1872 Peter French brought a half dozen Mexican *vaqueros*, among them Vicente Ortego, Juan Charris, Chino Berdugo, and Prim Ortego, to the Blitzen Valley (Slatta, 1975). Slatta reports: "Many ranches in southeast Oregon employed Mexican cowboys through the 1920's when the large outfits broke up and most *vaqueros* disappeared" (328). One of those Mexican cowboys, M. Morales, made a name for himself through his saddle-making business in Pendleton, Oregon (Morales 1925).

While migrants from Mexico to the United States in the early twentieth century generally found their way to California and the Southwestern states, there were always intrepid souls who ventured into less familiar territory in the Pacific Northwest (Saenz 1991). Given the nature of Mexican migration patterns—less visible undocumented entries paralleling documented ones—exact numbers of migrants reaching the northwest periphery, and specifically Oregon, are elusive. Gamboa (1990) observes that by 1910, if the Southwest were excluded, Oregon ranked seventh among states with Mexican-born residents. Gamio uses the number of money orders sent from the United States to Mexico as evidence of the number of Mexican nationals in the United States. He lists fifty-three Mexicans present in Oregon in 1900, eighty-five in 1910, eight in 1920; the total number of money orders sent from Oregon to Mexico in the first two decades of the twentieth century was 445 (24). Between July and August of 1926, 299 money orders were sent from Oregon to Mexico (4). The number dropped substantially in January and February 1927—ninety-eight are listed—suggesting that the migrant flow was seasonal then, as it has been in more recent memory. Judging from the size of the towns from which the money orders were issued, Gamio speculates that the majority of those sending them were employed in rural areas, most likely in agriculture. However, the Oregon Railroad and Navigation Company, the Union Pacific Railroad, and the Oregon Short Line were also recruiting mexicano workers to the area in the years before World War I (Compean 2008), though the record on their presence is lean. Gamio's figures, of course, do not include Mexican American workers, that is U.S. citizens of Mexican descent who migrated seasonally from Southwestern states and on occasion settled out. The Oregon census provides some valuable additional information, enumerating 569 Mexicans under the category of "foreign-born adults" in 1920. Carlos Gutierrez's father came to Oregon in 1919 and must have been among those listed in that census. Carlos was born in Oregon in 1920 and was still residing in Albany in 2007. In that same census, eighty-three Mexicans are listed as World War I draftees. The majority of them—thirty-seven—resided in Multnomah County (Oregon Census). Peterson del Mar (2003) notes that the 1930 census recorded more than fifteen hundred people of Mexican descent in Oregon, and García and García (2005) cite the exact number at 1,568, noting that this figure does not include individuals present in the area only part of the year.[4]

Notwithstanding the opposition by leaders of the National Quotas Act to unrestricted Mexican migration, the Gunn Supply Company of Portland was actively contracting Mexican workers. According to Gamboa, "This Oregon city, along with Denver and Los Angeles, 'the great Mexican peon capital of the United States,' was one of the company's principal areas of recruitment for Mexican laborers" (1990, 9). The sugar beet industry in Idaho and Eastern Oregon also drew large numbers of Mexican workers to the Northwest (Gamboa 1990). Certainly many of these recruits were from Mexico, but many others were from the Mexican American migrant stream. It was not uncommon for *mexicanos* recruited from Colorado and Texas to work in the beet fields in Idaho to make their way across the Oregon state line to work and eventually settle in Malheur County.

According to Dority Elguezabal, "Mexicans immigrated into Malheur County as early as 1918 but the majority came around 1937" (n.d. 1). She attributes this to the completion of the Vale and Owyhee irrigation projects in 1930 and 1932 respectively, and to the opening of a sugar factory in Nyssa in 1937. According to Elguezabal, a family by the name of Jaramillo was the first to settle in Malheur County. The couple left Guanajuato, Mexico, by train in 1918 and traveled to St. Louis, where for a short time Mr. Jaramillo worked for the railroad. They then hitched a ride west and ended up in Juntura, Oregon. Their granddaughter and her husband—the family of the latter settled in the area in 1943—opened the Gonzales Tortillería in Ontario in 1954. Their grandson, John Jaramillo, owned and operated a farm in the Treasure Valley for many years, and he eventually opened Casa Jaramillo, a restaurant in Ontario, Oregon. Today they figure among the prominent Hispanics in Nyssa.

Lupe Rivera Castro, another early settler in this region, tells us that as a child she came with her family by train to the United States (Oregon Council for the Humanities Hispanics in Oregon Oral History). Her father and eight other men who migrated as a group tried to stay together. After mining in Montana, they eventually moved to Nyssa. She recalls that her father initially worked with a machete in the sugar fields before moving on to work in the sugar factory in Nyssa where there were only three Mexican workers at the time. They brought friends and relatives one by one to work there and thus the Mexican population in the area gradually increased. In the labor camp at Adrian, the family of eight, which eventually reached eighteen, lived in a cabin with two bunk beds. She recalls her parents setting up a stove by the field and leaving her and her sisters to watch over a pot of beans. At lunch break their mother would come out of the field to make tortillas, and together the family would enjoy their lunch break. In Nyssa, Rivera Castro recalls, Mexicans lived on the east side in the early years of their settlement. They didn't have money to buy property in other parts of town. Later, when she was interviewed in the nineties, she observed that three quarters of the population was Hispanic and that they now lived in all parts of the town. When asked if she had felt discrimination growing up in Nyssa, Rivera Castro was magnanimous in her reply: "We are all discriminated. Humans make errors. Growing up and in school, I felt it. Maybe it was just a lack of cultural understanding" (Oregon Council for the Humanities "Hispanics in Oregon" Oral History). She recalled with pride that if there was one lesson she learned from her parents it was this: "they taught us to work hard."

Mary Thiel's family migrated to Idaho in 1929 (Gamboa and Baun 1995). By the time she was in high school they had moved to Vale, Oregon, where the family of seven worked as a crew in the beet fields. There can be no doubt that social and economic inequities deeply affected their family, particularly in terms of health. Mary's mother died of tuberculosis when she was in high school, and Thiel herself was forced to leave the fields because of illness. As hers was one of only two families in Vale, locals didn't pay much attention to them. But as more and more *mexicanos* moved there during the war she recalls that "people started focusing on the Mexican people" (134). Isolated as they were within their ethnic enclave, they experienced the kind of discrimination historically directed at immigrants. In Adrian, where Thiel's life-long engagement with her community began when she started teaching English in a labor camp, it was much more apparent; she remembers "being deeply hurt by things people said and did," and going home in tears (134). Wistfully, she recalls that her language class was soon taken over by a ministerial association. Feeling displaced, she dropped out only to see her program abandoned after a short time. Apparently this community was not yet ready to accept the idea of self-determination for its marginalized members, nor were the latter in a position to claim their rights.

As is evidenced by the cases discussed above, there are instances of settled-out *mexicanos* in Oregon in the first half of the twentieth century, particularly in Eastern Oregon. As more families arrived and settled, they struggled to make a living and to cope with social isolation and prejudice. However, the more usual pattern at that time was seasonal migration. Temporary, seasonal migration presented few stresses to existing social patterns and allowed discriminatory practices that would remain unchallenged over time by established communities. Seasonal workers tended to tolerate difficult conditions because they knew they were not permanent. This is a reality that must be taken into account if we are to understand the historical social positioning of *mexicanos* in Oregon, a state with a long history of itinerant agricultural workers.

Furthermore, Oregon has long served as an overflow delta for surplus migrant labor in California. For those workers who became most adept at stringing the crops together—tomatoes and grapes in California, then on to cherries, hops, and pole beans in Oregon, over to Washington to pick apples—in a work pattern that if plotted out on a map would resemble a beaded rosary, jobs could always be had on Oregon farms, even during the Depression. Some of these migrants became permanent residents, but as Gamboa (1990) observes, their situation was not an enviable one:

Necessity moved these migrants north from southwestern communities during a decade that witnessed major regional social and economic benefits from the New Deal. Since they were Mexicans and seasonal migrants, they had no other recourse but to depart as poverty stricken as when they arrived. Federal state relief was not extended to them, and the opportunity to escape the migratory cycle through the resettlement program was beyond their reach.... "[T]hose Mexicans who became permanent residents in the Northwest and elsewhere had no significant choice but to retreat into the backwaters of the depressed rural communities of the 1930s." (Gamboa 1990, 21)

Thus—out of sight, out of mind—early Mexican migrants in Oregon and the offspring of early settlers remained shadows in the official historical annals.

This was to change with the advent of World War II, when the institutionalization of the Mexican Farm Labor Program, popularly known as the *Bracero* Program, was to bring a good deal of publicity to Mexican migrant workers. Furthermore, their experience here was to pave a discernible path for the sustained presence of *mexicanos* in Oregon, a presence that has contributed to what Peterson del Mar (2003) has called the gradual "browning" of the state.

Braceros *Come to Oregon*

Oregon's fertile soils, aided by irrigation and rural electrification, had by the 1940s turned the state into a cornucopia of a wide variety of crops. These auspicious growing conditions resulted in the substantial production of commercially valuable perishable goods that required the availability of "a large pool of labor in order to rush crops to market at the optimum point of maturity and command the highest prices" (Gamboa 1990, 5). Over the years, local labor had been supplemented by the recruitment of workers from the Southwest and Mexico. However, it became increasingly apparent that a shortage of farm labor in Oregon was about to impede the state's ability to harvest and get its flash crops—now considered munitions of war—to market as World War II progressed and the exodus from rural areas swelled at an alarming rate (Ogden 2005). As available young men were drafted or volunteered to fill the ranks of the armed forces, remaining men and women flocked to urban centers to join the more lucrative war production industry.[5] A crisis indeed was in the making in Oregon, as it was across all the major food-producing regions of the country. Several unsuccessful attempts were made to resolve the labor shortage through local community participation. Such efforts in Oregon are described in some detail later in this chapter.

As early as 1941, growers in Texas, Arizona, and New Mexico requested permission from the Immigration Office to import workers from Mexico (Craig 1971). This request, however, was to go unheeded until the following year, when the United States and Mexico entered negotiations to implement a wartime emergency labor program. The resulting executive agreement was ratified in Mexico City on August 4, 1942, and in April 1943 it was extended to include railroad workers.[6] Only the railroad program—under increasing pressure from labor—would be terminated at the end of the war as initially intended; in areas other than the Northwest, where it was formally terminated at the end of the war, the agriculture program would last for another two decades, "reviv[ing] traditions of migration that had largely lapsed during the depression years" (Massey et al. 1987).

Driscoll (1999) sees this period as one of the few moments in history when Mexico was in a position to negotiate on an equal footing with the United States. Both countries had special interests and needs that could be met by wartime collaboration. Roosevelt's Good Neighbor Policy, with its tenets of non-aggression and non-intervention, had done much to encourage inter-American solidarity and set the stage for calling on Mexico to support the Unites States' war effort. However, Driscoll underscores the fact that despite its claims of encouraging Pan-American solidarity, this policy represented "negotiable economic dominance" of the United States over Latin America and central to its intent was the creation of strong economic relations that would guarantee the flow of raw materials from south to north and of goods and capital from north to south (1999). Initially reluctant to enter into this agreement, Mexico became more motivated to collaborate with the United States after Germany in June 1942 destroyed some of its naval vessels in the Caribbean, an event that compelled its declaration of war against the Axis powers (Galarza 1965; Driscoll 1999). Moreover, Mexico could ill-afford to antagonize its primary client for agricultural and mineral products (Scruggs 1988). Under these conditions then, "the development of the [railroad and agricultural] *bracero* programs during the war as a binational effort to secure Mexican labor for U.S. agriculture and railroads was entirely consistent with the thrust of U.S.-Mexican relations at the time" (Driscoll 1999, 39).

Hundreds of thousands of men responded to recruitment calls for this program. González and Fernández (2003) observe that many went into debt to fund their journey to the recruitment centers in Mexico. Some sold their small plots of farmland, so desperate were they to escape the poverty of their villages. A Mexico City *bracero*, who joined the railroad program at the National Stadium in that city, gives a lively account in his memoirs of the actual enlistment process:

> *Upon entering I realized that the organization was admirable. Each form was filled out by a friendly, well-paid and flirtatious bilingual typist who in addition to working quickly, carried out her duties in a most efficient manner. There were almost forty of them behind a long counter in a large hall that had been outfitted with all the accoutrements of a proper office. Our picture was taken and by the time we left it was printed and dried.... One could not ask for greater efficiency or organization from the Americans.... When I passed to the far end of the hall, a young, athletic American, of a playful and jolly nature, took my right arm and yanked me with his lion-like*

paw. Were it not for my physical strength, which allowed me to react quickly, I would have landed on all fours and this man would have manipulated me like a puppet. He then began to feel my biceps and he checked my hands, giving signs of satisfaction. He did the same with the other men, and thus my induction into this guild of braceros took place (Peón 1966, 26, translation by EG-B).

Mexican migrant workers disembark in Los Angeles, CA, 1942. University of California, UCLA Library.

In Oregon, *braceros* arrived in the summer of 1943. Prior to their arrival, calls were issued in the name of patriotism to the citizenry at large asking that they step up to fill the labor gap in fields across the state. Appeals went out to women's clubs, labor unions, schoolchildren, civilian defense and other community groups to rise to the call, as well as to business establishments to share their workers (Ogden 2005). Against forceful community opposition, farmers in Eastern Oregon received clearance from the president to employ uprooted and interned Japanese American farmers (Gamboa 1990; Nishihara 2007).[7] In other areas, there initially was optimism regarding the ability of locals to take up the slack. *The Monmouth Herald* observed in the early stages of the crisis: "This problem is being given a great deal of attention and it now appears that with the complete cooperation of townspeople the situation will be relieved and may be entirely licked" (June 17, 1943). This optimism was shored up by the deeply felt need of all citizens to make a personal contribution to the war effort. For those who remained at home, harvesting the crops that would feed America's soldiers and allied troops was a noble way to demonstrate civic pride and loyalty. Linked to these patriotic motives were feelings of rural independence and self-sufficiency, which made the idea of imported labor anathema to national pride. Hence, resistance to Mexican labor in the Willamette Valley was strong indeed. *The Monmouth Herald* makes this stance unequivocally clear:

> *Local authorities as well as people generally are opposed to bringing in Mexican labor, which was already picking crops in California, except as a last resort. Many people have expressed their opinions that the use of Mexican labor is not to be sought as it is believed that our own people are patriotic enough and anxious to lend assistance to the great task facing us this season (June 17, 1943).*

One month later, *The Herald* may not have changed its position, but it certainly was open to the possibility of *bracero* labor in Polk County, and it states the facts, simply and directly: "Elmer McClure, overseer, of the State Grange, who was in Monmouth Wednesday on his way to Benton County Pamona meeting at Alsea, said that Mexican labor is available to farmers and orchardists in Polk County" (July 15, 1943). One week later it announced: "500 Mexicans will join housewives, children, and a large number of evening work [sic] who are otherwise employed in day-time." These Mexicans, *The Herald* observed, were part of the fifty thousand allocated to the United States by the Mexican government, four thousand of whom would make up Oregon's quota. The newspaper assuaged public concerns by assuring readers that "in every community where they have been used they are exceedingly well pleased with them and have requested more than could be allotted to them", adding, "They are turning out very efficient work after they have had a chance to learn how the work should be done when they are not familiar with the work assigned them" (July 22, 1943). Implicit in early articles was the concern—real or imagined—that Mexicans were deficient in their knowledge of farm labor. This concern may very well have been instilled in the media and general public via statements issued by disgruntled farmers whose past free-wheeling recruitment practices had been interrupted by the inopportune intrusion of the Mexican and U.S. governments (Scruggs 1988; Gamboa 1990). An example of such a statement appeared in *Northwest Farm News* in the early months of 1943:

> *Somebody in our government with a lot of high ideals went to the Mexican government and made an agreement to send laborers to the*

*United States. They arranged to have a contract which would deal
with each laborer as a free agent and put in all sorts of conditions
which the farmer who had to hire him had to agree to.... But instead
of sending over experienced farm laborers, the Mexican government
gathered a lot of ne'er-do-wells and hobos (February 4, 1943).*[8]

If journalists at the *Salem Statesmen* were swayed by arguments of this sort,
by July of that year they certainly had experienced a change of heart: "*The
Oregon Statesman* has to revise its fears regarding the use of Mexicans for
farm labor. The reports from all over the state were the Mexicans employed
are uniformly good. The men are chosen from the farming region of Mexico,
are friendly and cooperative, and their work is very satisfactory" (July 18,
1943, 4). The fact that this writer highlights the social characteristics of the
Mexicans implies that initial fears went beyond the pragmatic issue of whether
or not they possessed farmwork skills. This declaration was probably a relief
to a public whose only exposure to Mexicans may have been the stereotypes
of Mexicans as indolent, crafty bandoleers, projected by dime novels and by
Hollywood. The latter played an important role in broadcasting racialized
notions about the "Mexican character."

Housing the increasing number of workers in the Willamette Valley
presented a special problem. One plan was to house workers arriving in
Marion County at an unused sewage-disposal plant in Salem; this plan
was scrapped when the War Food Administration promised to make a site
available for a camp. But even as this new camp—the site of which was
still unknown—was approved, *The Oregon Statesman* revealed the covert
resistance of locals to having these imported workers living anywhere near
them: "This much may be said: The proposed ground is state-owned and is
close enough to the city to be within reach of certain services of sanitation
and supply. It is not in the center of a thickly-populated area." This last
statement addresses the concerns of North River Road residents, who called
what the journalist reported as an "indignation meeting" to express their
objection to housing Mexican workers in their area. That their objections
may have been motivated by fears of the "racialized other" is suggested as
the subject of "race," and ways employed to deal with it, is subtly introduced:
"if Mexicans come here they will be used in comparatively few hop yards
and prune orchards, all of them large establishments which will use full
crews of the dark-skinned laborers, and will keep them separated from
other workers" (*The Oregon Statesman*, August 13, 1943). Throughout this
period, the media—perhaps sensitive to the watchful eye of the Emergency
Farm Labor Supply Office—was generally circumspect in its treatment of
braceros in racial terms. This might come as a surprise to readers familiar
with the lack of racial diversity in Oregon and its history of exclusionary laws

pertinent to Chinese and African Americans. Racial discrimination, however, was certainly an issue that *braceros* had to contend with, and one that the Mexican government grappled with throughout the length of the program, particularly in Texas. Gamboa (1990) finds that such discrimination also was present in the Northwest. He cites one particular case in Medford, Oregon, where a Mexican worker was beaten by five young men, then arrested and charged for drinking in public, when in fact he was staggering from the beating he had just received.

Small growers also were resistant to the use of Mexican labor. But their opposition was never expressed in terms of "race." Rather, their expressed concern was that locals, who had done their patriotic duty by taking up the slack, would be replaced by Mexican labor and thus be made to feel that their efforts were not appreciated. *The Oregon Statesman* assured Salem citizens that the *bracero* program "would not relieve local people of the responsibility of carrying most of the burden. It would merely be a small supplement to the local labor forces, but one which may be badly needed" (July 18, 1943). Indeed one of the provisions of the agreement stipulated that Mexicans would not replace local workers (Rasmussen 1951); this is stated repeatedly in articles acknowledging the need for Mexican laborers.

The expressed fears and reservations of Oregonians did not, however, impede the importation of Mexican labor to Oregon. Polk County received its first cadre of five hundred *braceros* in July 1943 (*Independence Enterprise* July 23, 1943). Walter Leth, in a speech made to the Polk County Historical Society in 1974, recalled their arrival. That this program was beneficial not only to farmers, but to *braceros* as well, is implicit in Leth's recollection of their departure a few months later. Viewed through the prism of the United States as the land of opportunity and plenty, Leth is certain that *braceros* were better off for having had an opportunity to work in the United States:

> *The war period was kind of tough on us and we had a hard time getting enough work performed.... Then we imported 1100 Mexicans during that period. And you really got a thrill seeing those Mexicans come and get off the train out here past Eola a little ways. The train stopped there and all these Mexicans got off and the kind of gear and everything they had was a surprise. When I went down to the train to see them off when they went back to Mexico, they all had nice new suitcases, brand-new hats, good shirts and good clothes and so on. They were a different sight from the ones who had gotten off the train when they were so poor coming out of Mexico (Latino Oral History Project).*

The first group to arrive immediately went to work at the Horst hop ranch, and one hundred of the men were made available to prune farms at harvest time. In August of that same year, 585 *braceros* arrived in the Salem area. They were housed in a "tent city" west of the Salem fairgrounds, and they began harvesting hops and prunes (*The Oregon Statesman*, August 25, 1943).

According to Gamboa (1995a, 41), "the tent cities were typical of the labor camps provided for workers throughout Oregon: The braceros were housed together, sometimes in mobile tent camps or in permanent farm labor camps that dotted the farming areas from Ontario to Salem and Hood River to Medford. As a rule, six workers lived together in a 16x16-foot tent that was furnished with folding cots, one blanket per person, and heating stoves when available."

Sleeping quarters, 1944. Oregon State University Archives.

The *Hood River News* is a good source of information regarding the experiences of the roughly six hundred *braceros* stationed in this region. Ogden (2005), drawing from this newspaper, writes that when there was a break in availability of orchard work, the Apple Growers Commission changed the rules to allow Mexican workers to do other kinds of work, primarily for private homeowners, the county, and the lumber industry. She notes also that virulent racist attitudes toward the Japanese citizens of this community invariably were extended toward Mexican *braceros* and that these attitudes were expressed primarily as opposition to their remaining in the area once their contracts were fulfilled: "The fact that practically all of the Mexicans have returned to Old Mexico, at least until spring, has put an end to rumors that the dangers of them becoming permanent residents had any foundation" (*Hood River News* cited in Ogden, 146). *Mexicanos* were considered an ideal labor force in that they were most likely to return home. There was, however, always that subliminal fear that these inassimilable aliens would choose to stay.

Living quarters, 1944. Oregon State University Archives.

As the presence of *braceros* became a reality in Oregon farming communities in other areas, newspapers played an important role in shaping the attitudes of local residents toward these once unwelcome guest workers. *The Oregon Statesman* reports, on August 25, 1943, "County Agent Nibler said that judging from the experiences of other Oregon communities in which Mexican groups have worked this year, they will prove to be excellent workers and quiet citizens who will have little inclination to visit in nearby cities, though they are free to do so and may occasionally come in to buy clothing or make other small purchases."[9] Obviously the writer walks a fine line here, as he attempts to address the divergent interests of wary citizens and pragmatic businessmen willing to overlook the stigma of foreignness in the interest of commerce.

Noteworthy in the literature of this period is how quickly the press passes from a stance of reluctant acceptance to one of enthusiastic commendation.[10] An August 29, 1943, headline on the first page of *The Oregon Statesman,* in very large print, hails Mexicans as " 'Good Neighbors' Here to Aid Farmers." Ironically playing off the war rhetoric and imagery of the day, the article includes a large photo of the "Foreign Army of Invited Invaders" (photo caption) marching like a troop of trained soldiers down Capitol Street.[11] In general, however, the press given to *braceros* once they had arrived and proved their mettle is quite positive. This may have been influenced by the Emergency Farm Labor Supply Office, which administered certain aspects of the Mexican Farm Labor Program out of the Agricultural Extension Office at Oregon State University, then known as Oregon State College. Part of this agency's job was to mediate between the federally funded program and rural communities in the state and to educate the latter regarding all aspects of the Emergency Farm Labor Supply Program. To this end, it engaged in a carefully orchestrated publicity campaign that included extensive use of flyers, news releases, photographs, radio advertisements, and farm labor radio programs. The following dialogue from a transcription of a radio program gives a clear idea of the approach:

> Beck: *And we should mention another source of labor. We know local sources will supply about 90 percent or more of farm labor requirements in Oregon this year. But 1944 production could not be harvested without the aid of Mexican nationals who have been transported into the state by the war food administration. Harold, I notice you haven't mentioned wanting any of these.*

> Rumbaugh: *I wouldn't be able to make use of them very well, although I understand they do excellent work. However, our community can use local labor better because we do not have enough concentration of jobs at any one time to handle a camp of Mexicans.*

Mr. Beck positively acknowledges the farmer's situation, but does not miss his chance to plug *bracero* labor as an integral and necessary element of the work to be done during this crucial historical moment:

> Beck: *Yes, that's about the lineup as I see it today. We have farm labor offices in every county and farm labor assistants on the job in all counties where early labor is needed. Oregon farmers are doing their utmost to raise the biggest volume possible of the many kinds of war crops that Oregon produces. We hope the emergency farm labor service of the extension service will help out by recruiting every bit of local labor possible where it's needed. Then on top of that we hope to*

> *have enough Mexican labor to put into the twenty or more districts where extra help must be had. We know it's a big job and all of us in Oregon are working together to get it done. (Bracero Files, Oregon State University Archives)*

This was not a spontaneous radio conversation. In fact, the script was written at the Extension Office, and then sent to the office in Washington D.C. for editing and approval before it was broadcast. The carefully worded nature of these broadcasts demonstrates the deliberate and controlled manner in which this federal program used the media to encourage citizens to toe the line—a line clearly drawn by the state department—in this time of war. And toeing that line included swallowing one's biases and accepting foreign workers.

September 16th celebration, ca. 1942–1947. Oregon State University Archives.

During the first year of operation of the *Bracero* Program, Mexican Independence Day celebrations held at the various camps in Woodburn, Dayton, and Salem were amply covered by the press.[12] Articles called attention to decorations of red, white, and green streamers, the Mexican flag raised alongside the U.S. banner, Mexican food, and choruses of "*Viva Mexico*" and "*Viva los Estados Unidos!*" (*The Oregon Statesman*, September 17, 1943, and September 26, 1943).

One news item reported that, in Dayton, "[g]irls from the war food administration office in Portland acted as partners" at the celebration dance (*The Oregon Statesman*, September 19, 1943). Several journalists expressed mild surprise regarding the men's orderly behavior, suggesting that it ran counter to their preconceived notions of how these workers might behave: "According to reports, the men have been satisfactory and diligent workers. They stand field work in the hot sun better than the average Oregonian…. After showers and their night meal, they deport themselves in an orderly manner" (*The Oregon Statesman*, September 26, 1943). Another reporter wrote, "And though they celebrated with song and shopping sprees, the end of the day found not one in any sort of difficulty—a rare record for any group of men bound together simply because of their common interest in work" (*The Oregon Statesman*, September 17, 1943). Máximo Peón, in his memoirs of his stint as a railroad *bracero*, assures us that Mexican nationals, anxious as they were to accumulate dollars to take home, were also reflective human beings, conscious of the role they were playing in helping the United States and its allies win the war: "Among the *braceros* there were a few who were disoriented, but the majority was filled with a notorious enthusiasm for our cousins whom we hoped would win the war" (1966, 46). Peón encourages his compatriots: "What I am trying to say is that we should not go only for the dollar, but rather with the mystical and humanitarian ideal of supporting our country and enthusiastically help increase the production of our neighboring and allied country, of sustaining the war effort and helping the civil population as well as those who do combat on the war front, so they do not experience need because of a labor shortage" (45).

Though some two hundred and fifty workers remained in Oregon through the first winter season (*The Oregon Statesman*, December 24, 1943), most were on their way home by October. About 245 pickers of the filbert crop were bid farewell with a steak dinner topped with "20 gallons of ice cream of which the Mexicans are especially fond" (*The Oregon Statesman*, October 1, 1943). In their pockets they and every other *bracero* to have worked in Oregon would carry a letter of gratitude and greetings to their fellow countrymen signed by Governor Earl Snell and William Schoenfeld, dean and director of agriculture at Oregon State College. The *Independence Enterprise* carried part of this letter in its October 8, 1943, edition:

> *Neighbors of the Republic of Mexico, Greetings: The farmers of the State of Oregon salute you. They are grateful to you and your fellow country men who have labored in the production of the crops of this country .... We hope that your associations here have been congenial and that you have found it as profitable to you as it has been to us.... If similar cooperation in the war effort should seem desirable again, we would consider it a privilege to welcome you back to the state.*

Thus ends the first season of *bracero* labor in Oregon. But it was not to be the last. Eager to bring back a cadre of efficient workers who "completed a three-week harvest in two weeks," the Horst ranch applied for five hundred *braceros* shortly after their departure (*The Oregon Statesman*, November 4, 1943). On Christmas Eve, the paper ran a brief article announcing the return of Mexican workers beginning in mid-February.

And return they did. *The Oregon Statesman* noted that new camps would be established in the Western states in order to help avoid the "racial flare-ups" that had occurred the previous years on farms (March 10, 1944). According to Gamboa, these kinds of racial incidents happened primarily at sites that included Jamaican workers who also came to this country as *braceros*. "To some extent, employers simply resisted the Jamaicans because they were black and their very presence among other workers led to disruptive racial problems and jealousies over jobs" (1990, 64). This observation sheds some light on the position of *mexicanos* in the racialized social pecking order of the state. Jamaicans were openly discriminated against by virtue of their African provenance. *Mexicanos* were still viewed through the socially discriminating prism of color, but the fact that they were "brown" rather than "black" moved them several degrees toward "whiteness" and shielded them somewhat from the racial discrimination reserved for African Americans in Oregon. In an attempt to prepare the community for this new wave of imported workers, a member of the county agricultural committee reported to the Lions Club in Salem that these workers "need to be here again.... They come purely as a wartime answer to a food harvest problem and they were called upon when it became apparent other labor could not save the entire fall harvest" (*The Oregon Statesman*, March 17, 1944). That year there were

Working in hops fields, Polk County, OR, 1943. Oregon State University Archives.

camps in the Willamette, Hood River, and Rogue River valleys, in Central Oregon, and in Klamath and Malheur counties. The largest concentration was at Salem, Independence, and Dayton on hops and prune farms.

Playing poker after work, 1942. Oregon State University Archives.

It is clear that Oregonian women took the responsibility for creating a bridge between Mexican workers and the communities they served. In April 1944, *The Oregon Statesman* reports that a Mrs. George Phalen talked to the Women's Salem Club "about the work done with the Mexico land army which has been here for the past two years. The local people, she said, taught them English and at the same time acquired a speaking knowledge of Spanish" (April 29, 1944). These efforts must have been greatly appreciated by *braceros*, who had little to do when they left the fields. These men were, after all, in a foreign country, the language of which they did not speak. They were far from their families, living with strangers in uninviting camps, eating strange food and, according to Gamboa, "treated worse than Italian and German prisoners of war held in northwestern farm labor camps" (1990, 129). Women in Salem also sponsored musical entertainment provided by local citizens for the men on Thursday evenings. In addition to the workers, a few locals also attended the programs, showing signs of greater acceptability of *braceros*. The American Association of University Women also helped plan the 1944 Independence Day celebration in Salem. They expected three thousand workers to show up at noon, then leave for a larger celebration to be held in Portland (*The Oregon Statesman,* September 14, 1944). The mayor, a state supreme court judge, and a representative from the governor's office attended the Salem celebration. Each worker was once again given a letter of appreciation, written in Spanish, in which the governor extolled Father Hidalgo, who set off the struggle for Mexico's Independence in 1810 (*The Oregon Statesman,* September 15, 1944).

Braceros returned in 1945, but anticipating an end to the war, the message of the Emergency Farm Labor Supply Office was a clear attempt to assuage any fears regarding the possibility of *braceros* remaining in the country: "Just as fast as men and women from the war plants show a desire to take over the jobs the Mexicans are now doing, the Mexicans will be repatriated" (*Farm Labor News Notes,* August 16, 1945, 2).[13] But the growers would much rather hire Mexican nationals. They certainly valued them over Jamaicans, whom they tagged as "troublemakers" (Gamboa 1990); given the historical attitude in the state toward black people, this comes as no surprise. However, it is noteworthy that they also preferred Mexican nationals to migrants of European descent, pointing to some flexibility in Oregonians' notions of racial hierarchies but also to the intersection of race and class. An editorial in *The Oregonian* minces no words regarding this preference among some

Farm workers at their camp, ca. 1942–1947. Oregon State University Archives.

Cafeteria Service, ca. 1942–1947. Oregon State University Archives.

farmers: "Fruit growers of the Hood River Valley, hop growers of the Salem area and other of the state's agricultural community have experienced almost unanimous satisfaction with the southern workers. Some declare their preference of the Mexicans to the jalopy brigade of white migrants that followed the crops in pre-war days." (September 29, 1943). Another article in the *Farm Labor News Notes* makes the following derogatory reference to "jalopy riding" families, as it tactically makes a subtextual case for continued importation of Mexican labor at the end of the war: "Roy Donaldson, farm labor assistant at Hillsboro, reports that contrary to popular opinion two weeks ago, cessation of hostilities abroad so far has not resulted in any influx of job seekers on the Washington County farm front. He says rather, workers seem to have vanished, as some farm labor people forecast. Roads seem to be filled with an endless ribbon of old jalopies bedecked with bedding, vacation equipment and carefree motorists" (August 27, 1945).

The alleged passivity of Mexican workers and their supposed "inherent" capacity for stoop labor had become legendary among growers, and this argument was used frequently to justify hiring them over other workers. Reisler's summary of the arguments of defenders of Mexican labor highlights the essentializing rhetoric that made *mexicanos* the ideal farmworker in the minds of growers: "Not only did the Mexican's mental outlook attune him to outdoor work, but his physical attributes allowed him to be a perfect stoop laborer. Because the Mexican was small in size, agile, and wiry, growers explained, his ability in the fruit, vegetable, sugar beet, and cotton fields far excelled that of the white man" (1976, 138). The fact that the growers could pay

Mexican workers lower wages than Americans was perhaps a more realistic motive for this preference, as was the fact that migrant workers of European descent had options not available to Mexican workers and hence they were more likely to abandon the fields when better job opportunities arose. The writer of the piece cited above from *The Oregonian* was right on mark in stating: "Consideration there, however, appears to be that the southerners, who are on loan from the Mexican government to ours, stay put, whereas the native transients are here today and gone tomorrow" (September 29, 1943).

Whatever the incentive for employers, local communities did not appreciate the hiring of Mexicans over American workers, particularly as wartime industry jobs dried up and workers returned to their rural communities, only to encounter job displacement. Gamboa documents the response to one such incident: "At the Dayton Farm Labor Camp in Oregon, nineteen Anglo families circulated a petition urging that Mexican contract workers be excluded from the camp on the grounds that whites remained unemployed while farmers hired the *braceros*" (1990, 64). The Emergency Farm Labor Supply Office, however, made every effort to assure that the crops got picked by domestic workers and volunteers whenever possible. In 1945, for example, one hundred patients at the U.S. Naval Hospital at Corvallis worked as hay hands in Benton and Polk counties, and four hundred G.I.s from Camp Adair gave up their Independence Day furlough to work at a hops farm in the area. Throughout Oregon, thousands of elementary school children helped pick crops as "Victory Farm Volunteers." In Milton Freewater, forty-five stores and businesses closed for several days so clerks and stenographers could work on farms; one ninety-year-old joined them. When thirteen hundred expected Mexican nationals did not show up because the Mexican government put a hold on recruitment for a week, prisoners of war were used to replace them[14] (*Farm Labor New Notes*, July 23, 1945; July 30, 1945; August 6, 1945; September 13, 1945).

Braceros returned to Oregon in 1946 and 1947. Gamboa (1993) writes that over fifteen hundred Mexican nationals brought their *brazos* (arms) to do contractual farm labor in Oregon between 1943 and 1947. During their stint in the state, they "thinned 25 percent and harvested 40 percent of the sugar beets, thinned 50 percent and picked 10 percent of the apples, and thinned 60 percent and picked 30 percent of the pear crop. They also harvested 25 percent of the asparagus, 20 percent of the onion crop, 60 percent of the cucumbers, and 60 percent of the peas" (57).

Their productivity should not, however, obfuscate the fact that this work did not always get done without a good measure of conflict and resistance by *braceros*. Demonstrating a strong sense of agency, despite constraining conditions, they frequently engaged in strikes and work stoppages to protest ill treatment, bad food, low wages, and other forms of exploitation. No sooner had they arrived in Oregon in 1943 than a platoon of *braceros* in Medford staged a work stoppage to protest the fact that they were being paid by the box instead of by the hour. The conflict was resolved when "[t]he growers then agreed to pay them 75 cents an hour instead of 8 and 10 cents a box" (*The Oregon Statesman*, August 13, 1943). Without the contractual protections insisted upon by the Mexican government, such actions would not have been possible.[15]

While the *Bracero* Program was extended at the national level until 1965, Gamboa (1990) says that Oregon growers ceased to employ *braceros* after 1948. There is evidence, however, that *braceros* were indeed brought to Oregon in 1952, when 1,014 picked crops in Umatilla and Jackson counties and in Hood River and Medford (*The Oregonian*, May 17, 1953). And in 1958 *braceros* were again brought to Medford to harvest the pear crop (Oregon Assembly Interim Committee on Migrant Labor 1958). Gamboa (1990) asserts that administrative changes in the *bracero* program, introduced in 1948, accounted for the reluctance of growers to continue their dependence on imported workers. Moreover, he found that Northwest growers were less than pleased with the assertive actions and numerous work stoppages of *braceros*. Particularly unsettling was the fact that growers would now have to bear the full cost of transporting workers from the interior of Mexico (Gamboa 1990; Loprinzi 1991). The high cost of transportation for so great a distance encouraged growers in Oregon to begin to look for a new source of labor. The *braceros'* work ethic, their low maintenance, their social manners, and their overall effectiveness endeared them to Oregon growers. Consequently, even though they refrained from participating formally in the government-sanctioned guest-worker program after the war, Oregon growers would seek other methods for bringing Mexican workers to the fertile valleys of Oregon, as we shall see in Chapter 2.

The Bracero *Legacy*

In a personal diary kept by an undocumented immigrant from Oaxaca, its author muses:

> *It didn't take a lot of thinking for me to decide to make this trip. It was a matter of following the tradition of the village. One could even say that we're a village of wetbacks. A lot of people, nearly the majority, have gone, come back, and returned to the country to the north; almost all of them have held in their fingers the famous green bills that have jokingly been called "green cards"—immigrant cards—for generations. For several decades Macuiltianguis—that's*

*the name of my village—has been an emigrant village, and our people
have spread out like the roots of a tree under the earth, looking for
sustenance (Pérez 1991, 12).*

These words vividly bear testimony to a legacy bequeathed to future
generations in Mexico by the millions of men who came to the United States
as contract workers between 1942 and 1964.[16] This is no less true for Oregon
than it is for other areas that employed *braceros*. Beyond the desire among
Mexican nationals to follow in the footsteps of their *bracero* fathers, the
Bracero Program created a massive data bank that played no small role in
encouraging migration to the United States. Never formalized, published, or
appropriated by the government of Mexico or the United States, information
regarding the who, where, what, and when pertinent to migrating north was
stored in the vaults of personal experience and passed on by word of mouth
to family, *compadres* (extended kin), friends, and *paisanos* (members of
one's village). The social networks through which this capital was, and still is,
distributed were dense, prolific, and beneficial, because "each time a *bracero*
departed, social capital was created among his circle of friends and relatives,
and that social capital in turn reduced the costs and risks of their own
international movement and increased their access to U.S. jobs" (Massey et
al. 2002, 42). *What is the climate in Oregon? What is the attitude of natives*

Workers playing guitars, 1942. Oregon State University Archives.

toward Mexicans? What are the expectations of employers? How do work habits in the United States differ from those in Mexico? How does one make a phone call? Which crops provide the best wages? Which crops should one avoid if possible? What would life be like for one's family in Oregon? Answers to these questions make up the information stored in the wealthy folk data bank that has provided the social capital, distributed through dense social networks, crucial to successful immigration during the last half century, and which has been crucial in bringing *mexicanos* to Oregon.

---

1. One such scholar, Robert Foerster, a professor of economics at Princeton University, was commissioned by the Secretary of Labor to issue a report on this question. In his study, Foerster (1925) concluded that in the interest of maintaining the well-being of American citizens, admission should be denied to dubious races that for several generations would reproduce prolifically, thus affecting the future stock of the nation. The designers of the Treaty of Guadalupe Hidalgo (1848) had agreed that Mexicans would henceforth be registered as whites—for purposes of bringing Mexicans conquered in the war of 1846 into a nation that extended full civil rights only to white individuals—but the reality of their *mestizo* heritage did not escape eugenicists like Foerster; and it was, the latter argued, the Indian portion of their heritage that made them inferior to whites.

2. Acuña argues that Mexicans were in fact demonstrating permanency, and he cites the increasing rate of home ownership as indicative of this trend: "The 1930 census showed that 18.6 percent of Mexicans in L.A. owned homes.... Home ownership did not infer moving up the economic ladder, but it suggested a state of permanency" (2004, 205).

3. This lack of attention notwithstanding, David Weber (1998) calls attention to a Spanish galleon that, in 1707, crashed at Nehalem Beach, just south of the mouth of the Columbia River, leaving sixty tons of beeswax deposited in coastal waters. The ship's castaways, Weber writes, remained among the native people in the area long enough to leave descendants.

4. A specific count of Mexicans for 1930 is accessible because the U.S. Government, for the first and only time, included a "Mexican" category in the census. Prior to this, native-born Mexican Americans would not have been registered as a separate race, given that since the signing of the Treaty of Guadalupe Hidalgo in 1848 they were treated as Caucasians. The practice of counting them as a separate category was discontinued after the 1930 census because of the opposition of Mexican American groups, who feared that counting them as a separate racial group would place them in an inferior social position similar to that of African Americans (see Foley 1997).

5. In Oregon, the primary employing war industries included ports of embarkation, ship-building yards, and aluminum plants.

6. In his recent work on Mexican immigrant labor in the Pacific Northwest, Jerry García (2005, Mexican and Japanese...) writes that railroad camps throughout the Northwest employed *braceros* as maintenance workers. However, the administration of the railroad program was separate from the farm-labor program, and virtually no attention is given to this facet of the war guest worker program in Oregon's newspapers.

7. Wayne Rasmussen addresses this issue in his 1951 history of the Emergency Farm Labor Supply Program: "Almost immediately after the Commanding General of the Western Defense Command had announced that all people of Japanese descent would be evacuated from the West Coast, large-scale agricultural interests, particularly sugar-beet growers in the Rocky Mountain United States, requested that the evacuees be made available for work in the beet fields and in other season agricultural work" (101).

8. Gamboa (1990) claims that the screening process was rigorous and "ensured that only able, experienced, and healthy individuals received contracts" (52).

9. One of the provisions of the labor contract stipulated that workers would be free to purchase personal items wherever they chose. The Mexican government, no doubt, insisted on this provision in order to avoid the kinds of abuses practiced by hacienda *tiendas de raya* [company stores] with which it was too familiar.

10. Gamboa points out the irony implicit in the high praise given to Mexican workers, even as the latter were creating all manner of problems for their employers through frequent work stoppages and "bootlegging." The latter term was used to refer to the practice of taking side jobs at farms that had no contract labor; these jobs were attractive because they paid cash at the end of the day. "Skipping," or deserting their contractual positions, was another common practice that resulted from worker dissatisfaction with food, housing, low wages, and ill treatment by employers. Gamboa states that it is "estimated that 10 percent of all *braceros* abandoned contracts" (1990, 68).

11. The newspaper also carries a photo of a *bracero* playing the guitar as one of his companions reads a girlie magazine titled *Burlesk*. Given that racialized discourse tends to project men of color as lascivious characters from whom women of the dominant culture must be protected, inclusion of this photo suggests to this reader some residual ambivalence regarding Oregon's "good neighbors."

12. These celebrations were sponsored by the Emergency Farm Labor Supply Office and were planned and carried out in conjunction with residents and leaders of various white communities (Oregon Farm Labor Report 1943, Oregon State

University Archives). The costs for these celebrations, however, were borne primarily by the workers themselves, who were charged an entrance fee of one to three dollars (Gamboa 1990).

13. The issue of hiring Mexicans over locals had already been dealt with in Oregon in 1944 when the cannery workers' union opposed the hiring of Mexicans in canneries. "'Not because of opposition to Mexicans as fellow workers would objections be raised,' representatives of the union declared, but 'because we are convinced that there is enough labor right here to handle the job if the labor in turn, is handled correctly'" (*The Oregon Statesman*, July 28, 1944). In Washington and Idaho, the hiring of *braceros* over locals in canning companies resulted in open protests by the affected communities (Gamboa 1990).

14. In response to alleged claims of discrimination, particularly in Texas, the Mexican government on numerous occasions threatened to end or curb the program. Reverberations of problems at the Texas border apparently were being felt in Oregon, as the Mexican government threatened to cut back the total number of *braceros* allowed to come to this country if Texas did not take care of its problem.

15. It is important to note that the Mexican government was not satisfied with just writing worker protections pertaining to salary, food, housing, etc. into the contract, but it also helped enforce them through their consulate offices in the United States. For further discussion on this topic, see Gamboa 1996. González and Fernández (2003), however, argue that the Mexican government exploited rather than protected *braceros*.

16. Craig (1971) states that 4,216,754 contracts were issued. *Braceros* were eligible for contract renewal, so this figure may not represent the net number of individuals who participated. It does, however, give us an idea of the scope of the program.

Chapter 2

Sojourners and Settlers: Tejanos *and* Mexicanos *in Oregon in the Mid-Twentieth Century*[1]

In the 1950s, the *Bracero* Program and its attendant albatross, illegal immigration, continued to come under severe scrutiny from various fronts. The press played an especially important role in shaping negative public opinion regarding the "invasion of illegal hordes streaming in from Mexico" (García 1980, 151).

Mounting pressure regarding illegal immigration led Congress, in 1952, to pass Public Law 283, which made it a felony to import or harbor illegal aliens (Craig 1971). Employers, however, were exempt from the law! In her assessment of this period, Calavita (1992) notes that the detailed exposé *What Price Wetbacks*, published in 1953 by the American G.I. Forum of Texas (an association of Mexican-American World War II veterans)[2] and Texas State Federation of Labor, and the vitriolic Cold War rhetoric of McCarthyism influenced significantly the national agenda regarding undocumented

Undocumented Mexican immigrants being searched by U.S. Border Patrol, LA Times, *May 2, 1950. University of California, UCLA Library.*

immigration. These pressures led to the drastic actions taken in 1954 when "the Border Patrol launched the greatest maximum peacetime offense against a highly exploited, unorganized and unstructured 'invading force' of Mexican migrants" (Samora 1971, 52). Under the leadership of General Joseph May Swing, Operation Wetback, as the campaign was called, was launched. This campaign pulled together federal, state, county, and municipal authorities, the

Illegal immigrants being deported, May 1953. Oregon Historical Society.

FBI, and the Army and Navy, employing aircraft, watercraft, automobiles, radio units, and special task forces to round up and deport undocumented immigrants first in California and Arizona, then in Texas and the heartland (Samora 1971). Through its militarization of the border and deployment of massive round-ups and mop-ups, Operation Wetback was successful in reducing substantially the number of illegal workers, especially along the border (Calavita 1992) and the number of apprehensions dropped from 1,075,168 in 1954 to 30,196 in 1959. In the process, however, Operation Wetback strained the precarious relationship between Mexican Americans and their host society, and it allowed sectors of U.S. society to dehumanize undocumented workers by "shroud[ing] them with names and labels that reeked of derision, racism, and denigration" (García 1985, 231). While the Department of Labor took a strong stance against illegal immigration, it was not uncommon for the Immigration and Naturalization Service to raid a field, to take the arrested workers across the border, and deliver them to the Department of Labor, which, as the on-the-ground management arm of the *bracero* program, immediately processed them as now-legal *braceros* and sent them back to the very fields where they had originally been apprehended (Massey et al. 2002). This procedure meant that workers who had been queuing up to enter as legal workers were bumped in favor of workers who had transgressed the very policies shored up by immigration policy. While we have found scant evidence of the deployment of Operation Wetback strategies in Oregon, we do know that undocumented workers supplied a good portion of the workforce in agriculture in this state, as they did in the Southwest and Midwest; an article in the *Oregonian* points to this practice: "In addition to the Mexicans brought into this country legally, Oregon gets its share of the illegal hordes of wetbacks who sneak across the border to collect the American dollars U.S. farmers are glad to pay them" (May 17, 1953).

This non-authorized migration from Mexico, which had run parallel to contractual labor migration during the 1940s, had by the 1950s begun to squeeze Mexican Americans in Texas, known amongst themselves as *tejanos*, out of farm labor in the Lower Rio Grande Valley (Fuller 1953). Furthermore, land consolidation, irrigation, and mechanization resulted in a significant reduction of jobs in that area (Wells 1976; Loprinzi 1991). The results were to have an enormous impact on Oregon, to which *tejanos*, unable to find work

in Texas, gradually made their way. Not unlike *braceros* before them, this group of workers arrived to cultivate and harvest and they left when the season was over, creating few wrinkles in the social fabric of the state (though in due time they began to settle out in Oregon). These *tejano* migrants were joined by Mexican American workers from other Southwestern

Mexican workers crushed by crowds at the U.S.-Mexico border, Mexicali, Feb. 2, 1954. University of California, UCLA Library.

states, and by former *braceros* who, although their formal contract program had ended, continued to come without authorization to places they had visited as contract workers. "In this sense, the *bracero* program never really ended, it simply went underground" (Cornelius 1978, 18).

From Sojourners to Settlers, 1950-1986

Agribusiness, Oregon's leading industry (including nurseries), generated more than one billion dollars in 2000. The nursery industry alone had a gross income of $642 million. Given this tremendous economic power base, it stands to reason that these industries would also have significant political clout in the state. In this regard we find persuasive Robert Dash's assertion: "The 'rightful' claim to an adequate labor force resonates particularly with Willamette Valley growers because of the labor-intensive nature of their agriculture. Not surprisingly, therefore, Willamette Valley growers have been militantly protective of the labor supply and control system that has historically serviced their needs" (1996, 13). This militancy repeatedly has been employed by growers to maneuver the legislative process in such a way as to allow them to "maintain a surplus labor market to keep wages low and prevent unionism, to secure government aid, to keep unwanted laws from being passed while keeping the enforcement of existing restrictions lax"(Loprinzi 1991). The entrenched position of Oregon agriculturalists was aided by the supply factor, as Slatta observes: "Although growers realized the importance of the migrant to the harvest, little was done to upgrade living conditions, regulate wages, or provide for the schooling of children because of the relative surplus of migrant labor" (1975, 329).

Perhaps the strongest example of agribusiness's political clout was demonstrated in 1961, when the industry persuaded the Oregon legislature to pass a law which "prohibited the picketing of farms which produced perishable agriculture crops while such crops were being harvested (unless the picket had been a regular employee in the farm immediately prior to beginning of picket)" (Dash 1996, 12). Arguing in favor of extending this law in 1963, farmer Kenneth Lafont affirmed: "We are concerned that a 'manufactured' dispute and 'stranger' picketing might result from outside sources instead of our normal work force" (*The Oregonian*, April 1, 1963). Furthermore, growers have controlled labor through the implementation of very deliberate strategies and tactics that go beyond the law-making process. As discussed in Chapter 1, the decision by growers in Oregon to diminish their reliance on the *Bracero* Program in 1948 stands as an early instance of the unbending will of Oregon agribusiness to get and keep its labor on its own terms.[3] In the post-*bracero* period, concerted recruitment practices that took labor contractors to economically depressed areas of Mexico and the Southwest, together with the tight operation of income-generating labor camps, formed the foundation of a highly structured process that guaranteed workers during the peak season, and encouraged their return on a yearly basis (Dash 1996). A report issued by the Oregon Bureau of Labor in 1958 found that there were four major contractors operating in Oregon who together handled 5,750 workers. In addition, there were nine lesser contractors who handled 1,735 workers (6). Suggesting that contractor practices were coercive, the words of teacher Connie García, whose migrant family settled in Independence in 1961, give us an idea of the tactics employed by contractors to ensure that workers completed the job:

> *We came to Horst Ranch and moved into the main labor camp. At that time, Horst Ranch had several labor campsites, but the main one was quite large. It had two community baths and outhouses, a "community center," a small park, and even a restaurant. We were*

assigned a section. Each family worked a couple of acres of asparagus, and we were paid a percentage of what that piece produced. Sharecropping is what it was. Another percentage was withheld until the season was over. If we didn't stay to finish the season, we didn't get the "bonus," as it was called (Latino Oral History Project).

The contracting process was crucial to the management of this exploitative labor system. In many cases the contractors, or their subcontractors, were themselves *mexicanos* from the Rio Grande Valley in Texas.[4] Their knowledge of the people and their social conditions gave the subcontractors certain advantages in selecting from the migratory labor pool. This practice is confirmed by Elena Peña, who came to Oregon with her parents in the 1960s and whom we interviewed in her home in Independence; she told us, "[T]hey always looked for [the] hardest-working families" (interview with Gonzales-Berry, 2004).

An informative record of a contractor's work is found in the testimony of Julián Ruiz, one of the first *tejano* contractors in the Willamette Valley:

Thereafter, every year I signed up other area farmers. I initially ran four small labor camps but this increased. Two of the largest camps that I ran had thirty to thirty-five cabins. Each of the cabins house a family of five or six. "El campo verde," so named because it was painted green, was one of the larger camps I operated outside of Woodburn. As I gained more farming contracts, the number of workers I contracted also increased. My contracting went beyond San Pablo and even into Independence, Brooks, Gervais, and Woodburn. In the beginning, there weren't any legal restrictions to be a labor contractor. During the early 1950s you simply went about your business. It wasn't until the early 1960s that we started feeling the pressure in Oregon to get a state contractor's license (Maldonado 2005, 221-22).

Contracted groups of families called crews were transported in large trucks with canvas-covered beds and delivered as a cohort to various sites along the migrant trail. A poignant memory for Elena Peña regarding her family's first trip was spending the entire night wrestling blankets from fellow travelers as they slept piled together in the back of the truck. In some cases contractors delivered the workers to farmers but did not act as actual employers. In other cases farmers paid contractors a lump sum for all aspects of the labor provided by migrant workers, and contractors, acting as employers, were responsible for paying out wages and taking care of all paperwork and record keeping. In the former case, employers paid contractors a per-head fee for each migrant delivered as well as an additional contractor fee from the workers' wages, which was deducted at the rate of five to eleven cents per hour. This fee was distributed among the contractor, any subcontractors, and crew leaders. Transportation fees were also deducted from the workers' wages, as were rental fees. The average weekly earnings for a family were $84 and expenses amounted to $69. At the end of a seven-and-a-half-month season, a fortunate family would return to Texas with $235 to sustain them for the remaining three and a half months of the year (Oregon Bureau of Labor 1958, 9-10). Once they arrived at a work camp, the contractors frequently made arrangements for credit accounts for the workers with local store and tavern owners, from whom they collected a cut (Oregon Legislative Assembly Interim Committee 1958). Some contractors lent money to workers at high interest rates and made additional money by "dabbl[ing] in markets of prostitution, drugs and gambling" (Loprinzi 1991, 40). This particular finding by the Bureau of Labor in its 1958 preliminary report apparently created quite a flap in the state. The Bureau's 1959 report addresses this issue:

> *In pursuing the regular survey of farm labor contractors and crew leaders, we came across a beneath-the-surface situation involving marijuana peddling, prostitution, and other things which make better headlines than the vast amount of statistical information which was really our major contribution... . The unfortunate effect, of course, was that it created a defense psychology on the part of the rural residents and farmers who quite rightly felt innocent of the activities described on the front pages of the papers (Current and Infante 1959, 161-62).*

The shared vicissitudes of migrant life had a profound bonding effect on families. This in turn benefited contractors upon whom employers could count to deliver a quota of workers at the opportune moment. Given that their capacity for work was their only possession, migrant families frequently felt beholden to the contractor for finding them jobs, and they showed their loyalty by joining his labor caravan year after year (Maldonado 2005). Because many did not have access to private modes of transportation, opportunities for breaking away from this pattern were scarce. The use of family cohorts guaranteed substantial numbers of workers and facilitated bookkeeping and payment, as all wages were tendered to the head of the family. More important, this practice functioned as a control mechanism. A man obligated to shelter and feed a family—which found itself in an unfamiliar environment far from the usual support networks and unable to speak English—was less likely to engage in disruptive labor actions or, equally important, to break away from the migrant stream. Furthermore, family crews were delivered yearly to the same farms, thereby creating a sense of connection and perhaps even reciprocal obligation on the part of farmworkers. Findings by Wells in Wisconsin are instructive in this regard. She states that those who were able to leave the migrant stream were workers who did not "regularize ties with particular growers. Such bonds, usually reinforced by personalistic relations, provided a measure of economic security within the migratory circuit" (1976, 85).

A not insignificant component of the contracting system seems to have been a rumor mill that functioned as an alluring siren call. It was this mill that fed the dreams of the Leos family when they came to Independence in 1954:

> *Word came from other farmworkers that they were hiring plenty of workers up in Oregon in some place called the Willamette Valley. From what they were told, it sounded something like a paradise. The weather was always mild and never too hot, the landowners paid more, and there were plenty of opportunities for housing, and basically the water flowed like wine. It was all too good to be true. And when they got there they found it was. The employers didn't pay any more, it was often too cold and rainy for a human to be working outside, and there weren't that many more jobs. It was all just a rumor. But they decided to stay anyway since they were already there. There, they were given less than good housing for a price of fifteen dollars a month. All nine of them lived there and when each child got old enough to work, they would. This age was about five or six years old. (Latino Oral History Project).*

The son of Hipólito García reports that his father's family had a similar experience when they decided to make the move from Texas to Independence in the early '60s. In this case, however, the rumor had the ring of promise, for it was made by the man they trusted and to whom they were about to turn over their lives:

> *[O]ne of the reasons they decided to move to Oregon was because they were told, by a contractor, that with all the children that my grandfather had, they would be able to make a lot of money. They were told that they would most likely make enough money to survive in Oregon and also make enough to return to Texas for the next crop season.... When they first arrived in Independence they stayed in Green Villa Farms and picked asparagus and also irrigated the crops. When they were finished picking those crops they went to another camp that same year in Independence called the Long Ranch where they picked pole beans. When the winter came his family realized they did not have enough money to return to Texas. They realized*

that what the contractor had told them wasn't true. (Latino Oral History Project).

Apparently this practice was not uncommon. In 1978, migrants brought a class-action suit against two brothers, *mexicano* contractors, charging them with "fraud, false advertising, and breach of contract and minimum wage violations" (Loprinzi 1991, 58). The brothers had offered workers high wages, quality housing with hot water, televisions, recreation facilities, and more perks, all of which proved to be false promises. Actions such as these highlight the vulnerability of migrant workers not only to discrimination from members of the mainstream but also to exploitation by their own kind.

Conditions affecting the lives of migrant workers had become a priority item on the national agenda in 1950 when President Harry Truman, in response to pressure from labor unions, the NAACP, and numerous religious and social reform groups, formed the Commission on Migratory Labor. In its report to the President in 1951, the commission found that migrant families in Colorado were making an average wage of $1,424 per year, and this included the work tendered by women and children of the family. The report stressed that migrant workers enjoyed none of the protections—such as the right to organize, unemployment insurance, minimum wage—guaranteed to other workers in the United States (cited in Fuller 1953). Moreover, they were subject to all manner of calamities as reported by Fuller, who cites newspaper headlines to make his point: "A Truckload Of Workers Smashes Up And Many Are Killed; An Ex-Chicken Coop Catches Fire And Migrants Living In It Are Burned To Death; Laborers Of Migrant Families Are Reported To Have Died From Malnutrition And Neglect" (Fuller 1953, 11).[5] In short, the commission found that the lives of migrants were governed by "uncertainty, insecurity, poverty and filth" (Fuller 1953, 11).

The new spirit of migrant labor reform that overtook the United States in the 1950s significantly affected Oregon, with its heavy dependency on migrant farm labor.[6] This is not to say that migrant workers had been completely neglected before that date. The Oregon State Council of Churches had been active ministering to migrants as early as the 1940s (Gamboa 1995b). However, the Council did not specifically call attention to *mexicanos* until 1957 when it referred, in its annual report, to "Spanish Speaking" clients. In its 1959 report, reference is made to "Texas Mexican" migrants in Eastern Oregon. Activities designed specifically for these migrants included English lessons, sewing, home-nursing classes for adults, Spanish-language radio programs, recreational activities, and summer church camps for children. In 1958, the Council was joined by the Oregon College of Education in providing summer school programs for migrant children at various camps in the Willamette Valley (*Independence Enterprise*, July 3, 1958). The following year, the legislature provided funding to continue these summer school programs. In 1961, additional funding was allocated for permanent programming to accommodate migrant children during the regular school year. A year later, *The Oregonian* reported that "Oregon was one of a very few states that offer special school opportunities to migrant children" (July 23, 1962). The Migrant Education Program is still in existence today and was cited in a recent study as an important factor in the achievement of sons and daughters of immigrants in Oregon (Gonzales-Berry, Mendoza, Plaza 2006-07).

Newspaper coverage reveals that many of the children attending summer school were *mexicanos*. Regarding the role of migrant summer school, *The Oregonian* reported: "They are, in a secular sense, out to save the souls of these children by developing in them a desire for learning some positive attitudes toward the world that lies outside migrant camps and a sense of belonging in this outer world" (May 23, 1962). The mission of the Council of Churches is summed up in the words of a ministry leader who told an *Oregon Journal* reporter, "The migrant needs a faith in God that gives meaning to life, guidance of ethical standards, and warmth of friendship and belonging" (July 31, 1963). The Council's focus on spiritual and social salvation notwithstanding, the Council became a strong political voice in advocating for social change for migrant workers. Among its major accomplishments was its success in lobbying the state legislature for the establishment of an Interim Committee on Migrant Affairs and for the enactment of legislation beneficial to migrant workers. In its twenty-fifth-year anniversary report, the Council lauds its own efforts and those of the United Church Women in stimulating "active support for the passing of the bills" (Oregon Council of Churches 1960, n.p.). Loprinzi, perhaps undervaluing this level of political work by the Council of Churches, reports that in later years Christian activists "moved from part-time charity to direct and constant involvement at the community level... . These later activists sought to change migrant conditions, desiring to help more than the spiritual needs of the migrants to which the Migrant Ministry of the 1950s and 1960s had confined itself" (1991, 102).

The State Council's sister organization in Portland, the Greater Portland Council of Churches, turned its attention to social action in matters related to civil rights of urban African Americans living in Portland in the '60s. Eventually, however, it too turned its attention to farmworker issues by joining the United Farm Workers grape strike and boycott, thereby trying to influence social action on behalf of Oregon's *mexicano* community.[7] As might be expected, this action was met with resistance and internal conflict. The freedom of church organizations to advocate for social change is often curbed by conservative constituents, who not only support the preservation of existing social hierarchies, but who also provide a good deal of financial support to churches. Members of the business community strongly resisted the GPCC's involvement in the grape boycott because, as Nelson reports, "numerous local lay members of churches which belonged to the GPCC had large invested interests in the supermarket being picketed and hurt by the Boycott. Because the pragmatic intensity of the issue *directly* affected their economic well-being, many of its own members vigorously questioned the GPCC's stand" (1974, 136). The limits of mainstream organizations in achieving radical social change are indeed apparent in this case.

The Catholic Archdiocese also became involved in ministering unto the spiritual needs of *mexicanos* in Oregon, the majority of whom were Catholic. In 1952, in an action predating a mandate from the Vatican to have Mexican priests accompany *braceros* to the United States in an effort to avert the danger of Protestant proselytism (Craig 1971), the Oregon Diocese recruited its first priest from Mexico, Father Ernesto Bravo (Loprinzi 1991; Gamboa 1995b). The Church recruited additional priests from Mexico who soon became involved in "providing culturally relevant masses, sacraments, and spiritual retreats to Mexican Americans in the Willamette Valley. In this way, Catholic parishes like St. Luke's in Woodburn started to emerge as the hub of the growing Mexican-American community" (Gamboa 1995b, 48). The Catholic Migrant Ministry Office, established in 1955, however, might have been a bit reluctant to advocate for migrant workers and risk antagonizing farmers, many of whom were members of the Church and contributors to its coffers. Loprinzi suggests this possibility in her assessment of the mission of the Migrant Ministry in its early years: "In their 1955 report the Migrant Ministry clarified its position, documenting that their members were only there to conduct research and provide religious services, not change conditions" (1991, 104). Eventually, as the Church became transformed by the liberal reforms of Vatican II, and its clergy increasingly influenced by the new ideas of Latin American Liberation Theology,[8] it was to become a catalyst for political activism among settled-out *mexicanos* and migrant farmworkers.

At this time, several government-sponsored agencies also began to work on migrant labor reform issues in Oregon. In response to pressure from the Oregon Council of Churches and the Oregon State Bureau of Labor, the legislative assembly created a Legislative Interim Committee on Migratory Labor in 1957. Subsequently, Governor Robert Holmes created an Oregon Interagency Committee on Migratory Labor.[9] These two groups generated three reports between 1958 and 1959, one of which was a substantive summary of a statewide, in-depth survey commissioned by the Bureau of Labor and carried out by three hundred volunteers whose services were coordinated by the Oregon Council of Churches, the Portland Archdiocese of the Roman Catholic Church, Willamette University Sociology Department, Mount Angel Seminary, and the Latin American Club. The project sampled growers, contractors and crew leaders, Anglo and "Spanish-American" [10] migrant workers, community members, and agency personnel. The final report covered a broad range of topics, including working and living conditions, wages, education, health, lifestyle, recruitment and contracting practices, transportation, migrant morale and morals, community attitudes toward migrants, the question of Mexican nationals, and vice. The reports included recommendations that resulted in passage of four legislative bills covering labor contracting, worker transportation, housing standards, and an education pilot program for migrant children. The Bureau of Labor's assessment of their work follows:

> *There is no question that Oregon has passed the most comprehensive and balanced and studied legislative program for the welfare of migrants ever enacted by any state at one time.... Lest Oregon sound like a Utopia for migrants, let it be said that many problems remain unsolved and that even the problems for which there now seems to be some hope of solution will require attention year-in and year-out for the foreseeable future (Current and Infante 1959, 162-63).*

This relatively optimistic view notwithstanding, our reading of the reports, even those that reveal a marked empathy for migrant workers, suggests that a preponderance of the blame for substandard labor and living conditions is laid at the feet of contractors, thereby tending to mitigate grower responsibility.

Migrant reform also arrived in the field of health, and rightly so, as health problems besieged migrant workers, who more often than not had little choice but to accept death. Mary Theil, whose family moved to Eastern Oregon in the 1930s, recalls:

> *If you got sick, you died if it was a disease that would take your life. In fact, we lost three that way. They got sick and all you did was try to take care of them the best you could. We did go to a doctor. The doctors would tell you if you didn't have the money, they wouldn't take you. We did take a baby to a doctor with measles, and my mother didn't know how to bring the fever down and things of that nature, and the doctor turned her away. So she brought the baby back and it died that night (Gamboa and Baun 1995, 135).*

In 1963 the Migrant Health Act provided federal funds to establish migrant health programs throughout the country. The Oregon Migrant Health Project, funded under this act, had as its mission to provide diagnosis and treatment services to migrant workers and their families and also to oversee sanitation in the camps. Nurses tending to migrant workers throughout Oregon found that families suffered from skin infections, bedbug and lice infestations, and diarrhea. These conditions were exacerbated by substandard conditions in worker camps: filthy toilet and shower facilities, lack of drainage, infested mattresses, polluted drinking water, and lack of refrigeration. In field after field, inspectors found only one drinking cup provided for workers, thus contributing to the spread of infectious diseases (Oregon State Board of Health 1971). One positive outcome of this project was that, on occasion, inspectors were successful in shutting down substandard labor camps. Loprinzi's assessment of the Migrant Health Project, upon its cancellation in 1970, was that it was "the best program that had thus far existed for migrants" (1991, 74). This speaks well for the program, as Loprinzi's sense of government, and especially of politicians' actions, is that they talked the talk, but when it came time to act, they tended to bend before the powerful farm lobbies.

Under the auspices of the Oregon Migrant Health Project, David Laing, a graduate student in English at the University of Oregon, carried out a research project and wrote a series of articles for the local press in which he summarized his findings. Laing reported that one migrant stream that came to Oregon each summer began in Texas, moved through New Mexico, Arizona, and the Central Valley of California into the Willamette Valley, and on to Washington. There was also a stream that moved directly from Texas to Malheur County, and a smaller stream that came from Mexico (*Independence Enterprise*, July 16, 1964). In the fourth article of the series, titled "Rugged Camp Living Causes Vicious Circle," Laing does not dwell on the conditions of labor camps, except to say: "Each year the better part of 2,500 people lead a miserable existence in Polk country. While here their standard of living is far below that of permanent residents." He does, however, pose the question, "Why?" Laing tells the reader that from the grower's perspective there are several reasons: "He doesn't have the money. He doesn't have the time. He doesn't see why he should improve his camp, in view of the relatively short time it is occupied." Laing's own conclusions are: "Most growers are simply not concerned. They are not motivated to come to the rescue of a group of people from whom society needs, but cannot seem to find room for. They take refuge in the old myth which claims that every individual can make his way, no matter what the odds are against him."[11] While growers will not of their own accord solve the problem, workers themselves, Laing believes, are passive and unwilling to do anything for themselves. Hence they are trapped in a vicious cycle (*Independence Enterprise,* August 6, 1964). This assessment of migrant workers is refuted by scholars who have found instead that migrant workers are highly motivated, ambitious risk-takers seeking "to build better lives for themselves and their children" (Wells 1976, 272).

The work of these religious and state-sponsored agencies was certainly important in addressing the conditions that affected the daily lives of *mexicano* migrants, many of whom were choosing to settle out in various communities across Oregon. While agency reports and newspaper coverage give the contemporary reader an excellent overview of the work of these organizations and the conditions they encountered, the recollections of early *mexicano* settlers in the Willamette Valley speak powerfully regarding those conditions and the strategies employed by families to confront them, as they made the transition from the migrant stream to permanent residency during the fifties and sixties.

In one such recollection, Elena Peña recalls a journey from Texas to Oregon in the 1960s, and how everyone rushed for mattresses as families were unloaded at one labor camp, only to find them crawling with bedbugs. Her parents refused to allow their children to sleep on the infested mattresses, so they spent the night in their truck. The next day, her father negotiated with their employer to allow them and another family to camp out by the river. They did so for a week, sleeping in their truck and in a tent. At the end of the week, the work at that farm was completed and the two families moved on to another crop. Peña stresses that having their own vehicle gave her family a measure of independence as well as additional money, because now they did not have to give the contractor a cut of their wages.[12] Their independence also facilitated the process of settling out in a shorter period of time. In 1967, just five years after arriving in Independence, Peña's parents, Monserrat and Antonia Vásquez, bought a small house on an acre of property. They still live in that house, and Elena and her husband Raul Peña have constructed their home next door to the original property purchased by her parents four decades ago.

Raul Peña's assessment of his life as a migrant child is interesting when viewed in relation to Laing's "cycle of poverty" theory, which sees migrant workers as victims lacking in agency, with only their hard work and faith to sustain them. The life of the migrant child, Raul recalls, was a life of adventure, one that involved the entire family. For a child who thought "going north" meant a trip to Plainview, Texas, rolling across the vast Western landscape was exciting and educational. He recalls winning a geography bee, not because he was the smartest kid in his class in Reynosa, Texas, but because, in addition to knowing the names of the state capitals, he actually had passed through scores of states and their capitals. Raul's buddies, excited because a Mexican kid had won the contest, expressed their jubilation by carrying him on their shoulders throughout the auditorium. Peña, who recently retired from the Oregon Department of Labor, where he worked as a labor compliance officer, added,

> Yeah, we were poor. Actually, I didn't know we were poor but my father sure knew it. If I had stayed in Texas my life would have been very different. I would probably still be working in the fields, or I would be pushing drugs or in jail for pushing drugs, or I would be dead. Coming to Oregon increased my life chances. But what I learned as a child of migrants is to value work. My father taught me that no matter what the job was, I was being paid for it, and I was obliged to do it the very best I could. "If your boss asks you to dig a ditch," my father told me, "ask how deep and how wide" (interview with Gonzales-Berry, 2004).

The Peñas, like other *tejanos* in the migrant stream, were not foreigners but U.S. citizens or long-time residents and so they had a sense that in this country one could get ahead through hard labor. However, the enduring colonial mind set in Texas—stemming from the foundational myth of the Texas Republic, the battle at the Alamo—made Texas a difficult place for its Mexican-origin population. Extreme poverty and racial discrimination locked *tejanos* in brutal poverty and segregation. Life in Oregon would represent a change, as we can glean from Elena Peña: "The teachers were so nice to us. We weren't used to this in Texas. We were even afraid to speak Spanish because we thought we were going to get spanked. To me, that was really different. We would speak Spanish whenever we wanted…. The school system was better. They treated us nicer. There was a lot more curriculum…. That's when I got the idea of what going on field trips was about." These changes had a lot to do with her family settling in Independence. "My dad saw how happy we were, that we were speaking more English and more involved in school, and he was more involved in school. In Texas he didn't feel welcome." Furthermore, she found joy in interacting with Oregonians, something that was out of the question in race-conscious Texas. Her mother likewise enjoyed exchanges with white women because "they were so nice to her."[13]

Historian David Montejano addresses the effect of Jim Crow laws on Mexicans in Texas, pointing clearly to the deeply entrenched racialization of Mexicans, a practice that put them on a par with African Americans in that state:

> "Jim Crow" may appear to be an odd description of the situation of Mexicans in Texas. There was no constitutionally sanctioned "separate but equal" provision for Mexicans as there was for blacks. According to the prevailing jurisprudence, Mexicans were "Caucasian." But in

political and sociological terms, blacks and Mexicans were basically seen as different aspects of the same race problem. In the farm areas of South and West Texas, the Caucasian schools were nearly always divided into "Anglo schools" and "Mexican schools," the towns into "white towns" and "little Mexicos," and even the churches and cemeteries followed this seemingly natural division of people. This was not a natural phenomenon, however, but the cumulative effect of local administrative policies. In the farm districts, the result was a separation as complete—and as "de jure"—as any in the Jim Crow South (1987, 262).

Under these conditions, "people stayed on their side of town," (Raul Peña, interview by Gonzales-Berry, 2004) and speaking Spanish in public was akin to committing a crime.

Women in costume ride in unidentified parade, Independence, OR, ca. 1965. Oregon Historical Society.

Connie García, who also came to Independence with her parents in the 1950s, gives a vivid image of the life of a Mexican child in a Texas school:

The next year I joined my older brothers and sister in school. All I remember of that experience is that we were all herded into one room with a whole bunch of other kids and we moved around a lot, singing "picking up posies, puttin' them in a basket, picking up posies, puttin' them in a basket." I think we really weren't in a school, because the following year, my mom walked me to school and we met with the principal. His name was Mr. Barron. He told my mom to tell me

I was not to speak Spanish at school at all. We then went down a
corridor to a room down the far end. The teacher took me in and sat
me down, and there I stayed, completely mute, silent for almost three
years (Chicano Literary Group 2000, n.p.).

In a story reminiscent of a scene from the movie *Giant*, Raul Peña recalls the
time he, his father, and his uncle were refused service and asked to leave a
restaurant in Texas. Peña is thankful that his father did not teach him to hate.
Instead he told him, "It's all right. We'll just go to the other side and be with
our people." In a joint interview with the Peñas, Elena acknowledged that
not all *mexicano* settlers felt this way. "They see a different story, because
they had probably already been poisoned with that attitude." She is of
course referring to the resentment that frequently develops among victims
of bigotry in response to the pain of rejection and discrimination. But for
tejanos like the Peñas, accustomed as they were to a life of segregation and
deeply entrenched racial discrimination in Texas, Oregon indeed was a
welcome change.[14]

Ironically, the state of Texas seemed quite concerned with how Texas
mexicanos would represent the state as they left to work elsewhere. In a letter
given to migrant workers by the Texas Extension Service in 1946, emigrants
were warned:

> *"The eyes of Texas are upon you, all the live long day. The eyes of*
> *Texas are upon you, you cannot get away." No matter where you go, to*
> *the people of other states you represent Texas. All Texans are proud*
> *of their citizenship and their fellow Texans. All Texans are interested*
> *in what their citizens do when they get to other states. We want to*
> *see them make good. We also want to see that they are treated right*
> *wherever they go.... Lets [sic] stay by our contracts. Lets do a good job*
> *so that those who stay in Texas can always say that they are proud of*
> *the Texas Latin Americans (Latino Oral History Project).*

If migrants felt liberated from the humiliation of the Jim Crow environment
that prevailed in Texas upon their arrival in Oregon, that is not to say that
Oregonians were beyond prejudice and discrimination. The son of Raul
Leos, who came to Oregon in 1954, reported the following incident: "When
Raul Sr. and Anna were putting the children to bed they heard a noise
outside the window. They both went out to check and what they found was
a letter tacked to their door reading, *Leave wetbacks*" (Latino Oral History
Project). In their 1959 report, Current and Infante found that in one county
the practice of "price-jacking" was common, with prices of staples increasing
by 15 percent once migrants arrived. In another county, one tavern made it
a practice to refuse service to "Spanish-American" migrants, though other

migrants were not turned away. The law-enforcement official in this same county counseled "businessmen and townspeople to handle the 'Mexicans' with extreme caution and give them no chance to start anything. As far as he is concerned, all 'Mexicans' are dangerous" (116). At another location, a police officer, speaking of migrant youth, affirmed: "If we see the young boys dating white girls, we tell them to go only with their own" (123). In 1962 Gilbert López reported to *The Oregon Journal* that "transient workers in the Boise Valley area of Eastern Oregon were unable to meet socially because of discrimination against them by bar and club owners." Everywhere they turned, he reported, "they are met with signs stating 'No Mexicans allowed'" (July 19, 1962).

Sign posted in businesses in the Southwest in 1950s. From the collection of E. Gonzales-Berry.

We could argue that the treatment of these migrant workers was simply because Mexicans and Texans of Mexican descent were outsiders, and that these patterns differ little from the discrimination suffered by other immigrant ethnic groups. However, on numerous occasions we have found in the public record of Oregon allusions to Mexicans' skin color and alleged character. This acute consciousness of "darker skin color" supports our argument that Mexicans historically have been viewed as a racialized ethnic group, and that it is the very process of racialization—the attribution of negative characteristics based on physiognomic features—that justified the differential treatment and discrimination of this population. The words of one education official who declared in an annual school report, "I have noticed that if the children are more on the Indian side, they are slower in learning than those who are more on the Spanish side" (Infante and Current 1958 supplement, 7) sustains our argument. This thinking harkens back to the racialized discourse that accompanied the annexation of half of Mexico's territory to the United States, and which we believe set the stage for embedding *mexicanos* within the ideology of a racial hierarchy that historically defined the relations between peoples of European, African, and indigenous descent in this country.

Despite displays of bigotry, the Texas migrant stream increasingly was finding Oregon a better place to be, and they were settling out in increasing numbers. In 1965, Mrs. Kenneth M. Walker, member of the Migrant Community Center of Independence, conducted a survey of the "Spanish-American" residents living in the area. Walker reported that sixty-three families had left the migrant stream to settle in the area. The families interviewed by Walker met their housing needs in the following manner: twenty lived in housing provided by their employers on ranches; twelve were renting; six lived with other families; and twenty-five were in the process of purchasing homes. For the latter, their migratory lifestyle was indeed coming to an end (*Independence Enterprise,* April 22, 1965).

The Oregon Interagency Committee on Migrant Labor noted, in what could be interpreted as a mildly acerbic and warning tone, this settling-out pattern and called attention to the problems the *tejanos'* settlement augured for Oregon, unaccustomed as the state was to diversity:

> *Some of the migrant workers who have been coming to Oregon the past few years have selected to stay here. As citizens of the United States this is their privilege. However, the transition poses some problems for the state and its communities. Having spent most of their lives working in agriculture, they are not prepared to obtain jobs other than that type of work. Beginning in November the workers find little to do. It is after a lean Thanksgiving and a bleak Christmas they can again be used in preparing for another berry and bean season (1966, 14).*

If *tejanos* came here prepared to get ahead, the very nature of seasonal work presented tremendous obstacles. Hence, in addition to handicaps related to their ethnic outsiderness, their class status as workers virtually trapped in a labor structure that precluded vertical movement contributed to their marginal condition in Oregon. And this in turn contributed to generational poverty and discrimination.

Like Independence, Woodburn became a mecca for the Mexican-origin population in the early fifties. Miguel Salinas, whose father jumped off a train he was riding in the Willamette Valley in 1947, considers his family one of the earliest pioneer families to settle in this area. Salinas, who has done much in recent years to record the history of *tejano* pioneers, recalled, "When I was growing up you would walk through Woodburn and see maybe one brown face. Today you don't see any white faces." The enterprising young Salinas finished high school with the certain knowledge that he would get a job. However, he was turned away time and again "for lack of experience." Finally he offered to volunteer at a gas station in order to get experience.

Within two weeks, this young man had proven his mettle and was hired part time at a wage of $1.25 per hour (interview with Gonzales-Berry, 2003).

By the end of the '50s there were sufficient *mexicanos* in Woodburn to make it profitable for the local theater to run Spanish-language movies once a week. Moreover, Woodburn had the only Department of Motor Vehicles office in the state which administered the driver's license test in Spanish. Current and Infante (1959) report that "Spanish-Americans" from all over the state traveled to Woodburn in the '50s to get their driver's license.

By the '60s, *mexicanos* in Woodburn were beginning to form a critical mass. Sal Cantú (personal conversation with Gonzales-Berry 2007) recalls that the gas station owned by a fellow *tejano* was the hub of community life and a center for social networking. *Mexicanos*, including those driving past Woodburn, stopped by the station for gas, coffee, to catch up on the latest gossip, and to exchange information regarding jobs and working conditions. By 1964, the large presence of *mexicanos* prompted the Chamber of Commerce to organize its first Mexican fiesta "for the purpose of recognizing 'the many Spanish-speaking peoples in the area for the harvest season' " (Dash and Hawkinson 2001) and to create "reciprocity between these two cultures" (Flores 2004). Because Mexican Americans were not counted as a separate category in the U.S. census prior to 1970, we do not know how many *tejanos* settled in Oregon in the decades following World War II.[15] Decades later, thousands of descendants of *tejano* migrants live in Woodburn today. With the largest percentage Latino population in the state, the city is the epicenter from which much of the state's activism on behalf of *mexicanos* and Latinos—both early settlers and recent immigrants—continues to emerge.

Mexicano families were also settling out in Washington County in the early '60s. The Hinojosa family started coming to Oregon in 1959 from Harlingen, Texas. In 1961 they stayed the entire year, living at a labor camp. That year the camp burned down and the second year there was a severe ice storm. In 1962 they decided to remain in Oregon, because the three young sons had "fallen in love with Oregon's natural beauty" (Héctor Hinojosa and José Jaime, joint interview with Gonzales-Berry, 2004). The entire family worked in the fields, and the boys also worked at a car wash. Eventually the Hinojosa brothers got year-round employment at $1.25 an hour. They and their parents pooled their money and were able to buy a "little place, where Mom still lives, for $10,000—$104 a month for ten years. The owner carried the contract." A number of local churches organized to help people settle; each church adopted a family for six months, helping them find jobs and acquire money to buy a house. Hillsboro community activist José Jaime, reported, "That's how several families here were able to buy homes and settle out." Héctor Hinojosa recalls the challenges young people faced in these times:

There were a handful of us who went to school together all the way through the sophomore year, which is when I dropped out. But until that point I tried to get some of my peers to come to high school, but they were seriously discriminated against, for things that ranged from speaking Spanish, to attendance, to dress, to need for school supplies. So they would end up dropping out, the majority of them. In fact, that's why I ended up dropping out. I was the one that had to translate for everything for my parents, medical problems, work, everything; and I had to miss a lot of school. A new attendance policy was put in effect. You could not miss more than ten days in a school year in order to graduate. The second quarter, I dropped out because I knew I couldn't graduate anyway. The school was not very culturally or linguistically sensitive to our needs.

Hinojosa's observation is one that still applies to the education of *mexicano* children in Oregon. Although Hinojosa's generation has carved out a space in which their children and grandchildren can succeed, today new immigrants find themselves in the same position. Jaime added, "Dark-skinned and people with little English-speaking skills are the ones who suffered more discrimination."

Eastern Oregon continued to draw *mexicanos* throughout the second half of the twentieth century, giving Malheur County the second largest concentration of Hispanic population today, as evidenced by the 2000 census. In 1954, Nyssa held its first Mexican fiesta, and by 1959 it had a baseball team organized by migrants from Eagle Pass, Texas, a bilingual mimeograph newspaper, and Spanish-language broadcasts (Current and Infante 1959). By 1964 there were three hundred and thirty settled-out families in this county (Oregon State Board of Health 1971), forcing school districts to give some thought to how they could best serve migrant children. The Nyssa School District, for example, encouraged parents to send their children to school and to assuage fears regarding their treatment:

We believe your children should attend schools while they reside in this Community. We have no prejudice against any Nationality, Race or Creed. A child is a child as far as we are concerned and we treat them all alike... . You may be assured that your children and you, if you accompany them for registration, will be treated courteously and kindly (Oregon Legislative Assembly Interim Committee on Migratory Labor 1958, 54).

The letter sent home to parents would, of course, have had greater impact had it been written in Spanish.

Tejanos were also settling out in Northeast Oregon. Queli Martínez's family started making the trek from Texas to Washington, Idaho, and Oregon, settling in Hermiston in 1963. Queli said:

> *I was little, I was like five years old when we came from Texas. So all I remember is playing in the yard and the relatives and all this kind of stuff, you know, because that is where our family is from, Eagle Pass, Texas. And then one day mom told us after school that we were going to Oregon because she had a sister, two sisters, actually, that lived here in Hermiston at the time—that there were better jobs and things like that. So we came up to Oregon. And that was very different for me, to come to Oregon. Because there were maybe four, maybe five families total, in Hermiston that were Latinos. And like I had said, I had never seen a blue-eyed, blond-haired person before. I had never seen a red head with freckles. That was all very different for me. I had always seen brown eyes, brown skin, brown hair. That's all I'd seen. So it was very scary to me as a child when I was growing up. Going to school, I was one of those that would cry because I was so scared. You know. And like I said, I just had myself and then I had a cousin in the same room. They put us together because I couldn't communicate (interview with Gonzales-Berry, 2007).*

The cultivation of onions and the potato-packing companies in this area have attracted a steady stream of *mexicanos* over time, and today there are noticeable pockets of *mexicanos* in this area.

While there was not a *mexicano* population on the Oregon coast, we did find evidence of one highly respected citizen. Just about the time that Operation Wetback was winding down in the mid-fifties, a Mexican national arrived and settled in Lincoln Beach, Oregon. Samuel B. Zarate was born in El Oro, a mining town near Mexico. His father, a music teacher, began instructing eight-year-old Samuel in flute, which he played in his father's traveling orchestra. Later he started to play the violin and enrolled at the National Conservatory in Mexico City, and he studied there until he received a scholarship to study music in Paris. There he met his wife, a singer and dancer from Madras, India. The couple formed a musical duo and together "Zarate and Paquita" performed across Europe, and after World War II, in Canada, Alaska, and the United States. In 1959 they settled in Lincoln Beach, where they established a culture center where they taught music and gave dance lessons and ran a small restaurant called "The Gingerbread House" (Zarate papers, North Lincoln County Historical Museum). After his wife died, Zarate built the All Faiths Chapel in her honor. He was greatly admired and respected in the coastal communities of Central Oregon, so

Violinist Samuel Zarate. Courtesy of the North Lincoln County Historical Museum.

much so that Gleneden Beach paid special tribute to him, declaring September 22, 1996, "Sam's Day" (*The News Guard,* October 9, 1996).

Mexican Nationals Join Tejano Settlers

The seventies and early eighties witnessed the continued arrival of *mexicanos* to the state, most of them coming under the same circumstances as the early settlers of the fifties and sixties: as migrant workers. But larger numbers of these migrants came from Mexico (Loprinzi 1991). The "Mexican miracle"[16] was by then coming undone, resulting in low wages and scarce jobs. Mexico thus became fertile ground for recruitment by Oregon farmers. The case of Hood River farmer Eugene Euwer, as reported in *The Oregonian* (April 26, 1987) is instructive in this regard:

> *The relationship between Gene and the men of Mezquital began in 1970 when Tony's friend José Santillán and his two cousins, Arnulfo and Francisco Santillán, met Gene and asked for work. Gene hired them, weaving the first thread between Mezquital and Hood River. Tony went to work for Gene two years later, and dozens of other men followed. Each year their lives became more tightly knit, bound by personal, economic and emotional ties. In some ways, the relationship between Mezquital and Hood River is not much different from that of hundreds of communities throughout Mexico and the United States where two cultures, two languages, and thousands of lives have become entwined.*

When this article was written, Eugene Euwer's orchards had been tended for 17 years by workers from Mezquital. The pattern was (and still is) a familiar one: yearly a crew leader delivers workers from his village—relatives, friends, other acquaintances—to farms in Oregon. A tight web of relations and reciprocal obligations was established that satisfied the needs of growers, supported the lives of their families, and boosted the economy in Mezquital but, more importantly, this practice guarantees a known and dependable labor force for the agriculture economy in this state.

In addition to the yearly return of recruited work crews selected through community social networks, thousands of other workers from Mexico followed the migrant stream on their own, picked crops in California, Oregon, Washington, and Idaho, and returned home once the harvest season ended. In the early 1970s, by most accounts, Mexican nationals began settling in the Mid-Columbia River region in Oregon. While some of these early settlers were older and more experienced and other workers arrived with their families from California, Texas, and New Mexico, the majority of these newcomers were young single males from Zacatecas, Jalisco, Durango, Michoacán, Hidalgo, Baja California, and Yucatán. These laborers were employed seasonally in the harvest of cherries, apples, peaches, and pears, doing farm work like pruning and thinning, packing and processing fruit crops and grapes for wineries. They formed communities around the camps, and settled-out families sent their children to school, worshiped at churches, and used the services of community health clinics and migrant centers, while Mexican entrepreneurs in Hood River opened restaurants, *taquerías*, *tiendas*, and specialty stores to serve the ethnic communities.

In 1978, researchers at Oregon State University interviewed ninety-three Mexican workers accessed through stratified random sampling of the Hood River Valley's orchard operations (Cuthbert and Stevens 1980) and found that Mexican migrant workers in Hood River were earning six times more than they would have earned in Mexico. This differential was reduced to three times more than earnings in Mexico when accounting for total

Illegal aliens getting inside U.S. territory on the U.S.-Mexico border, 1984. University of California, UCLA Library.

expenses in Oregon, including round trip transportation, housing, food and other expenses.

The Bermúdez (pseudonym) family is an example of Mexican families who settled out in the late seventies. The experiences of this family, as related by eldest daughter María (interview with J. Otañez, 2003), are in many respects typical. However, the central role taken on by the women of the family is noteworthy, for it belies the stereotype of the Mexican woman as a passive and subservient victim of the equally flagrant stereotype, Mexican "machismo." María Bermúdez's family first moved to McAllen, Texas, from Gomez Palacios, Durango. From there, her family came, "like animals in a trailer truck," with nine other families to Jefferson, Oregon. When they arrived there were no jobs, but the contractor kept charging them for rent and other expenses. Her father and another family broke away and headed to Woodburn, where they were able to hook up with another contractor who found them work in the strawberry harvest. The whole family worked to get ahead and eventually bought a car. The family mitigated the effects of alienation linked to relocation in the same way that others before them had done and continue to do today. They linked up with other Mexican families and formed a small, bonded community upon which they could rely for mutual support. These eight families joined together and borrowed $15,000 each to build homes. The federal loan required that each borrower contribute six hundred hours of labor toward the construction of the home. The families pooled their efforts and all were able to move into their own homes in a shared neighborhood within a few years of their arrival in Oregon. Bermúdez's father suffered from ulcers and other complications and passed away when María was fourteen. As the oldest of four children, she had to help her mother, who worked in the fields to support the family. "Study and work, study and work, study and work" was what she recalls about that period of her life. After graduating from high school, María continued studying and working until she got married. Her husband was "very *machista*" and did not let her continue her studies. María stayed home, had a family, and eventually left her husband, from whom she received no assistance, so she returned to work to support her family. She held two jobs, one in the daytime and one at night, sleeping only four hours. Today, María works as a teacher's aide and also owns her own commercial cleaning business. She is particularly pleased that having her own company allows her to set her hours and be her own boss. Her only regret is that she was not able to attend college. However, this disappointment is offset by the knowledge that her eldest son had just received his bachelor's degree when this interview was conducted. Looking back at her life, María Bermúdez proudly proclaims: "I have always worked and have not asked the Americans for anything, because I have exerted myself to get where I am. All of my life I have worked for the little that I have, and I have done it with my own sweat."

The Valley Migrant League and Community Empowerment

During this period of settling out, many social agencies turned their attention to *mexicano* migrant families. Of the many organizations and agencies that arose to serve the needs of migrant workers, the Valley Migrant League stands out for its overall impact on *mexicano* communities—both settled and newly arrived—and, more importantly, for the role it played in training and empowering cultural brokers (educated, English-speaking Latinos who mediated between migrants and mainstream agencies and individuals). Article II of the league's Articles of Incorporation clearly lays out the intent of this organization: "[Our mission is] to assist the migrant and seasonal agricultural worker and his family to deal effectively with their own problems of poverty so that they need no further assistance" (*El Relámpago*, April 1971). The VML's first action was to secure a $700,000 grant from the U.S. Office of Economic Opportunities. Regarding this victory, Rev. Ken Lawrence, one of VML's founding members, reported to *The Oregonian*: "[The money] will make possible a program of education and social service, unparalleled in the United States and previously impossible in Oregon" (March 20, 1965). Over the years, and with numerous hefty federal grants, the VML set up opportunity centers at Woodburn, Hillsboro, Independence, West Stayton, and Dayton; sponsored summer school programs for migrant children in fourteen communities; ran a day care program and nursery facilities;[17] and oversaw a corps of Vista Volunteers. At its various centers, it offered adult education programs in English, citizenship, health, childcare, home making, and credit management, as well as vocational, social, and legal skills. Their Head-of-Household Program helped migrant workers get a college degree at Linfield and Mount Angel colleges in three years; many of today's leaders in *mexicano* communities in Oregon came through that program (John Little, interview with Gonzales-Berry, 2004). Another successful initiative was a self-help housing program, which helped migrant workers (such as the Bermúdez family discussed above) get low-interest government loans for homes and involved them in the actual building of these homes. In addition, VML administered a migrant health program and sought to convince growers to improve their labor camps (*The Oregonian*, August 11, 1965).

The growth and impact of the VML took place during the emergence of a powerful socio-political movement that had taken hold in Mexican American communities throughout California and the Southwest, spread to the Pacific Northwest, and found willing participants among VML workers. In fact, it was the VML that sent thirty to forty *concilio* members to California to a Chicano training conference in the late sixties. John Little, who later became director of the VML, recalled that event in his 2004 interview: "It was a great training session. What was so great was that they went down there and met with Corky Gonzales. They met with César Chávez. They met with all the great leaders at that time. They all stayed in this camp and established a good spirit. When they came back, all the area directors were now Chicanos." While in California, this group of VML workers was exposed to the Movement discourse of cultural and social revolution, and they returned with a burning thirst for community organizing and self-determination. As Chicano leadership developed, more *mexicanos* were added to the VML staff. Tensions soon arose between "conservative, charity-oriented volunteers and ex-migrants" and between growers and religious activists within the organization. John Little's words again are instructive in helping us understand the power struggles that developed within the VML:

> A lot of the people in the VML were either old bureaucrats or do-gooders. So what happened was they were going to help people. We had one bureaucrat who was a social worker and he gave a training lecture in which he said, "[I]t's like these people are sick and we're the doctors. We're going to get them well." We had people there, for example, who were working as job counselors. They were Anglos. They didn't know the language; they couldn't talk to the workers. Like the one I inherited. He was so incompetent he couldn't go around and get a job, so his assistant Sonny Montes was the one who was going around and getting the jobs and talking to the people. And the guy was doing nothing. Sonny was getting minimum wage and this guy was getting big money.

A statement made by a VML assistant director to *The Oregonian* lends credence to Little's harsh observations: "They [migrant workers] naturally mistreat facilities... . They haven't any idea of respect for their own, much less someone else's property... that's why the Valley Migrant League was created... . We're trying to educate the migrants" (August 11, 1965).

Little's philosophy, influenced greatly by Paulo Freire and Maryknoll missionary values, [18] played an important role in determining the direction taken by the VML. He came to the director's job knowing full well that this was a bureaucracy and as such there were limits to what it could accomplish. Nonetheless, his stance was the following: "What I was saying was I'm here to change the institution. You can make the institution friendly to self-organization, then the people have to take charge and take responsibility for the decisions. But the institution has to permit them to make those decisions." In fact, it was his own philosophy that forced him to step down as executive director to make way for a Chicano. He recalls, "When I took the job as Executive Director, I said 'I will only take this job on one condition. That is, I will take the job until we can find somebody who can survive in Washington D.C. and who is from the *raza* [the *mexicano* people], preferably an ex-migrant worker.'" Frank Martínez was identified as his potential replacement and was brought in as a staff member. He was given the responsibility of organizing the Poor Peoples' March in 1969 and, as a result of the strong leadership exerted in that capacity, he was hired to replace Little.

With Martínez's appointment, it was just a matter of time before Chicanos took control of the organization. In 1972, the VML bylaws were amended to require that 51 to 100 percent of the board members be migrant representatives. Community response to this action was jubilant: "The crowd of over a hundred and fifty Chicanos and supporters of VML packed inside Jason Lee Church then cheered wildly. After nearly seven years, farmworkers had finally taken over complete control of the Valley Migrant League" (*El Relámpago*, February 13, 1972). Martínez triumphantly observed, "This is probably the greatest victory for farmworkers in Oregon's history. No longer will it be possible for the Establishment to manipulate the VML. The day when the bureaucrats in Washington could tell VML what to do is over ... This means that the man who gives slave wages and the man who runs the slave market will no longer have a say in formation of VML policy" (*El Relámpago*, February 13, 1972). To the broader Oregon community, Martínez earlier had sent a simple message, revealing that the fundamental principles of the Chicano movement—community empowerment and self-determination—had indeed found fertile ground among Oregon's *mexicano* communities: "Whenever the dominant society thought about us, it was in terms of 'Oh, these poor migrants. Let's take them some cookies and old clothes'... Well, we are tired of cookies and old clothes" (*The Oregonian*, January 24, 1971).

Without doubt, the Chicano Movement played an important role in politicizing *mexicanos* and in giving them the tools for empowering their communities. However, this movement was not as radical in Oregon as it was in California, New Mexico, Colorado, and Texas, where nationally renowned grassroots leaders achieved near-legendary status. First of all, the communities were much smaller in Oregon and, as we pointed out in the introduction, in the main, the population tended to be seasonal and there was not a long-standing "colonized" population, carrying as it did the proverbial resentment of its social positioning, to fan the flames of radicalism as occurred in Border States. *Tejanos* would of course qualify as such a demographic group, but their own marginalization in migrant labor and their imputed status as "outsiders" limited their ability to create the kind of radical social movement that evolved elsewhere.

Grassroots Organizing in Washington County

Washington County provides additional examples of grassroots organizing led by migrants and cultural brokers, some of whom were trained by the VML. Ruby Ely, who had worked for the VML in Woodburn, became the director at the VML Hillsboro office in 1966. Growing increasingly disillusioned with the power structure of this organization, she became interested in finding ways to facilitate community leadership development, which she saw as essential for grassroots mobilization. She brought José Jaime, a seminarian from Mexico, and José García, another seminarian from California, to work with her during their summer break from Mount Angel Seminary in Oregon. José Jaime was a program aide, and José García, who in prior years had worked as a labor organizer in Chicago, eventually became the temporary executive director at the Hillsboro VML. As their education in the seminary progressed, these two young men increasingly had come to understand that spiritual service was not enough for *mexicano* communities, bereft as they were of adequate educational and social services. Finding themselves, in José Jaime's words, "converted by the people," they actively strove to interweave "faith and practice." Their exposure to Saul Alinsky's agenda[19] for social change had given them a clear understanding of how structures of power operated, as well as how to access resources for their community. Hence, they clearly saw themselves as cultural brokers who could play a useful role in linking community members with activist inclinations to resources and in helping people acquire skills necessary for operating within mainstream structures and institutions, albeit from a firm grassroots position. Crucial to their advocacy work was the identification of potential community leaders who could replace them when they returned to the seminary, though they continued to work in Hillsboro on weekends during the academic session and, indeed, Jaime ended up staying permanently. He still lives in Hillsboro and continues to be an advocate for the rights of *mexicanos*.

Jaime and García found their leaders in twelve *mexicano* families in Washington County that had already come together to "do something for the community." Under Jaime's mentorship, in 1966 they formed *Los Amigos Club*, which became an incorporated organization in 1971. The main purpose of this club was to help community members buy homes and to assist them in time of need, particularly with shipping the remains of deceased individuals to Mexico or Texas for burial, as was customary among *mexicano* families.

The idea of self-determination spawned in this small circle of families took root in Washington County. VIVA (Volunteers in Vanguard Action) was founded by Emilio Hernández and Ruby Ely after they splintered off from the VML, and their actions influenced the formation of *El Hogar del Campesino*, another program that sought to empower migrant workers. Its director Guadalupe Bustos did not mince words when he stated: "One of the most difficult jobs we have is trying to convince all state and private agencies that work for betterment of migrant worker conditions that among the workers there are people who can lead and direct if given the opportunity" (*The Oregonian*, August 19, 1968). Staff member José Morales added, "Nobody can do it for us. Only we who have experienced it can end this so-called war on poverty." Bustos, under the auspices of VIVA, was also instrumental in starting up a cooperative full-service gas station for *mexicanos* in Hillsboro. Hector Hinojosa, who was then a young boy living in Hillsboro, recalled with relish, "This was unbelievable for 1969, *el concepto de hacer una cooperativa entre mexicanos* [the concept of starting a co-op for *mexicanos*]. Across the street was Texaco. There were gas wars between us" (interview with Gonzales-Berry, 2004). He recalls also working at the co-op, where he learned about bookkeeping, inventory, and purchasing at the age of fifteen. Bustos and Morales, both college-educated sons of migrant workers from Texas, clearly represented the new breed of cultural brokers engaged in helping *mexicano* communities take control of their lives.

The next step for this community was the founding of a cultural center. Again, Hinojosa recalls what a monumental accomplishment this was: "The first time I heard of this concept of the *centro cultural* was from my parents, coming home from the meeting of *El Club de los Amigos* and talking. Our need was for education, for having a resource center, a place for celebrations. Then the fund-raising started. *Vendiendo* [selling] tacos, *tamales, bailes* [dances], in order to raise funds to first purchase the property—two properties—one house in Cornelius and an old house here. We needed a safe haven from *la migra* [border patrol]." Hinojosa assured us that it was not just the men leading the way: "It was both the men and the women. Couples always worked together." In 1972 they opened Washington County's first *mexicano* community center in Cornelius. The center's mission, as stated in its bylaws, was "to help provide basic emergency needs and to promote economic development, education, and cultural awareness between the diverse groups that make up our community. To provide a cultural and educational bridge, where rich and poor, young and old, educated and illiterate, could meet to discuss and find solutions to common problems" (Hinojosa family papers lent to authors by Hector Hinojosa). Activities at El Centro included "instruction in Mexican art, sewing, typing, languages, canning, adult basic education, and vocational training. The latter component, vocational training known as ORMETEX, is cosponsored by Tektronix, Inc., of Beaverton, and other local companies, to aid low-income people, principally ex-farmworkers, in making the transition to technical, industrial employment" (Slatta 1975, 332).

As El Centro grew in strength and influence, it spawned several new initiatives. The most impressive of these was the Virginia García Memorial Health Center. In 1973, young Virginia García stepped on a rusty nail and her foot became infected. She was refused medical attention at the community hospital because the family had no insurance. She was then taken to St. Vincent Hospital where she was treated, given medication, and sent home. Because the family did not receive treatment instructions in Spanish, they did not administer the medicine as indicated, and young Virginia died. It became clear that medical care was a critical problem for the *mexicano* community, and El Centro, which was about to start a training program in auto mechanics, rose to the occasion. They had the space for the garage and had bought the tools. However, when the community mobilized around the death of Virginia García, the board decided to use the resources for a training program to start up a health clinic. With support from Tualatin and St. Vincent hospitals, El Centro founded the Virginia García Memorial Health Center, which is still in operation today, serving thousands of patients each year.

That *mexicanos* were successful in building community in Washington County is further attested to by the existence of a bilingual newspaper called *The Rural Tribune.* This newspaper, now defunct, was linked to the Washington Community Action Program and it stood as a strong voice of advocacy on behalf of *mexicanos.* It was particularly vigilant of the community's rights and frequently registered abuses of those rights by law-enforcement agencies as well as incidents of conflict and discrimination. One article reported on a meeting of the Forest Grove School Board, at which citizens engaged in heated repartees that clearly demonstrate tension between *mexicanos* and other residents. One citizen claimed that "Ninety percent of the Mexican-Americans don't pay taxes because they work in the summer and then buy brand new cars with chrome wheels and then go on welfare." Rebuttal came from a Chicano who replied, "We do pay taxes, just like everybody else—gas tax, income tax, state tax. And when we buy a brand new car, who do we buy it from? An Anglo businessman." Tensions and abuses were such in this county that *Oregonian* journalist Robert Olmos, a Chicano from East Los Angeles (Slatta 1975), who had established himself as a media spokesperson for *mexicanos* in Oregon, wrote a scathing article that opens with the following line: "To be a Chicano in Washington County is to be, if not ignored and disregarded, harassed, insulted and generally made to feel like a second-class citizen. So say some of the Washington County Chicanos" (February 18, 1973). Olmos goes on to document numerous cases of harassment of young males by police; the lack of Chicano employees in service agencies, the police department, stores, restaurants, or banks; the expulsion of three young men from a local bar because they were speaking Spanish; and the mistreatment of *mexicano* children in the public schools. Given this history of tension surrounding the presence of *mexicanos* in Washington County, it comes as no surprise that the most active anti-immigrant association to emerge in Oregon in recent years has its home in this county. Oregonians for Immigration Reform—following in the footsteps of the incendiary national organization Federation for American Immigration Reform—strongly advocates against "illegal" immigration and seeks to undermine the efforts of pro-immigrant groups.[20]

PCUN, a Labor Union for Mexicano *Farmworkers in Oregon*

César Chávez began unionizing farmworkers in California in the mid-1960s. By 1968, his efforts had reached Oregon, and a local branch of the United Farm Workers was formed. In the early seventies, while visiting Oregon to rally support for the UFW boycott, Chávez publicly deplored farmworker conditions in Oregon. But Chávez's union—perhaps due to the migratory nature of the bulk of farm-workers—did not take root in this state; instead a home-grown organization, the Willamette Valley Immigrant Project, led by Cipriano Ferrel, Ramón Ramírez, Larry Kleinman, and Juan Mendoza, began to represent farm and reforestation workers by responding to increasing INS raids and deplorable wages, opposing a new guest worker program, and advocating for amnesty for undocumented immigrants (Stephen and PCUN 2001). This organization was the precursor to PCUN (*Pineros y Campesinos Unidos de Noroeste*), which was founded in 1985 by eighty farmworkers under the leadership of Cipriano Ferrel. Ferrel had grown up in California with César Chávez's children. His connection to Chávez was instrumental in that he was able to seek out Chavez's advice regarding his efforts to organize farmworkers in Oregon. After Ferrel died, Ramón Ramírez, a former student at Colegio César Chávez, assumed the leadership of PCUN, which continues to be a strong voice, not only for farm, nursery and reforestation workers, but for immigrants in general. Two decades after its founding, PCUN boasts forty-five hundred members. From its very inception it has represented a strong voice for workers' rights, has engaged in collective bargaining as a "means to redress power imbalance between growers and workers," and has led the way in community organizing in the Mid-Willamette Valley, (www.pcun.org). PCUN's success is owed in large part to Ramón Ramírez's commitment to collaboration and alliance building and to his firm belief in the need to engage in mainstream political venues and processes. Under Ramírez's leadership, PCUN keeps a vigilant eye on labor camps, it pressures both agribusiness and the state legislature to give these workers their due, and it offers numerous services to its members, including translation and information on labor and immigration issues. More recently Ramírez has been successful in establishing *Radio Movimiento, La Voz de Pueblo*, PCUN's twenty-four-hour FM radio station in Woodburn. He also supported the UFW campaign at Threemile Canyon Dairy in Eastern Oregon, which won the first large-scale collective bargaining agreement in Oregon agriculture and the first employer acceptance of the "card check" and mandatory and binding contract-arbitration processes (personal communication to Gonzales-Berry, 2009). Moreover, under Ramírez's leadership, PCUN has become a national leader in the struggle for immigration rights and reform, regularly testifying in Congress and in the Oregon legislature. Regarding his impressive record of accomplishments, Ramírez allows that "organizing farmworkers is the most difficult task in the labor movement, primarily because farmworkers are not covered by the national labor relation law. It wasn't until César Chávez started organizing the 1960s did we see major changes in the way farmworkers were treated. While we have created many positive changes for farmworkers in Oregon, we are a long way from realizing our dreams" (personal communication to Gonzales-Berry, August 2009). When asked about his greatest challenges as a labor organizer Ramírez mused:

> *My greatest challenge has been overcoming my own fears and insecurities as an organizer. In this society we are taught that making errors or admitting setbacks are a sign of weakness. I feel it is good for your development to commit mistakes and errors as long as you admit them and learn from your mistakes. At this point I would say that my greatest challenge is preparing the young generation to take over the leadership of PCUN and continuing the struggle for farmworker rights in Oregon. I want to leave the movement stronger than I found it. I am motivated to do the work even if it's difficult because I truly believe social change is possible and that we can build a society based on equality and respect for all (personal communication, August 2009).*

PCUN has an active core of female members and has been instrumental in helping women organize *Mujeres, Luchadoras y Progresistas*, an organization that assists in the creation of economic opportunities for immigrant women. If Woodburn is the mecca of the Oregon *mexicano* community, PCUN is its heartbeat and its unrivaled champion.

A College of Our Own

The formation of a college, *El Colegio César Chávez*, aimed at educating primarily migrant workers and other working-class people, was yet another example of community empowerment led by cultural brokers. Sonny Montes, who had gained solid leadership skills working seven years with the VML, went to work for Mount Angel College in 1971. His job was to direct the Ethnic Studies program and to recruit *mexicano* students for the financially strapped but socially conscious institution. When it became apparent that the school could not meet its financial obligations, Montes proposed to the archdiocese that it permit him to attempt to form a Chicano college, a "college without walls" that would give credit "for prior experience gained outside the classroom" (interview with Gonzales-Berry, 2004). Hence, the only Chicano college in the nation was founded on an auspicious date, December 12, 1973,[21] but with, according to Montes, an inherited "debt of almost one million dollars ... from the former administration," as well as a hefty debt owed by the Benedictine Sisters to HUD (*Rural Tribune*, April 6, 1974). From the beginning, César Chávez, who was regularly visiting Oregon to promote the UFW's grape and lettuce boycott, was supportive, and the college was named in his honor. Montes fondly recalls the time when Chávez, who happened to be in Washington D.C. when administrators from the college were attempting to negotiate with HUD, showed up and used his masterful organizing tactics to influence the outcome of the meeting. Within a year, the *colegio* had 125 students, most of them migrants from the Mount Angel area. *El Chavista*, the college newspaper, provides a clear sense of the strong influence of Chicano Movement grassroots, bilingual discourse among its student body:

> Colegio *is a living picture of* la familia, *a constant reminder of the rural, urban and migrant* barrios. *It is a spirit of* carnalismo *[brotherhood]. It is a mirror of you and us and of all* raza. Colegio *represents our admiration, acceptance, understanding, respect and love for our* padres y madres *[fathers and mothers], for our* abuelitos *[grandparents], our* principios *[principles]. Who are we? We are the people who do not accept any less than your fullest potential in living, in learning, in creating. We are the people who will help the chicana/chicano to get a GED Certificate, and to get a college degree. We do not accept that a chicana belongs in the kitchen. We recognize that women, too, must contribute their fullest to* la raza. *If you are not afraid to defend our people and the poor, if you really believe that you should participate in decisions which affect our people, and if*

you truly believe that in unity there is strength, then you should come to colegio *and learn to become a leader of our people (*El Chavista, *March 1979).*

Despite the passion that moved the *colegio*'s student body and the administration's success in both gaining accreditation candidacy and establishing an educational program that was relevant and empowering for the student body, the college's financial burdens simply could not be overcome (José Romero, interview with Gonzales-Berry, 2004). Consequently, this inspiring experiment came to an end in 1983. Montes enthusiastically recalls those years:

Teníamos muchas ganas de hacer cosas *(we had the desire to accomplish things) and considering that we had paid our quotas it was a perfect fit for those days, because one thing that we didn't lack was energy and knowing people here and there. I remember when they said the only way you're going to be able to have financial aid is if you guys get some institutional self-studies. I didn't even know what the hell that was. So you know you do common-sense stuff. We asked Father Waldschmidt at the University of Portland if he could come over and talk to us about institutional self-studies, what they look like and all these kinds of things. And he did. So we put together a plan including twenty to twenty-five people. We started writing (laughs). A lot of people got involved in this. We submitted the report, with a request to the Northwest Accreditation Association for candidacy status. We went to a hearing in Idaho and we were on the news every day because we were kind of ridiculous. We didn't have any money, we didn't have accreditation. After the site visit and so on we made a presentation before the association and, lo and behold, they gave us candidacy status. It turned out to be a brand new ballgame after that, because they had to release some federal monies. So it worked out. It worked out. But again it was the effort of a whole bunch of people. A lot of struggles. It was hard. It was hard because—I'm not exaggerating or anything—but right after HUD started coming after us, we went about six, no maybe seven, eight, or nine months without any pay. How we were surviving was that any time I would go out and speak at different places, and I would say, we need to get paid. And then we had an agreement that anybody who generated monies would bring it back into a pot and we distributed among everybody else. But you know what ... fantastic experience. I don't think I'll ever go through that again. We never fought with each other. We were too busy trying to make the Colegio become a reality.*

We cite Montes at length because his words are testimony to the stuff those early *mexicano* activists and settlers were made of; they bear witness to the fact that through sheer will and hard work they were able to extricate themselves from paternalistic poverty programs and to take control of their communities. We must point out, however, that not all *mexicanos* view the accomplishments of the *Movimiento* with equal enthusiasm. Manuel Salinas, a retired educator whose family settled in the Willamette Valley more than sixty years ago, offered the following assessment of the activities described above:

> What we lacked was how to separate reality from fantasy and too many people were focusing on the fantasy and not the reality. You got the centro cultural that used to be over here a mile away [in Woodburn]. What happened to that? Well, when you don't have the business savvy, when you don't have the fundamentals to engage in some kind of business partnership, sometimes it's a lot of heart and not enough of the other. I think there has to be a balance. It's a shame to have a lot of this movimiento and not to have today, in the year 2005, not to have any tangibles (interview with Gonzales-Berry, 2005).

In our mind, however, there is no doubt that the settlers and activists discussed above, and others whose stories are not told here, laid a strong foundation for future generations. This foundation provides new migrants from Mexico[22] a foothold upon which to anchor their very vulnerable lives as they arrive daily in Oregon to continue picking our crops, washing dishes in our restaurants, making beds in our hotels, mowing our lawns, building our houses and, equally important, enriching our cultural landscape.

Descendants of Tejano *and* Mexicano *Settlers*

The descendants of the early *tejano* and *mexicano* settlers are scattered throughout Oregon, though they are primarily concentrated in Ontario, Nyssa, Woodburn, and surrounding areas; Independence, Washington County; and Medford and Portland. Their children and grandchildren are integrated into Oregon's mainstream society, but in general, their acculturation has been selective. Portes and Rumbaut (2001) characterize selective acculturation as a paced learning of the host culture accompanied by retention of significant elements and key values of the culture of origin. The individuals who are left of the first and second generation have sustained a strong ethnic identity linked to Mexican culture but also to their place of origin, Texas. In recent years *tejanos* have held reunions in

Washington County and in Woodburn. Miguel Salinas, the organizer of the bi-yearly *Tejano* Reunion in Woodburn reported to us that four hundred people attended this event in 2009 (personal conversation with Gonzales-Berry, 2009). Lorenzo Rubio from Hillsboro assured us that *tejano* identity runs deep in Oregon. He believes that *tejano* music, played on Spanish radio stations and featured in popular music concerts in Los Angeles and Las Vegas, has played a key role in sustaining that identity (interview with Mendoza and Gonzales-Berry, 2009). And although *tejanos* view themselves as separate and apart from Mexican nationals, the continual flow of migration from Mexico has been a source for cultural renewal that has contributed to the selective acculturation of *tejano* settler culture. In this regard, Oregon is beginning to resemble Southwestern states, which have a long-standing *mexicano* presence, which forms the bedrock upon which newer immigrants struggle to build their communities and construct their new identities as Americans and Oregonians.

The many individuals we have interviewed for this section speak of hard times, of struggle, of perseverance, and of community building. On the whole, they feel positive regarding their settlement in Oregon. However, we also have found numerous reports of exclusion and of blatant discrimination.[23] These practices have not disappeared with time but, in fact, have become more pronounced in recent years, encouraged perhaps by the anti-immigrant rhetoric spread through conservative talk radio and cable television that characterizes undocumented immigrants as aliens and criminals.[24] The underlying theme of anti-immigrant sentiment and its attendant handmaiden, social bigotry, in the history of *mexicanos* in the United States and here in Oregon cannot be divorced from the deeply entrenched racialized ideology of this nation. From their first entry into the nation as a conquered people and throughout their experience as new immigrants giving rise to second and third generations, *mexicanos* always already have been viewed as outsiders, and their national/ethnic/racial background has frequently been used as an excuse for marginalization and intolerance. The beating of two *mexicanos* by high school students at a park in Mulino, Oregon, in 2007 (*The Oregonian*, May 26, 2007) attests to the negative impact of this nativistic discourse and reminds us all that, although *mexicanos* have long been in Oregon and diligently have worked to carve out a niche for themselves and their families in the economic and social fabric of the state, we still have a long way to go before they are recognized as more than just the people who pick our crops.

1. A version of this chapter appeared in Xing et al. 2007.

2. The GI Forum is an advocacy group for Mexican American veterans of war. Its advocacy work, however, did not extend to undocumented immigrants, and the organization was not reluctant to speak out against immigrants when they felt the jobs or rights of *mexicano* residents or citizens were at stake.

3. In another case, "the Fruit Growers' League of Jackson County demanded to the state and to the politicians" that Bureau of Labor Director, Marco Antonio Infante, who was especially outspoken regarding migrant labor conditions, be fired, and "they framed him on trumped-up drug lord charges which they circulated in the press" (Loprinzi 1991, 53).

4. In its 1958 report, the Oregon Legislative Interim Committee on Migratory Labor attempted to tease out the distinction between labor contractors and crew leaders: "The purpose of the distinction is to ensure encouragement of the crew as a source of labor for Oregon. The detailed difference between the crew leader and the labor contractor is primarily legal. Customary usage of the terms varies in the United States and in different sections of Oregon. Generally speaking the crew leader is one who in addition to working in the crops himself aids the crew as spokesman and the farmer as foreman. The contractor usually seeks to handle a job for the farmer at a fixed price and then pays his workers less, keeping the difference for himself" (15).

5. For a touching story of these conditions see Rivera 1991.

6. A report issued by the Oregon Legislative Assembly Interim Committee in 1958 found that Oregon ranked sixth in the nation the previous year as a user of migratory labor.

7. Under the leadership of César Chávez, the United Farm Workers Union led a nationwide grape boycott beginning in 1965 and lasting more than five years. The boycott was successful in pressuring Schenley Industries and DiGiorgio Corportation into signing contracts with UFW workers.

8. The Second Vatican Council created an atmosphere that encouraged new ways of conceptualizing the world. In Latin America, theologians began to question the social problems affecting their countries. They also began to think about the relation between faith and poverty and to understand that the principles of Christianity, as espoused in the Bible, provided a blueprint for social justice. They encouraged the merging of theology with social praxis and this, in turn, prompted priests and nuns to engage actively in social movements. They named this movement "Liberation Theology."

9. This committee was made up of representatives from the departments of Agriculture, Education, Labor, Public Welfare, Industrial Accidents, Motor Vehicles, Health, and Employment Services. Their job was to "develop a cooperative program

to assist in solving the many problems facing the agricultural employer and worker" and to "cooperate with the Legislative Interim Committee on Migratory Labor … in studying the problems of the migrant agricultural worker" (Current and Infante 1959, 5).

10. As explained in the introduction, the term *Spanish American* was standard government and media usage in the first half of the twentieth century. In the reports issued by Infante and Current (1958) and Current and Infante (1959), the term Mexican is occasionally used, but always in quotes, as if to signal that this is not appropriate usage. Given that Infante was himself from Mexico, it is likely that he reserved the term Mexican for individuals of Mexican nationality, but found it inappropriate to designate United States citizens of Mexican origin, who could not lay legitimate claim to Mexican national identity.

11. Loprinzi finds the absence of concern among farmers stems from their lack of direct contact with workers, "because the use of contractors often allowed small and large farmers alike to be unconcerned" (1991, 49). In fairness to small farmers, she adds: "As the small farmer continued to struggle, and the larger farmer profit, farmworker conditions remained a low priority" (49). (Loprinzi believed that the large growers persuaded politicians and the public that the plight of the struggling small farmer was the plight of all farmers.) The words of one farmer, who spoke at a conference on migrant labor at Oregon State University, offer another perspective on the issue of farmer responsibility: "Within my financial ability, I can do things about wages, housing, and working conditions. I cannot do much for the chronic wino or the unskilled, uneducated father of eight children under the age of ten. Their problems are not agriculture's, and when society recognizes that I would hope society can stop shirking its collective duty by pointing its finger at farmers in order to expunge its own responsibility" (Ewer, *Perspectives on Migrant Labor in Oregon* 1968, 13).

12. Loprinzi (1991) notes that families who operated independently of contractors faced challenges that did not affect contract workers, such as arriving without funds and not being able to find work or not being able to buy items on credit. Despite these drawbacks, one report indicates that in 1957, of the total 111,760 Spanish-speaking workers running the migrant circuit to Oregon, 2,945 (not counting children) came independently of contractors (Oregon Bureau of Labor 1958, 9-10).

13. It would be very tempting to infer from these comments that Peña was a good candidate for complete assimilation. Her strong identity as a Chicana and a life of involvement and service to the *mexicano* community in Polk County belie such a speculation.

14. It was the kind of environment that the Peñas and García describe that prompted the Mexican government periodically to refuse to send *braceros* to Texas.

15. They were listed as Hispanics after 1970 because of civil rights legislation. A future scholar might want to explore school enrollment or church records to tease out these numbers.

16. Beginning in the 1930s, Mexico moved toward political stability and economic development that led to an annual growth pattern of about 6 percent. This period, which lasted through the '70s, came to be known as the *milagro mexicano,* or the Mexican Miracle.

17. This interesting note regarding childcare appears in *El Relámpago*: "Many problems face establishment of child care centers in the different areas served by the VML. Local citizens are frequently ignorant of the problems of migrant families. Farmers feel child care is somehow subversive. Some school and church boards whose facilities are badly needed feel the political pressures against child care and are reluctant to co-operate with the program. Many people simply do not understand the relevance of day care in solving the problems of migrant families" (April 1971, 1).

18. Paulo Freire, renowned Brazilian educator, espoused a philosophy that sought to empower disenfranchised and marginalized populations by encouraging dialogue as a step to recognizing their own social positioning and consequently defining their own needs and political agendas. The Maryknoll missionaries build communities of faith around the world, and they minister to the sick, elderly, orphans, and people with AIDS.

19. A community organizer who espoused radical social action, Saul Alinsky's philosophy is spelled out in his book *Rules for Radicals.*

20. Recently members of this group targeted the Centro Cultural in Cornelius, leading demonstrations against the center's day labor pick-up site. They were joined by members of the Minutemen, a self-styled vigilante group that maintains that "without the collective power of a national fraternity, immigration law enforcement advocacy groups cannot match the enormous clout of the combined influence of adversarial organizations who have banded together to force their way into U.S. territory in an effort to establish dominion over the United States of America by sheer numbers" (www.minutemanproject.com).

21. December 12 commemorates the apparition of the Virgin of Guadalupe to the indigenous youth Juan Diego. This date is celebrated yearly in Mexico and also in *mexicano* communities throughout the United States. In fact, a mass in honor of the Virgin of Guadalupe was the first event slated for the opening celebration of *El Colegio.*

22. We consider "recent immigrants" those individuals who began arriving in Oregon after the passage of the Immigration Reform and Control Act in 1986. Immediately after passage of this act, thousands of workers were given amnesty in Oregon, and

shortly thereafter, statistics related to demographic growth of "Latinos" in Oregon—the majority of them *mexicanos*—began to soar (see Chapter 3).

23. For a report on various incidents of discrimination against *mexicanos* in Oregon during the 1990s, see Brier, Ramírez, and Dash (1998).

24. The following, for example, appeared in an article in *The Sonoran News: "*Illegal aliens are not necessarily coming here to work. Lou Dobbs recently reported that 33 per cent of our prison population is comprised of non-citizens. Plus, 36 to 42 per cent of illegal aliens are on welfare. So, for a good proportion of these people, the American dream is crime and welfare, not coming to work" (April 4, 2004). Perhaps one of the more egregious claims regarding "illegal aliens" was the one made by correspondent Christine Romans on CNN's Lou Dobbs Show. Romans reported in 2005: "There have been 7,000 cases of leprosy in the United States in the last three years," and she attributed them to illegal immigrants. (The U.S. Department of Health and Human Services confirmed that there had been 7,000 cases in the last 30 years.) When Dobbs was called on this claim by a host of *60 Minutes*, Leslie Stahl, Dobbs, rather than correct the claim, said, "Well, I can tell you this. If we reported it, it is a fact" (*New York Times*, May 30, 2007). A recent report by Akdenizli et al. (2008), observes: "Since November 2003 when he launched his "Broken Borders" series, Dobbs has crusaded on the issue of illegal immigration with increasing intensity, reaching a crescendo during the 2006 and 2007 congressional debates with daily coverage. His focus on the illegal aspects of immigration is in keeping with tendencies evident in coverage by traditional news organizations over many years even if his explicitly biased approach to the subject, his lapses in verification and his haranguing style of presentation are obvious departures from the standards of journalism" (24).

Testimonio

by Celedonio Montes

This testimonio *comes from excerpts of an interview with Celedonio "Sonny" Montes in his office in 2004. At that time he was working for the Portland Public School District. The interview was conducted in English with smatterings of Spanish by Gonzales-Berry, and excerpts were selected, transcribed, and arranged by the authors.*

In California, I did farm work, and also for a year and a half I managed a *ranchito* of about thirty-five acres. In those days I made $1.35 an hour. My ex-wife had her family living up here in Cornelius. We came up and stayed at a camp and worked that summer. And by accident, I guess, some people from the VML had a presentation there at the camp. I asked a couple of questions, then the director, José García, came up to me afterwards and asked me if I wanted to work. He said, "Well, let me start you at such and such a month." I said, "Let me think about it because I can probably make more than that working in the fields." A couple of weeks went by. He approached me again, and I made a deal with him, because it was in the summer. What the old VML used to do was have a lot of camp meetings in the evening. So a lot of the work was visiting camps and making presentations to the farm-workers. So I thought, I'll make a deal. I'll work in the fields from 5:00 or 6:30 in the morning to 12:00, then I'll work from 1:00 to 10:00 at night. So that's how I got involved with the VML. They hired me as a program aide.

I think he [García] was the only Latino at that time—the only Latino area director in the VML. The sad part was that he left. He didn't last there too long. He hired me but then he left and that's when John Little came in. I believe in October of 1966. But John came in and then we became good buddies. He had just gotten back from Ecuador, and I started as a program aide. Then they offered me a job for $32 more as an assistant job counselor. Then John applied for the director's position, I believe in 1967. When he became executive director and I applied for his job, the area director's job in Hillsboro. I got lucky and I got it. And that's when all these changes came about... .

There was an organization called VIVA (Volunteers in Vanguard Action). At that time it was being run by an older Anglo lady [This would be the Ruby Ely mentioned in Chapter 2]. There was a group of families. Lydia Ramos was one of them, associated with her at that time. They were having some difficulties with the VML and the way it was being run and operated, very legitimate concerns by the way. Because in those days you had white people running the programs. All the administrators were white people; all the other directors were white people with a small sprinkling of Latinos here and there as program aides, which was the lowest-paid position in the organization. So, some of the concerns that they had were legit. But I think what happened in the process, once we started getting in there, and, to be honest, I think John played a key role in helping with the transition from an Anglo-controlled board and staff to a predominantly Latino-controlled board and the hiring of more Latinos into key responsible positions in the program. So that was one. I think if you look at some of the people who worked for the Valley Migrant League, the VML played a key role in the development of Latino leadership in the old days, and a lot of them are still involved in different activities.

And then that was one group. There was another group. There was a guy by the name of Guadalupe Bustos who was very critical of the VML. He had a radio program in Woodburn, and he was always bad mouthing the organization. And somehow or other—because I left the VML for a short period of time to go back to California—upon my return, John had worked out a deal with them. They called themselves the Farmworkers Forum. They were operating out of Washington County. They would get our funding, but it was a separate entity of sorts. A little more autonomous, but the same programs and so on. So upon my return—because I had resigned my position, and then I came back—I interviewed for a position because I needed work. He hired me as the education coordinator, so I worked there for a short period of time. Then there were some major conflicts between Bustos and José Morales and Emilio Hernández and they got into some blows actually. When that happened, we had a special meeting at Pacific University. Emilio and the other people told John to take the program back. Which I think he did. They asked me to run the program after that and I did that through 1971, then I went to the work at Colegio César Chávez.

Testimonio

by Maggie García

This testimonio *comes from excerpts from an interview conducted by Gonzales-Berry in 2004. At that time, Ms. García was a teacher at the MacLaren Youth Correctional Facility in Woodburn, Oregon, where the interview was conducted in English. The excerpts were selected, transcribed, and arranged by the authors.*

My parents were migrants. That's what they did. We came to Oregon, we went to California and Texas, and we did the whole migrant cycle thing. And then as we got older, my parents just traveled from Oregon to California, and then they added Idaho because it's close, for sweet potatoes. So we'd come to the area to pick strawberries, cherries, prunes, berries, do the hops. And then, around October, we would all go to California to do the citrus, oranges, grapefruits. And then we would come back to Oregon. And then, at one point, my father added Idaho. So then in October, instead of going to California, we'd go to Idaho because it's closer. We'd go from Woodburn to Idaho, to Jerome, Idaho, and pick potatoes. And that lasted about a month. When the potatoes were finished, we'd come back. One year we went to Arizona also. By that time we stopped going to Texas and settled out in the Northwest, Washington, Oregon, California, Idaho, and Arizona. And then just Oregon and Idaho. And then we just settled in Oregon. My father was told that there were a lot more opportunities for work here. The racial thing wasn't as evident as it was in places like Texas. And it was true, there was work everywhere. We'd work after school, all summer, on weekends, sometimes on Thursday, Friday, and Saturday. If there was work on Sunday, we'd work on Sunday. The only months that we didn't really do any work at all were November and December and most of January.

I remember a lot of times I didn't understand. But there was another thing that one always understands and that's prejudice. And I understood that, even as a child. Discrimination—I understood that as a child. One of my first feelings when I started school in Woodburn was the discrimination and the prejudice against Mexicans with the children and some of the teachers too. Just the way they looked at you or didn't; the way they helped you or didn't help you. But the kids, I remember some of the kids would say, "Go back to Mexico." "Where's that?" I was born in Texas. Those are my earliest recollections of school.

Of course things didn't get any better. It's just that I got smarter. You know, you learn to identify certain feelings for what they are. When you are a child you are innocent. You know that the feeling isn't right, and you know that there's something wrong, but you can't put a name to it. You just know where you're comfortable and where you're not, and school was not a place where I was comfortable. The school bus was even worse. I hated getting on that school bus, because I felt the discrimination was just so strong. I always felt the looks the kids gave us when we got on the bus. We were the only Mexican kids on the bus. And I always remember that I hated to go on the bus. It had to do with that, with the feeling that you were unwelcome and uncomfortable. But I always liked learning, and there was an occasional teacher that was nice... .

Then I went to college—my girlfriend and I. Her parents took us. I didn't even own a suitcase because we never traveled anywhere. When we did travel we packed in boxes, because you know, we were migrants. And then we stopped migrating, so we didn't need to pack anything. I don't even remember what I packed my clothes in. It was probably in boxes or bags. I might have even borrowed a suitcase from someone. So we took off for Eugene. I remember crying all the way from my house to Eugene. But I never turned back. I didn't say I wanted to go back. I cried, because I was excited. I was scared. I didn't know where I was going or what was going to happen to me when I got there. But I knew that I had to keep on going.

Testimonio

by Lorenzo Rubio

This testimonio *is composed from excerpts of an interview conducted by Mendoza and Gonzales-Berry in 2009 at Lorenzo Rubio's office at the Hillsboro Sheriff's Department where Rubio is a crime prevention officer. The interview was conducted in English with smatterings of Spanish. The excerpts were selected, transcribed, and arranged by the authors.*

I was originally born in Mexico, in a little town near Juarez. We came to the U.S. when I was about two or three years old. We moved to Texas, around the El Paso area. We lived there until I was five. Then we moved to New Mexico and we were in Artesia, New Mexico, until I was sixteen years old. The work there was mostly farming. A lot of alfalfa, cattle, that type of thing. We lived in a ranch for many of those years and when my stepfather and my mother separated, we decided that we were to come to Oregon for the summer, just to work for the summer because of the strawberry farm owner here. His name was Ron [Mr. Rubio did not provide a last name], I think he is still alive, you probably have heard about him. He sent some recruiters down to New Mexico to recruit families to come to Oregon for the summer to pick strawberries. They would bring the families up here and would send them back when the work was over. There were some families already here. These families were from Texas. On top of that Juanita, the wife of Ron, *era mexicana.* She lived in the same town, in Artesia, and I went to school with her brother, who was my age. So we knew the family and did not think that anything fraudulent would happen. We figured, well, we trust this family. So they recruited about twelve to fifteen *mexicano* families. Mostly everyone was from Texas or somewhere in Arizona. When they were down in Artesia, they showed my mother a picture with a little river or creek and they showed a guy fishing. It was a really nice picture in that setting, so my mother liked it. I just had gotten my driver's license and did not want to come for the summer and leave my friends. So I came under protest. The oldest was my sister, who at the time was eighteen. I was sixteen. We had three other brothers—two were developmentally challenged, so my mother had that stress.

We arrived here in two school buses. It took us about four days to get here. Of course the buses were full of people. You can imagine, we had six in my family. There were not enough seats for everyone. Some people had to ride standing because it was so packed. They told us that the money that we spent on the trip for food, they would reimburse us. It took four days. Back then there were no Arco or BP stores. It was only a gas station and they had some potato chips or a coke—that was the extent of the food that was available to buy. Every once in a while the bus would stop in a town or a city and we would have a decent meal but these were very few and far between, and the school buses were old and broke down a few times, but eventually we made it. North Plains was the little town we landed in. When we saw the shacks we were so disappointed, my mother especially. We got down from the buses, and we got a shack assigned to us and then the food was given to us. At that time the Department of Agriculture had food that [they] gave to the workers (canned meat, cheese, and peanut butter). We recognized what kind of food it was [welfare commodities] and thought this is not what we expected! But having no other options, we settled in. There were four bunk beds, so we had to make do. The little shack was probably five or six by ten and it had a little stove-top (a gas burner) and that was it. It was really a hardship for my mom thinking that we were to make some money and all was to be tax free. We were told that if we stayed up to the end of the picking season, we would get a bonus. Of course, we never saw that. This was the summer of 1969. We stayed and picked that summer, and towards the end of the summer the harvest was getting lower and lower, no more strawberries. This particular ranch would take us to other fields of other ranches to supplement the work and try to keep us busy, but we did not make enough money to go back home. Consequently, my mother lost the house that she had back in New Mexico, and we stayed in Oregon all that year. There was another family from New Mexico that decided to stay. We didn't have an option to go back because we didn't have any money, and the money that the rancher had promised that we wouldn't have to pay, it never got reimbursed. We were out of cash. We thought, well, at least he is going to give us some money to spend. We didn't get that. Eventually we were able to hook up with a man, Guadalupe Bustos, who worked for the Employment Office at that time and he heard our case. Bustos had a radio show. He was trying to help out people, a little political too. He hooked us up with an attorney. I can't remember his name. This attorney took our case pro bono. He helped us with a class action suit. My mom was named with one of those twelve families from New Mexico in the suit.[1] I believe we were successful in winning that class action suit but we didn't get any money. We had the honor of winning. We still couldn't go back home so we stayed that summer of 1969.

We moved to a little town near Salem (between Woodburn and Salem). There was a little ranch where they gave us some work and at the end of the summer we moved back here to Hillsboro and stayed for that one year. I went back to high school. My sister went to beauty school, trying to get a degree there. At the end of the following summer we got our monies together and got enough to go back to New Mexico. After getting back to New Mexico, I left my family and came back to Oregon on my own to finish high school. I was seventeen years old and came to live with another Mexican family whose kids I had become friends with. I met someone, we felt in love, and in 1972 we got married. At that time I was at Forest Grove High School and there were probably no more than fifteen *mexicano* kids in the school, we were very few. I remember not feeling very welcome. Consequently I transfered to Hillsboro High School, and I didn't feel more welcome there either. I remember that while I was at Forest Grove High School the counselors were trying to tell us, "Well, yeah, this is the kind of career that you need to go into. You need to learn janitorial work or mechanic, that type of jobs." I didn't like it. I thought that I was a decent student so I had higher expectations of my own but they didn't materialize. Now it's different but when my daughter was in high school, the counselor still wanted to give her basic classes that are not college preparatory. That is a credit that I give to my former wife. She fought very hard because she never had the opportunity to go to college—later on in years she did—but when my daughter was in high school she said: "No, the girl is qualified to learn the material," and she was able to get her in a college track. At that time when I just got married there were probably two dozen, no more, *mexicano* families in this area. We all attended mass at St. Mathew's Catholic Church and we had meetings and dances. There was a little club called Los Amigos. My mother eventually became part of that. It was our social network.

In terms of discrimination, it was always there. To tell you the truth, I never felt it until I came to Oregon. I remember at one point we were renting an apartment in Forest Grove and the landlord, who was drunk, kicked us out for no reason. Luckily my sister had been attending beauty school and she had met a German girl who was married to an Italian professor at Pacific University, so they became very good friends. When the landlord kicked us out, my sister called the only person who she thought could help us. Her friend's husband came, put us in a motel, and contacted the owner of the apartments. The owner fired the landlord and gave us a little better housing. I never forgot that professor. Later on in years I was working for a printing company as a sales representative. My former wife started as a secretary for the Valley Migrant League (VML). Then she became a teacher and had this position in the sheriff office that I have now. I also used to work at this social service agency, the Valley Migrant League. There was a farmworker program that came out of the VML called Oregon Rural Opportunities. I got involved with them. First I was a janitor while still in high school, cleaning their offices.

After I graduated from high school I became a board member, and after that I became an employee of the program. I used to travel from Hillsboro to Salem and my particular position was to help young Latinos who were about to graduate to get grants to go to college. With that I became involved in the political sense and started helping people who felt discriminated. When we were at the labor camp, one of the biggest things that struck me was how many social service agencies there were. Sonny Montes and others went to the labor camps to bring clothing, food, services, whatever ... but that farmer Ron would not allow those types of agencies to come in for whatever reason. I remember him calling the sheriff's office and the sheriff going up there and blocking the social service agencies from going in. The irony is that I now work for the sheriff's office and I go to the labor camps and offer services to the workers: "What can I do for you?"

When I got married, me and my wife were both working and were able to get a little bit of income, so we would go to stores and buy things. I remember very specifically that whenever you went—that taking into consideration that the majority of people here where from Texas, they were either second- or third-generation *mexicanos* that would come up here every summer and then go back, and then eventually decided to stay here—I felt that the stores didn't like our business. There was really no need for interpreters because the majority of the people spoke English, but as years progressed more and more monolingual people were starting to come up from Oaxaca and other parts of Mexico and Central America, so there was more need for interpreters. People didn't want the owners to hire bilinguals to deal with those customers. At times it gave me the feeling that they didn't want our business, but as the population grew things started changing a little bit and the owners started marketing towards the Latino community.

Back in 1972, I also got involved with the radio station here in Hillsboro, which I still love to do today. Back then, we used to provide music and public service announcements. We would do interviews with social service agencies, government agencies, to let people know what services were available to them. I remember I was seventeen when I got involved with the cultural center. They had offices in an old building. Whenever there was a problem in the community and the police got involved, we always gathered there and strategized. It was a very active community but there was a division within the *mexicano* community. At that time Lionel Lucero, Sonny Montes, and a bunch of others were more conservative if you want to label them; and there was Bustos and his followers who were more liberal. They had their own ideological concepts about what we should be doing there to help *mexicanos* and how to do it. They were more political, although in my view I don't think that the Chicano movement played out very well in this area, at least where

I lived. That would be more in the Woodburn area, in Salem. It was more regional. Most people in the circles I ran with or my mom ran with were more just trying to survive. The biggest challenge for me in those years was just to survive because we were really, really poor, and my mom was sick and not getting the adequate health care that she deserved, and there was nothing to help my younger brothers who were mentally challenged. All that weighed on me so much. It was very sad.

My former wife left the position at the sheriff's office and became a parole probation officer for Washington County, and then she moved on to the department that regulates law enforcement in the state of Oregon. Later, she was hired by the U.S. Department of Justice and went to work in Washington, D.C. That's when we divorced. I didn't want to move. But when we had 9/11, she decided to come home to Oregon. I think the political scene for *mexicanos* here was changing; but then there always remained those two factions. The new immigrants were coming to Oregon, mostly Mexicans and Central Americans, and they saw the Texans. Those guys didn't like the *tejanos* because they didn't speak Spanish well. The *tejanos* didn't like those people because they were always trying to correct them: "No, you don't say it that way ... you guys don't talk right." So that was mostly the division. It was the time when I got involved with the radio. *Tocábamos pura musica tejana*, and we would give public service announcements. I started getting more and more calls from *mexicanos*. I think that that really helped me to play the role of bridge between the *tejano* and *mexicano* communities through music, because music crosses any kind of generation and political beliefs that one may have. Music united us in this area.

The *tejano* community also grew to a point that we have a *tejano* community that loves *tejano* music. People say that *tejano* music is probably dying. Our generation loves it. We play it on the radio, dedicate hours to do it. We do conferences on *tejano* music and whenever there is a festival in Las Vegas, a lot of *tejanos* from all over the U.S. participate. We see people in Las Vegas on a yearly basis. In Sacramento, California, there is another festival of *tejano* music. Even here in Washington County a couple of years ago we did a reunion of early-arrival *tejanos* and that went very well. Hector Espinosa was there. We saw families that we had not seen in years. I think that for the most part their kids have integrated to the larger community. That was an interesting thing that we found out about at this reunion. We saw the kids of our friends and asked them: "What do you do?" They've got tech jobs, and they have good jobs. It was really interesting. If I see this young person on the street, I would have never guessed that I used to hang out together with her dad or her mom. Many do not speak Spanish, though. When my daughter was in college at the University of Oregon, she saw the other Latino kids and became more politically involved and more bilingual, so she learned Spanish. She has a lot more knowledge of our history now. In our generation we did not intermarry with non-Mexicans but we are seeing more of this with our kids. I see that a lot and it does not surprise me. My daughter for example got married with *el hijo de* José Romero. Unfortunately, it didn't work out but my daughter went on to the University of Oregon, got a degree, and then went to the University of Washington and got a Masters in Communication. My ex-wife and my daughter were both working for the Mayor of Portland until he left the office. My daughter stayed working with the city. She is a policy advisor for one of the commissioners. I'm very proud of her. She's doing a lot of work in Portland. Now we are Oregonians *hasta las cachas*.

---

1. On December 14, 1971, *The Oregonian* reported the following regarding this lawsuit: "In a stipulated judgment, a group of migrant workers has been awarded a total of $8,000 in damages in a civil suit arising from a federal court decision of August, 1970, which found a Washington County farmer guilty of breach of contract. Defendant in the action was Ronald Tankersley, a berry farmer who had been accused of making false promises to induce Mexican-American workers to come to Oregon in 1969."

Chapter 3

Unintended Consequences: Mexican Immigration to Oregon after 1986 Immigration Reform and NAFTA[1]

There is a great deal of misunderstanding regarding the contemporary phenomenon of immigration. We believe that, in order to understand why the numbers of *mexicano* immigrants to Oregon increased dramatically between 1990 and 2007, it is essential to understand the larger forces that have created an undocumented international labor force that finds its way not only to Oregon but across the entire globe. Hence, much of the discussion in this chapter pertains to the broader national scene rather than to Oregon, and an understanding of this broader picture will create a greater appreciation of the local situation.

By the 1980s Mexican immigration to the United States had become a systematic, circular phenomenon that met the needs of all involved. This migration initially came "from a small subset of communities in seven or eight Mexican states" (Cornelius 1992). It developed in response to global macro-economic forces that changed the American labor market, and simultaneously shaped life in Mexican villages. Meanwhile, social and economic micro forces affected people's decisions at the personal or familial level. Mexico's inability to provide sufficient jobs to accommodate the size of its work force; the demand for cheap labor in the United States; a legacy of migration engendered by the bi-national labor agreement signed by Mexico and the United States during World War II; vigorous labor-recruitment practices by U.S. agricultural interests; the desire of Mexican families to enhance their life chances—all were compelling factors that spurred migration from Mexico to the United States. While some families did make the journey north, it was primarily young and single males, "the sons and brothers of former *braceros* who were able to garner sponsorship through family connections" (Cerruti and Massey 2004), who journeyed to *el norte*. Their willingness to risk travel to a foreign land—whose language they did not speak, whose customs were inaccessible, and which long had exhibited a hostile attitude toward their kind—guaranteed U.S. employers, particularly in agriculture, a seasonal labor force. Mexican workers, on the other hand, were able to divide their time between earning money in the United States and spending time with their families during the off season.

The social networks that evolved during many decades of migration provided migrants with crucial information, material and emotional support, job references, temporary lodging, and warnings regarding potential pitfalls. These networks facilitated migration and decreased its attendant risks (Portes and Rumbaut 1996; Massey 1990; Chávez 1992a). When workers returned home between jobs, they could make their earnings work for them by investing in small family-operated businesses, or by buying equipment and fertilizers for their land; or they could apply them to more personal enterprises such as adding a second story to their home, or begin a courtship that would eventually allow them to start a family in their home villages. Jesús shared with us the goal that motivated him to come to the United States at the age of seventeen: "What always passed through my mind was that I would come here to study and like everyone else make loads of money in a short while. I wanted to study and learn English so I could get a good job. And another thing that I wanted to do was buy my father a pickup. That was an idea I always had. It was what motivated me to work." Because Jesús was young and he was still not responsible for a family of his own, his motives were tied to a need for recognition and the desire to enhance his self-esteem: "The first thing I did with the money I earned was buy a truck for my father and when I returned in 1994 I took it to him. I had a lot of plans: study, work, and make money. And be someone. I wanted my parents to be proud of me as they were of my brother" (interview with S.J. Acosta, 2003).

Circular migration, which kept workers connected to their hometowns in Mexico and discouraged them from settling in the United States, had its own logic: it was regular, systematic, and predictable; in short, it functioned like a well-oiled machine (Massey et al. 2002). Isías lived in a small *rancho* in Guanajato when he started coming to the United States in 1979, and he engaged in circular migration for years before settling in Oregon. He recalled his various crossings and his dogged determination to return despite frequent setbacks. Isías was deeply aware of the toll exacted by this life style.

> *I came with a cousin and a coyote. He crossed us at Tijuana. In one and a half hours we were at our destination. We worked the fields and slept in the mountains. We were afraid because we didn't have papers. People brought food up and sold it to us. We made $2.90 an hour. In 1980 I got a raise to $3.10. Another time, the migra rode on horseback and they chased us and herded us down. I was stopped three times. Two times crossing through the hills and one time at the airport. The first years I came, the safest place was a bar or a pool hall because the streets were so dangerous. I had never seen that in my village. In 1989 I came to Oregon. Here it was difficult. For three*

months I couldn't find a job. Some boys I knew were working and gave me food. One time I went to a ranch to look for work and they chased me off. I cooked for my friends because they helped me out. I never thought about staying or returning. All I knew is that I had to help the family. My father wrote me that my family needed me. My ambition was to help them more, so I didn't think of going back. Things got better, but it's not a way to live separated from family (interview with S.J. Acosta, 2003).

Immigration reform legislation passed in 1986 (Immigration Reform and Control Act) and again in 1996 (Illegal Immigration Reform and Immigration Responsibility Act), and the subsequent militarization of the border would change the pattern of circular migration (Andreas 1998; Massey et al. 2002; Cerruti and Massey 2004; Richter et al. 2005). At the same time, an expanding global economy would dislodge an international work force, the likes of which had never been witnessed before. Nationally, this phenomenon spurred increasing demands for hemispheric economic integration, resulting in the signing of the North American Free Trade Agreement in 1994. It is apparent that the social realities associated with neo-liberal economics and the immigration policies of sovereign nation states do not mesh; in fact, for the United States, the disconnect is so great that it has created the "immigration crisis" that currently bedevils politicians and citizens alike.

The Unforeseen Ramifications of Immigration Reform Legislation

The economic and political climate of the early 1980s created unfavorable conditions for immigrants from Mexico and Latin America. The United States had just recently retreated in a deeply wounded condition from Viet Nam and faced a harsh period of economic recession as European and Asian economies hurtled past our own. Guerilla warfare against oligarchic regimes supported by the United States was spreading in Latin America, raising the proverbial flag of a "communist threat" at our borders (Massey et al. 2002). Moreover, production jobs were dwindling, the service sector expanding, and labor casualization becoming ever more pervasive (Sassen 1996). These conditions called for increasing numbers of low-skilled workers precisely when the U.S. working population was aging and the U.S. birth rate decreasing (Bustamante 1992). Massey et al. (2002) maintain that this historical moment of instability and self-doubt led U.S. citizens to clamor for change; they forced that change through the election of Ronald Reagan. In addition to taking a sharp conservative turn, the Reagan administration resorted to a pattern common in the history of the United States; it sought someone or something to blame for the distressing conditions that plagued the nation, and it looked no further than the Mexico-U.S. border to find a scapegoat (Bustamante 1992; Massey et al. 2002; Nevins 2002). Popular radio talk shows played no small role in characterizing the border as "out of control" and in characterizing those who crossed that border without authorization as criminals. In their analysis of media coverage beginning in the last thirty years, Akdenizli et al. (2008) maintain:

> *The cumulative portrait drawn by nearly 30 years of American journalism emphasizes illegal or uncontrolled migration rather than the much larger movement of people that has been legal and orderly. This emphasis on illegality applies not only to the means by which people enter the country but also to their activities once here (24). The subtext of this discourse was and continues to be that failure to curb illegal immigration threatens the economic, political, and cultural integrity of the United States.*

By the mid-80s, and with nativists fanning the ideological flames, many leaders in Washington jumped on the anti-immigration bandwagon. After several iterations, the originally named and controversial Simpson-Massoli Act (then the Simpson-Rodino Act) was passed through Congress as the Immigration Reform and Control Act of 1986.[2] This piece of comprehensive immigration reform legislation unleashed "an internal migratory flow within an international one" (Zuñiga and Hernández-León 2005, 126). This flow would bring scores of migrants to the United States—as evidenced by their growing numbers, documented in the 1990 census when the dust of IRCA was beginning to settle—and eventually it would scatter them to new destinations within the country.

IRCA, as it popularly came to be known, had the following objectives: 1) to make illegal crossing less attractive by tightening up the border; 2) to discourage the hiring of undocumented workers by imposing fines of $250 to $10,000 on employers and possibly imprisonment;[3] 3) to grant temporary amnesty to individuals who had been in the country continuously since at least 1982, provided they apply by 1988 (Massey et al. 2002).

Congress at first anticipated that at least a million individuals would apply for amnesty. However, as the proposed legislation was examined and debated, anticipated numbers oscillated wildly, reaching figures as high as twenty million. The latter figure was offered by Representative Hal Daub, a strong opponent of amnesty. Representatives Henry Hyde and F. Sensenbrenner went so far as to predict that one third of Mexico's population would be drawn to the United States by IRCA (Ong Hing 2004). In the end, almost three million applied for authorization to be in this country. Of these, 1.7 applied for amnesty and another 1.3 million applied for regularization under a provision that dealt specifically with agricultural workers, the Seasonal Agricultural Worker Program (SAW), although only two hundred and fifty thousand had been anticipated in this category. SAW provisions granted temporary legal residence to individuals who worked in agriculture at least ninety days out of each twelve-month period during 1984, 1985, and 1986. A second round of SAW required only one ninety-day stint of farm labor in 1985-86 (interview R. Ginsburg, 2007). Viewed as separate from "amnesty," and intended as a "fast track" to legalization, these provisions were influenced by the agriculture lobby, which employed primarily seasonal migrant laborers, many of whom did not have records of longer term continued residency necessary for amnesty. Of the nearly three million individuals who applied for legal status—either amnesty or temporary residency through SAW—under IRCA, 74 percent were from Mexico and 21 percent from Central America; among them, 83 percent were already employed in the labor market (Library Index n.d.). With both groups—SAWs and amnesty seekers—combined, a total of just fewer than 2.7 million applicants from all countries were granted legal status. (The actual processing of applications and appeals, however, went on past 2000.)

With a more secure border and the erasure of illegal status for hundreds of thousands of "aliens," national leaders anticipated that the "immigration crisis" would be solved, all of this in preparation for passage of a Free Trade Agreement in 1993. NAFTA would allow the United States the benefits of free trade without the untidy, trailing, international labor force which already was being unleashed across the globe in the wake of globalization.[4] Individuals who were granted amnesty could then apply for visas for their spouses and children. In 1990, the Immigration Act granted legal temporary residence to one hundred and sixty thousand spouses and children of amnestied workers; as was true of all amnestied individuals, they would become eligible for permanent residency status in three years. However, these dependents were not included in the official IRCA count. It is also a fact that many families, fearing that the border would be permanently shut down, rather than waiting out the time required to do the paperwork for a formal visa as required by amnesty provisions, came without authorization. SAW applicants, however, were not included automatically in the family reunification process; they could not secure authorization for their families through IRCA, but they were eligible to apply for visas through the regular visa allocation system should slots become available. This might involve returning to Mexico and applying to the U.S. Consulate there. Because it was a cumbersome and drawn-out process, and actual slots rare, many men brought their families without documents (interview R. Ginsburg 2007).[5]

That the number of families heading to the United States in this period was increasing is attested to by the fact that more women and children than ever before were apprehended at the border (Cornelius 1992). In 1990, on average, fifteen minors aged five to seventeen were apprehended daily at the Tijuana crossing (Cornelius 1992). Those who evaded apprehension began to be counted in the 1990 census at which time we witness a dramatic increase in the number of *mexicanos* present in Oregon and in other areas of the country.

The Consequences of Immigration Reform Legislation in Oregon

The enactment of IRCA created a wrinkle in the usual pattern of migrant labor in Oregon. Some potential migrant workers were concerned that the newly imposed sanctions stipulated by this legislation would keep employers from hiring them. Others were deterred by the propaganda spread by the Mexican press, which declared: "Mexico-U.S. Border in State of Siege" (Bustamante 1992). Oregon, with its lowest unemployment rate since 1973, felt the brunt of the "wait and see" stance assumed by workers who for years had ventured north to pick the seasonal crops. In May and June of 1987, Oregon newspapers sounded the alarm: "Oregon's proclaimed labor shortages have catapulted the state, which has less than 1 percent of the country's population, into the unusual role as a bellwether of the effects of the nation's new immigration law. The problem, according to farmers, is that strawberries are dying on the vine. Farmers and state officials warn that cherries are next. Then apples and pears, and with those fruits will go $300 million" (*The Oregonian*, June 11, 1987). One indignant farmer exclaimed in frustration, "I blame the government. And the people in Oregon are the ones who are going to pay" (*The Oregonian*, May 24, 1987).

At the time that this legislation was enacted, undocumented workers in Oregon were in need of immigration reform. In several areas of the state, there were reports of violence and intimidation toward agricultural workers and individuals advocating for their rights. Immigration attorney Richard Ginsburg believed, "What we've seen over the last year or two I would call peonage; it borders on slavery" (*The Oregonian*, August 22, 1986). One would expect that these exploited undocumented workers would have welcomed the opportunity for legalization, with hopes that it might improve their treatment. However, when IRCA was first implemented on May 5, 1987, they did not storm the official processing centers. Immigration officials expected a hundred thousand applicants for regularization, particulary under the SAW provisions, in a state whose undocumented labor force was estimated to be as high as 90 percent; but three weeks into the program only seventy-five individuals had filed applications in the two legalization offices in Oregon (*The Oregonian*, May 24, 1987). Undocumented workers may have been wary of setting foot in an INS (Immigration and Naturalization Service) office. *Mexicano* immigrant workers were accustomed to living in the shadows and made every effort to remain invisible. An outreach campaign, which assured confidentiality and safety, was carried out through Spanish-language radio, newspapers, and cultural centers. In addition to the official processing centers of the INS, the government also authorized QEDs (qualified agencies and volunteers) and CBOs (community agencies) to process applications. The immigration counseling service associated with Catholic Archdiocese of Oregon was one such QED that processed large numbers of applications (interview Ginsburg 2007). The farmworker union, PCUN, also became heavily involved, processing thirteen hundred cases between June 1987 and June 1988 (Stephen and PCUN 2001). Private lawyers were also permitted to process applications, and like the CBOs, they dealt mainly with more complicated cases involving documentation problems and the like. The expectation was that CBOs and QEDs would be more effective in attracting individuals who were fearful or distrustful of the INS, but Ong Hing (2004) reports that the collective goal of all involved entities was to get as many people authorized as possible. Richard Ginsburg recalls the abuses that emerged in connection with this program. One of the most common forms of fraud was the selling of letters confirming length of employment and, not infrequently, it was employers who engaged in these practices. One berry farm allegedly gave away or sold up to four thousand letters (interview with Gonzales-Berry, 2007). Ginsburg reported there were also instances in which individuals were told by personnel at the legalization offices, "We don't think you're eligible," and were turned away. Often these cases were appealed. Ginsburg noted also that he was still working on IRCA cases in 2007: "Some of these cases went through an appellate process and that took time. We have a couple of cases that we won on appeal so they got remanded back to immigration service. There's hardly anyone at the immigration service who remembers the programs so they don't have the expertise anymore and they're exceedingly slow in processing these cases." Nonetheless, this lawyer's overall assessment is that IRCA was a fairly administered program.

According to Stephen, Mendoza, and Magaña (2008), 23,736 Mexicans and some Guatemalans were authorized under the Seasonal Agricultural Program in Oregon in its first year of operation; additional workers were given temporary residency status in the following six years (Mason et al. 1993). Once amnestied and SAW workers were regularized, many were joined by their families, including wives, children, siblings, and parents. In the narrative cited below, Edith Quiroz Molina (whose life will be presented in greater detail in a *testimonio* that follows Chapter 6) recounts her family's trek north after her father acquired legal immigration status:

> *My father was a cherry, apple, and pear picker in the Hood River Valley and The Dalles during 1985. He always thought he would come and go from Mexico to the United States. However, his family was not here in 1987 when he applied for the residency papers, which resulted in his wife and children's papers being stalled at the headquarters of immigration in Ciudad Juarez, where he filed. When I was ready to send my college application and to apply for one of the most valuable scholarships of that time, the Laurel Scholarship, which was a full-tuition-paid scholarship for four years, the Permanent Resident Alien number was asked for. "What is that?" I asked my counselor. He looked at me with concern and said, "Well, are you a U.S citizen?" "No," I responded. "Well then, you might be a permanent resident, which means that you are here legally and that you have a number that is similar to a visa, or do you have a visa?" I was confused and a little nervous. I knew that I did not have a visa because I never carried one, but I was not 100 percent sure that I had a green card number. "Dad, I need my green card number," I demanded. "Oh, I don't think you have one. I applied for the whole family when I received my papers in 1986, but I think we have to do more. I have no idea how to get your number. Maybe you should try to find out what happened with your papers" (personal essay, 2006).*

As happened with this family, workers who had been regularized under the terms of SAW frequently brought their families as quickly as they could, thus avoiding the tightening up of border control, and they either did not bother to apply for visas for their families or did not follow through with the application process.

A comprehensive report on the impact of IRCA on farm labor in Oregon indicates that the supply of workers increased as a result of this legislation. It also notes that the SAW provisions of IRCA were particularly effective in addressing the adequacy of the labor supply in the state, and that "labor supplies also have increased as SAW workers bring their families to the United States. These family members are often employed illegally in agriculture" (Mason et al. 1993, 144). While growers appreciated the availability of this labor supply, they also resented the fact that they had to serve as an enforcement arm for IRCA. They were especially fearful "of hiring illegal workers and being fined; on the other [hand], they fear they could be accused of discrimination if they don't hire a particular [native born] worker" (Mason et. al 1993, 144). This report stresses that there was a noticeable exodus of workers from farms to other types of work after passage of immigration reform, and other scholars agree. A federally sponsored report issued in 1991, however, argues, "On a nationwide basis, there is no evidence that workers of any legal status group (except a small heterogeneous group of 'other legal') is leaving agriculture" (Mines and Gabbard 1992, 1). In Oregon, the nursery industry was a direct beneficiary of IRCA, as it was able to attract workers with papers who now had the kind of security that permitted them to seek year-round employment. Francisco, interviewed by Gonzales-Berry in 2007, first came to work in Oregon agriculture. Currently, he has year-round employment in a nursery and has been able to bring his family with legal visas. His wife works as a custodian at Hewlett Packard. Their joint salary allows this family to rent a lovely home in Corvallis and to enjoy a more secure life than others who continue to work in seasonal occupations. Santiago was also given residency status through IRCA. He now works for a gas company and he, his wife, and child are beginning to harvest the promise of the "American Dream" in Philomath (interview with Gonzales-Berry, 2007).

Militarization of the Border and the Failure of Deterrence Policies

By 1990 the number of *mexicanos* entering the U.S. began to increase once again, and continued to do so for more than a decade. Mexico's economic crash of 1994 played no small role in "pushing out" workers for whom there were not enough jobs. These increased numbers caused some concern in the U.S. Moreover, negative publicity attached to Haitian "boat people" and Cuban "*balseros*" (rafters) arriving in large numbers on the Florida shores. Nativist responses included Peter Brimelow's *Alien Nation* (1995), with its warning that the very character of the United States would be transformed through immigration, and the anti-immigration discourse of right-wing talk radio hosts "resonated across the land" (González 2001).

In 1996, Congress passed and President Bill Clinton signed new immigration reform legislation, Illegal Immigration Reform and Immigration Responsibility Act (IIRIRA). Lynn Stephen summarizes one of the act's most onerous stipulations:

> *Under this act, undocumented family members filing for residency in the United States after January 1998 were punished if they tried to file while undocumented and living in the United States. They had to leave in order to file for residency, because they could no longer apply in the U.S. If they did leave, then they could trip a bar of up to ten years before they could apply to change their immigration status (if they had been in the United States illegally for more than a year since*

April of 1997 and there was evidence of that). If families wanted to remain united, they had to take the risk of remaining undocumented in the U.S., thus replicating the pattern of families with multiple statuses among their members (2001, 196).

The IIRIRA also included severe penalties for apprehension and provided hefty increases in the U.S. Border Patrol budget as well as escalating militarization of the border.[6]

Deterrence programs such as Hold the Line and Operation Gatekeeper certainly prevented unauthorized migrants from crossing at traditional sites such as Tijuana and El Paso. However, they merely dispersed them to new entry points. Immigrants began to forge new paths in isolated desert locations and inhospitable mountain terrain, introducing the possibility of death from dehydration and hypothermia (Andreas 1998). The INS had anticipated that, as crossing became more fraught with peril, workers would choose to stay home rather than rely on *coyotes* or *polleros* (the guides leading migrants across the border), who would raise their prices substantially to adjust for new hazardous conditions. But migrants did turn to *coyotes*, whose sophisticated smuggling tactics increased their chances of successful crossing. The use of fraudulent documents also increased. These responses to border militarization thwarted the anticipated deterrence effect of a militarized border, but not without tragic consequences. The World Immigration Web site reports that 1,954 deaths occurred between 1998 and 2004 and lists the number of deaths in 2004 at 325 (www.en.allexperts. com/e/i/im/immigrant_deaths_along_the_u.s._mexico_border.htm). Border activist Enrique Morones tells of much higher numbers of tragic deaths. The names of many of these individuals have been recorded, although the organization founded by Morones, Border Angels, estimates that about one thousand unidentified migrants have died attempting to cross the US-Mexico border (www.borderangels.org).

In view of these consequences, Ong Hing had harsh words for this facet of U.S. immigration policy. Referring to the California border enforcement program, he wrote: "Operation Gatekeeper is not simply a law enforcement operation that has created a harsh result. Gatekeeper is a law enforcement operation that imposes a death sentence on individuals, principally Mexicans, who are simply seeking a better life because of economic imbalance or seeking to be with family. Operation Gatekeeper is a moral outrage, and our nation has lost its soul in supporting it" (2004, 102). Throughout this text we have demonstrated that both in terms of national policy and national attitudes, historically, Mexicans have been viewed as puppets in an economic and political theater. It is true that other immigrant groups have also faced indifference and harsh conditions. However, these conditions eventually came to an end for them. What is so disconcerting about the Mexican case is the pervasive nature of their inferior social position in American society—beginning in 1848 and still going on today—and this is true even for citizens of Mexican origin. Their case, in fact, resembles more that of African Americans than that of European immigrant ethnic groups, and this is so precisely because they have been cast as players in the racialized ideology of the nation, though it is rarely acknowledged that the black/white race construct is inadequate for accommodating a discussion of the racism experienced by Mexicans in the United States.

The architects of "hold the line" strategies seriously miscalculated the resolve of *mexicanos* (and Central Americans) determined to reach *el norte*. Higher costs and greater risks, both in terms of physical danger and more severe apprehension penalties, did not keep unauthorized workers from crossing over. But they did discourage them from engaging in the customary seasonal treks; instead, the workers prolonged their stay in the United States, thus increasing the probability of settlement. According to one scholar, the length of stay for unskilled workers rose from eighteen months to eighty-four months, and for skilled workers from forty months to one hundred and twenty months, beginning in 1993 (Kandel 2004). The disruption of circular seasonal migration—which for decades had allowed workers to spend part of the year working in the United States and part of the year tending to their families and their business at home—encouraged undocumented workers to bring their families to live with them. Once families come over, settlement becomes a tempting option, thereby ending the tradition of workers eventually returning to Mexico for good (Andreas 1998; Massey et al. 2002).

It is clear that the immigration reform acts of 1986 and 1996, the supposed panaceas for fixing a "broken border" and curbing undocumented immigration, failed to achieve their objectives. Immigration scholar Douglas Massey and his colleagues did not mince words in their indictment of these reforms:

> *If the United States had set out to design a dysfunctional immigration policy, it could hardly have done a better job than what it did between 1986 and 1996. U.S. tax payers now waste at least $3 billion annually in essentially useless border enforcement while the efficiency of the Border Patrol operations is in rapid decline. Despite its extravagance, the expensive post-IRCA enforcement regime has had no detectable effect, either in deterring undocumented migrants or in raising the possibility of their apprehension. It has been effective, however, causing at least 160 needless deaths each year. It has also lowered wages for workers—native and foreign, legal and illegal—and exacerbated income inequality in the United States.*

> *Furthermore, it has guaranteed that these negative externalities are widely felt by transforming a seasonal movement of male workers going to three states into a national population of settled families dispersed throughout the country (Massey et al. 2002, 140).*

These and other scholars also acknowledge that immigration policies have failed precisely because they do not take into account the existence of an international labor market that has been created by the politics and ideology of global economic integration. We would add that the historical failure, beginning in 1848, to accord Mexicans their full humanity has also played a role in the creation of ad hoc and ambivalent immigration policies formulated by this country vis-à-vis Mexico.

North American Free Trade Agreement: More Unintended Consequences

NAFTA, spawned by neo-liberal economics that swept the world in the late twentieth century, was signed in 1993 and went into effect in 1994. If IRCA had failed to deter immigration from Mexico, NAFTA promised the final solution. Supporters of the treaty believed that hemispheric economic integration would invite greater investment by treaty partners in Mexico, resulting in the expansion of Mexican exports and in the long run spurring Mexican job growth and decreasing out-migration (Acevedo and Espenshade 1992). In anticipation of this trade agreement, the U.S. International Trade Commission concluded in a comprehensive study that a free trade agreement "is likely to decrease slightly the gap between real United States wages and Mexican wages of both skilled and unskilled workers combined, but a greater share of the wage adjustment would occur in Mexico than in the United States. As wage differentials between the United States and Mexico narrow, the incentive for migration from Mexico will decline" (cited in Acevedo and Espenshade 1992). Thirteen years after the fact, evidence to evaluate NAFTA's success in meeting its original goals offers a bleak picture. According to the World Bank, Mexico's gross domestic product (GDP) experienced an increase of 5 percent in 1996, 7 percent in 1997, 5 percent in 1998, 4 percent in 1999, 7 percent in 2000, and 0 percent in 2001, but this after a drop of 6 percent in 1995. Moreno-Bird and colleagues have noted, "In 2001-2003 the Mexican economy barely grew and registered a trade deficit once again of 1.5-2 percent of GDP" (2005, 1112-1113), and they conclude: "it is clear that the evolution of employment after NAFTA has not fulfilled the expectations that had been generated" (1114). The Carnegie Institute reported in 2004, "NAFTA has produced a disappointingly small net gain in jobs in Mexico; it is clear that jobs created in manufacturing have barely kept pace with jobs lost in agriculture due to imports. There has also been a decline in domestic manufacturing employment, related in part to import competition and perhaps also to the substitution of foreign inputs in assembly operation" (Audley et al. 2004, 12). The same report highlights also that "agriculture has been a net loser in trade with the United States and employment in the sector has declined sharply. U.S. exports of subsidized crops, such as corn, have depressed agricultural prices in Mexico. The rural poor have borne the brunt of adjustment to NAFTA and have been forced to adapt without adequate government support" (Audley et al 2004, 12).

While the assessment of various facets of the impact of NAFTA on the Mexican economy can at times be contradictory, the Carnegie Institute report is unequivocal in its overall assessment: "NAFTA did not create necessary conditions for the public and private sectors to respond to the economic, social, and environmental shocks of trading with two of the world's biggest economies. Mexico's most vulnerable citizens have been forced into malstrom of change beyond their capacity, or that of their government, to control" (Audley et al. 2004, 7). Richter and her colleagues (2005) argue the GDP growth that has occurred in Mexico has actually encouraged rather than discouraged immigration by providing capital for rural households to finance trips to the United States. Other scholars foresaw, even before NAFTA was passed, that it would contribute to undocumented immigration. Hinojosa and Robinson (1991) anticipated that workers—particularly those in agriculture—would become displaced as credit subsidies decreased and protectionist policies were removed. This displacement, they noted, would result in a period of increased migration, to be followed by a substantial decrease after a decade. A broader time-span was suggested by Martin (1993), who predicted that out-migration from Mexico would not begin to decrease until fifteen years into NAFTA. Fifteen years after the fact, it is clear that many national and regional leaders, nativists, and the mainstream media in the United States are outraged over the increase in undocumented immigration, and are not willing to wait until predictions regarding NAFTA and immigration play out fully before engaging in a major overhaul of U.S. immigration policy.

Mexican Population Growth in Oregon: The California Factor

Since the late 1980s, through the 1990s, and ongoing today, *mexicano* immigrant workers continue to settle in the state. Oregon's Mexican population increased 144 percent during the 1990s, and the Hispanic workforce grew 269 percent from 1990 to 2003, according to the Oregon Employment Department. The natural growth of the *tejano* settler population certainly accounts for part of this population increase in Oregon, but the spike in numbers can also be attributed to enhanced employment opportunities in agricultural enterprises and other industries such as hospitality, reforestation, construction, light manufacturing, and transportation. Events in California during this time may also have had an impact. In the early 1990s, California suffered a severe recession resulting from the closure of military bases throughout the state. At the same time the number of immigrants from Latin American and Asia was rapidly increasing and causing a saturation of the social networks that had connected immigrants to employment and housing. This mix contributed to the emergence of a potent anti-immigrant agenda unleashed by Proposition 187, a referendum designed to deny public assistance and education to unauthorized immigrants. As competition for jobs grew, and as immigrants were made to feel ever less welcome to the state, many of them began to look beyond California as potential work and settlement sites (Nevins 2002; Ong Hing 2004).[7] The neighboring state of Oregon, with its healthy level of economic growth in a number of sectors including its huge agricultural industry and its expanding nursery and Christmas tree industries, was certainly an attractive option. Those immigrants who "spilled over" from California during the past fifteen years, like those who arrived directly from Mexico, received assistance from social networks created by relatives, friends, and acquaintances who had settled before in the cities of Portland and Salem, or in small communities in other parts of the state. These social networks provide information, help finance trips, and assist in the job search. A wide range of individuals facilitate the arrival and settlement of newcomers, including labor recruiters and contractors, providers of transportation, landlords, immigration lawyers, auto sales, money-lending, and money-sending merchants (who may also cash checks and sell phone-cards), all of whom participate in a deep-rooted local "migration industry."

Mexicanos *in Oregon after IRCA and NAFTA:*
Motives, Networks, and Challenges

The testimony given below by José is instructive in helping us understand the conditions in Mexico that motivated its citizens to seek employment in the United States during the era of IRCA. His parents, a family of humble rural origin, moved to Mexico City so he and his siblings would have an opportunity to get an education. After finishing the college preparation program, José studied engineering at the university and progressed with high honors. One summer, he took time off from his studies and responded to a newspaper ad for a welder's assistant. He had experience in this area, and he believed his studies in engineering made him a perfect candidate for the job. Having left quite early for the interview, he was shocked upon his arrival to find seventy men already lined up waiting for the interview to begin. While standing in line, he spoke to other applicants and learned that there were men present who had years of work in this trade and had reached the highest skill level attainable. He could not believe they were applying for this assistant job. He spoke wistfully of the epiphany he experienced while standing in that line:

> *Upon seeing this I realized that, no, it doesn't matter if one graduates from college, there are no jobs. And that is difficult, because when you are in school that is your goal. Like me, I come from a family of eleven children and my parents are illiterate; it was very difficult growing up. So upon seeing there was no future, I decided to come here and also because my brothers told me they would support me if I came. I worked here in 1986, in the fields. Then I returned, because my experience in the fields was very difficult. I worked cutting asparagus, and they stole a lot from us. We worked all day and they paid us little, $3 per box. Sometimes we earned only $5 for a whole day. People took advantage of us and that's a big problem. The people who are against immigration don't understand how the system works and how convenient it is for many for illegals to be here. It's a chain that begins with people who are crossing illegals and reaches to the consumers. It is a chain. I never, ever worked with an American person at my side. Always, we were Mexicans. When amnesty was passed, I decided to return. I collected all my information and qualified for the program. This time I returned with work papers and I started working as a janitor in a factory. After that I worked in a food processing plant. Then I went to an employment office and I was sent to a potato-processing plant here in Hermiston. And I've been working there since 1988. I'm a technician and I have a good job (interview with Gonzales-Berry, 2007).*

Immigration scholars recognize that social networking is the backbone of migration, and throughout our interviews we found this to be the case. These networks are configured primarily around immediate and extended family, though shared place of origin also plays an important role: "Migrant networks are an important source of social capital for people contemplating a move abroad. They are sets of interpersonal ties that connect migrants, former migrants, and non-immigrants at places of origin and destination through reciprocal ties of kinship, friendship, and shared community origin. They increase the likelihood of international migration because they lower the risks of movement and increase the expected net returns to migration" (Massey et al. 2002, 19).

Betita became aware of the importance of social networks at an early age, and they undoubtedly influenced her own decision to come to the United States:

> *I always believed that someday God was going to grant me the opportunity to come here to the United States. I used to listen to people about coming here and helping each other and it was something quite lovely. Later when I got married, my sister used to come yearly and she always encouraged us to come over so we could help ourselves. She knew that we needed to get ahead and she saw that the harvest wasn't enough to live on. There was a lot of lack (interview with S. J. Acosta, 2003).*

Within a network system, family members left behind are encouraged by relations already in the United States to join them, or individuals call on family members or acquaintances already in the United States to sponsor them. In some cases, the latter travel to the border to pick up their relatives, frequently after having paid a *coyote* to bring them that far. Agustín's experience bears testimony to the dense nature of social networks. Agustín's friend first called his father, who was working in Salem in 1978. The father was able to get them jobs in a mushroom plant with a social security card under someone else's name. Agustín worked there from 1978 until 1995, traveling to Mexico every fifteen months to see his wife. Eventually she insisted on coming, refusing to stay behind any longer. The couple now had a three-year-old son. In addition to his wife and child, Agustín brought his sister-in-law, a friend's wife and their four children, and the family of a man who was working in a plant in Oregon. They all took the bus to Nogales, where they were joined by two more migrants who worked in Salem. Agustín recalls that there were fifteen individuals plus two *coyotes*, but they had only one pickup truck. They crossed the women and children first. The *migra* (border patrol) stopped them and they all went back while the men were crossing on foot. The men arrived on the U.S. side only to learn the families had been sent back and the INS had taken the pickup. They huddled in a restaurant until a local man invited them to his home. The *coyote* then told them to pool their resources to buy a van. Agustín had $1,000 with which he bought a van with two seats in front. Eventually everyone passed "the line." They boarded the van and arrived in Salem on New Year's Day 1980. His final words regarding this experience are words we heard time and again during our interviews: "We've always believed in God and felt we would be safe" (interview with S.J. Acosta, 2003).

In other cases, such as that of Malena, *coyotes* bring individuals to safe houses at the border, where they must wait to receive money from their sponsors for additional transportation to the final destination point. Malena recalls having to wait for a month with her thirteen-year-old daughter at a safe house before her contact was able to raise the money to get her to Oregon. After their arrival, new migrants are dependent on the social network anchor for housing and transportation (interview with Gonzales-Berry, 2007). Tomasa recalls how uncomfortable she felt living with others when she first arrived: "What I remember was the language and the lack of privacy. In Mexico I had my own humble living space. But here, I had to share a house. I didn't feel comfortable when I got up. I didn't feel free to do what I wanted" (interview with M.A. Chávez, 2003). While many of the contacts house the newcomers only until they get on their feet, it is not uncommon for members of these networks who own or rent homes to rent a room long term to new arrivals. In this way they not only aid newcomers but they are also able to supplement their own incomes.

Networks at home also play a key role in aiding migrants in a number of ways. Eliseo, for example, points out the role of social networks in helping finance trips. "You don't think a lot before coming. You just decide and do it. Many have the means to do it, but those of us who didn't had to compromise ourselves, borrowing money from friends or from people who lend money and charge interest. And this is how we came; with time, things get better" (interview with S.J. Acosta, 2003). There are, of course, always individuals who are willing to make money off people in need. However, even if prospective migrants are forced to seek out money lenders beyond the family or circle of friends, prior connections are necessary and there must be an element of trust. We spoke to numerous individuals whose first checks, once they secured employment, were set aside to pay off individuals who had loaned them money to make the journey. During this pay-off period they are truly dependent on their network anchors.

Many adults would not be able to venture north if it were not for the fact that they are able to leave children at home with family members, who bear the cost of reproductive labor—the bearing and rearing of children and the nurturing of all household members so they are able to join the workforce (Stephen 2007). Ponciana recalls her own family's incremental migration: "My parents came to the United States in 1986 with my youngest brother. He was two years old. After a year my mom went back to Mexico for a year and took my brother with her, and then she came back to the U.S. and left my brother in Mexico with the rest of us. After two years they sent someone to get my oldest brother, my youngest brother, and myself. My other brother Andrés stayed in Mexico for three more years" (interview with J.L. Torres, 2002). In recent years, scholars have begun to explore the negative impact of this kind of family separation, particularly in terms of resentment toward parents by children who felt abandoned. Ponciana's words communicate clearly her own feelings regarding being left behind: "I felt that they did not love us, that they would never come back and that they were just going to leave us there forever with my grandma and aunt."

Finding a job is also facilitated by the immigrant networks. In fact, in many cases it is the employer who encourages migrants to bring family members or acquaintances from their villages to work for him or her. This kind of informal recruitment, in which the migrants bear the responsibility of getting to the U.S. and the employer reaps the benefits, has been singled out as one of the factors that creates competition between migrants and native-born workers, particularly those of marginal status within this country who have little human capital of their own. As dense social networks supply workers to U.S. employers, job slots are not made available to U.S. workers (Waldinger 1997; Bean and Stevens 2003).

Transportation is also a challenge to new migrants, and many workers, particularly women, are dependent on others to shuttle them to work and other places. Susana's shift at Hewlett Packard begins at 5:00 p.m. Her husband drives her to work when he gets home after putting in a full day at a local nursery. He spends time with the children before going to bed, only to get up after midnight to go pick up Susana, whose shift ends at 1:00 a.m. He sleeps an additional three hours and must get up at 5:00 a.m. to be at work at 6:00 a.m. This schedule, which expands the father's role to include the reproductive labor normally reserved to women, obviously creates burdens for all involved. However, without Susana's extra income, the couple reports that it "would not be able to *salir adelante*" [get ahead] (interview with Gonzales-Berry, 2007).

Irma was brought here in 1991 by her husband, who became a citizen after being legalized through IRCA. In Mexico, Irma was a teacher but in Oregon she became a victim of "brain waste" frequently tied to immigrant status. Initially she began working in the fields; she then moved on to a food-processing plant. Eventually Irma got a job in the Head Start Program in Hermiston. For years she was unable to drive and this caused her no small amount of anguish. "There were two obstacles I have not yet completely overcome. The first is the language. When my children got ill, I had to look for an interpreter. The second obstacle is not knowing how to drive. I didn't drive and I didn't speak English. This was very sad for me. If my husband was at work and my children got sick I had to look for someone to take me to the doctor or pay a taxi. Then I had to find an interpreter; this makes me feel so bad in this country" (interview with Gonzales-Berry, 2007). Very few of the women we interviewed are able to drive, and, like Irma, they cite this and the lack of English language skills as major obstacles to improving their situation.

Recent immigration reform proposals are adamant in making English a prerequisite to legalization, or in the parlance of the day, a "path to citizenship." Immigrants themselves understand the importance of learning English, and manifest a strong desire to learn the language. However, attending language classes after a full day of work—and for women after doing the additional domestic chores—is an enormous challenge. Schooling is not an experience that comes naturally or comfortably to workers who may average less than six years of education.[8] Moreover, sitting in a formal language classroom can be intimidating and frustrating. But a more serious issue has to do with the fact that in order to acquire speaking proficiency in a foreign language, one must have opportunities to engage native speakers of the language. It is a fact that current economic practices have created a bifurcated labor market in which immigrants form a large proportion of workers in the unskilled labor sector (Massey et al. 2002). Because immigrants in Oregon tend to congregate as a cohort in segmented labor structures, in a variety of agricultural and service industries they have few opportunities to interact with native speakers of English. This "ethnic closure" (Bean and Stevens 2003) diminishes their opportunities, not only for learning English, but for social integration into the host culture. But we would be remiss if we did not also acknowledge that factors emanating from the host culture certainly influence the potential for integration. Deeply entrenched notions of the inferiority of *mexicanos*, an accepted view of Mexican immigrants as dispensable, dehumanized cogs in a seemingly incontrovertible social order, and more recently, a growing fear of immigrants, who have been under a barrage of xenophobic attacks—in Oregon by right-wing talk-show hosts, politicians, and nativist organizations such as the Minutemen and Oregonians for Immigration Reform—all contribute to shape the conditions of marginalization, criminalization, and dehumanization within which Mexican immigrants must navigate as they help produce the wealth of our nation.

Diversity Within

Many of the people who come to Oregon from Mexico are from rural areas, and because they come without authorization, they find few employment options other than low-wage jobs, particularly in agriculture and the service sector. Among those of rural provenance, diversity exists. Beginning in the eighties, indigenous people, primarily Mixtecs and Zapotecs from Oaxaca, headed north from California to Oregon for seasonal work. By 1990 as many as nine thousand *mixtecos* were picking crops or working in nurseries and reforestation in Oregon (Dash 1996). Gradually they began to settle out and today there are settled communities of Mexican indigenous groups in the Willamette Valley (in the Woodburn area, in Canby, around Salem, in Junction City, Harrisburg, and in Eugene). Employers appreciate the work provided by indigenous farmworkers, and it is not uncommon for them to recruit heavily through indigenous foremen in communities in Mexico. Dash (1996) points out that these workers "may lack ... developed systems for helping each other find work and housing" and thus are especially "vulnerable to abuse and exploitation" (14). Many indigenous immigrants speak their native languages rather than Spanish—it is estimated that fourteen Latin American indigenous languages are spoken in Oregon (Stephen et al. 2008). When they come to the United States, they may be automatically lumped in with Spanish-speaking Mexicans. Schools and agencies may assume that their needs are being met through Spanish interpreters when in fact they do not have proficiency in that language.

However, given the kind of discrimination that they have experienced in their own home country—indigenous people live very much at the margins of national life in Mexico—they may be reluctant to lay claim to their indigenous identities and admit that they speak a language other than Spanish. We interviewed Agustín Valle in 2004. His family first migrated to Sinaloa before coming to the United States, and he recalls the treatment he received as an indigenous child in Northern Mexico:

> *There was a lot of discrimination and it was difficult. We had different customs and celebrations, like the Day of the Dead. We were very poor, a large family but poor. Then, because of the way we dressed, they looked at us in a certain way and it was hard. Sometimes when we were playing with other children they called me Oaxaca all the time, or Oaxaco. In the beginning, since I came from there, I didn't feel bad. But when we got angry or got into a fight and they called me by that name, I felt uncomfortable because I understood they said those things to make me feel bad (interview with Gonzales-Berry 2004).*

Julie Samples and Santiago Ventura, who are in charge of the Indigenous Peoples Project at the Oregon Law Center in Woodburn, pointed out that the same discrimination that occurs in Mexico may be transported to the United States, in which case discrimination and conflict may arise between immigrants of indigenous descent and other Mexicans (interview with Gonzales-Berry, 2004). The staff at the Oregon Law Center is very aware of this challenge, for all too often they see that indigenous immigrants do not have access to information necessary to make their way in the host culture. Consequently, they direct their efforts at providing materials through radio and on C.D.s or tapes for the indigenous communities they serve, as well as training translators, particularly for work in the courts.

Danza de los Diablitos *de San Mateo Tunuchi.* Guelaguetza *celebration, Salem, OR, 2009. Courtesy of Justo Rodríguez.*

The *Danza de los Diablitos* (Dance of the Little Devils), which was introduced by the Spaniards in the seventeenth century during the period of colonization, simulates a struggle between Good and Evil. During the conquest of the New Continent, elements of existing indigenous cultures melded with elements of Catholicism, which was brought through evangelization to the people of the "New World." "Pagan" elements mixed with religious iconography. The origin of this dance is found in the native *chareos.* Evangelists wanted to represent evil dressed in an elegant manner, choosing hairy goat skin chaps and a grotesque mask with horns that resembled the *idad cuauquisiqui,* a figure adored by the Mixtecas. In the final stages of the dance, called "The Moors and Christians," when the Christian St. James defeats and kills Pontius Pilate, the devils emerge to carry Pilate away to the depths of hell, wrapped in a Mixtec palm mat. The Dance of the Little Devils denotes elegance and good taste as indicated by goat skin chaps and pants, a suit jacket, and a tie. And of course the costume includes the famous devil masks, with carved wood horns and sometimes ram or bull horns. The masks are born from the imagination of the artist and vary from the most horrible to sad or happy devils (a translation of the Spanish text provided by Justo Rodríguez).

It is perhaps Ventura's own personal experience that has made him the dedicated worker he is on behalf of indigenous *mexicano* people in Oregon. Ventura was given a life sentence for allegedly murdering another migrant worker in 1986. He had served four years of his sentence when members of the jury admitted they believed Ventura was innocent and they may have made a mistake (*The Oregonian*, July 24, 1988; June 5, 1991). Ventura, a Mixtec speaker, barely had rudimentary control of Spanish, but a Spanish rather than Mixtec interpreter had been provided for the trial and he had not understood what was transpiring in the trial. The decision was overturned and Ventura was released from prison. He enrolled at the University of Portland and vowed that he wanted to help "wrongly convicted people. I want to help people in the same situation I was in" (*The Oregonian*, January 21, 1992). His work at the Oregon Legal Center has certainly given him that opportunity.

One striking characteristic of indigenous migrants is their ability to lead transnational lives (Stephen 2007). Because many adhere to communal values, they have found a variety of ways to remain connected to their communities of origin in Mexico. In some cases, they hold governance or social positions within their native communities that carry certain obligations. Their religious *cargo*, for example, may require that they serve as sponsors of the yearly religious celebration honoring the community's patron saint. Thus, they must return to their village to discharge this duty. They may also be responsible for their *tequio* or community service obligation. Failure to do so could result in the loss of their land. José (interviewed with Gonzales-Berry, 2005), the American-born son of Mixtecs from Oaxaca, reported that his father had insisted that he return to the village to carry out his father's social service. José was in college at the time and could not take time off from his studies to fulfill his father's demand. The issue was resolved by paying someone in the village to do the familial duty to the community. Agustín Valle told us how he used to believe that people were foolish for taking on the debts associated with social charges. However, after coming to the United States and receiving a college education, he has come to understand how important these practices are, not only in terms of solidifying social identity, but also in terms of accruing status within the community:

> *After I went to college I learned who I really am and how it was in our country. I was thinking about my father and the things he did and sometimes I didn't understand. I used to say, no, people are dumb. They are always poor. They work all year and when it comes time to carry out their cargo they have to borrow money. I used to wonder why they didn't just get out, but instead spent all their money or got into debt. I really couldn't understand what it means to someone to*

be a mayordomo and how this is related to who we are as indigenous people. When my father did these things for the community, even after we left, I didn't understand why he sent money to help improve the village. I used to say to myself, how can that be?

While immigrants from indigenous communities in Mexico are Mexican nationals, their ethnic identities are indigenous. They do not fit the preconceived notions and expectations that the host culture tends to have regarding Mexican migrants. According to Agustín, the experiences of indigenous Mexican people in this country are particularly difficult, and his people are completely dependent on social networks for their survival:

Yes it is truly difficult for an indigenous person, who cannot understand, who cannot speak Spanish, or who does not have much education. It is super difficult. The majority survive through the family or through friends or through other persons who have figured out how to survive here. For example, right now a cousin of ours has come from Oaxaca and she is working in Arizona. Her survival depends on our sending her information of where the jobs are. Wham, they go there where there is someone who will help them and that is how everyone helps each other. Otherwise they would not survive, because it is really difficult.

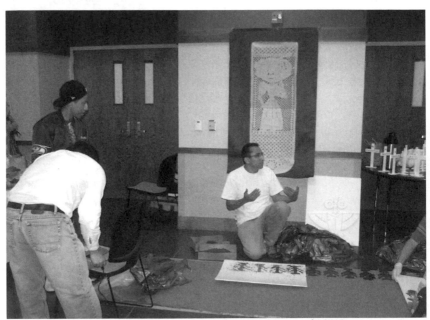

Día de los Muertos *celebration altar setup, Salem, OR, 2009. Courtesy of OCIMO.*

Other Mexican immigrants do not fit the historical profile of rural workers either. These are individuals who, discouraged by the lack of opportunities at home, many with higher levels of education, knowledge of English, and an understanding of middle-class values and expectations, headed north. Their accumulated human capital facilitated their transition to life in Oregon. However, even though they too must navigate difficult waters as they adjust to the local environments, many from this group became involved in serving *mexicano* communities here. Juanita, an English teacher and an education administrator before coming to Oregon from Tijuana, presents a good case study in this regard:

> *I understand that when you go to another country, you can't expect to have the same position you had at home. You have to earn it. I began as an assistant teacher because they didn't get my papers. It wasn't so obvious because although my position was as assistant I was the only teacher in the classroom. It was just me. It was hard after the position I had over there. But I knew I had to start at the bottom and that's what I did. My husband, who was trained as a lawyer in Mexico, spent three years coming and going and trying to sell our property. The first two years, he would say, "I'm going to return. As soon the kids finish, we'll go back." He didn't know English correctly, because even though he was born in the United States, they took him to Mexico when he was three and his education was in Mexico. For me and my children it was easier. We had studied at the border and we knew how to function and we were able to move, to study, to get ahead. But for my husband, at his age, he was already forty plus, it was harder. He kept working over there until he sold everything, and we opened a restaurant in McMinnville, but it was very difficult. With the payments for our property, we were going to keep up the restaurant. But this didn't happen. They gave us a down payment, and never paid us one more penny. Then we had to close the restaurant. And he had to return to Mexico to go through the courts. We recovered the property two years ago. But by then, he had already started a body shop, because he had been a car racer over there; cars were his hobby. He built race cars. So he said, I know cars. I know I'm not going to be able to practice law without returning to the university. So he started his shop, a tiny shop. Now he has a larger shop here in Salem. He's gotten ahead, and I kept studying. When they told me my papers weren't sufficient, I became an assistant for two years so I could learn the system. But then I took my papers to all the universities and I can say that I'm happy to have found this university. Of the eight*

institutions I went to, Oregon State University was the only one that would even look at my credentials, and would deal with me. This was how I was able to finish my career. Now I'm in the MA program. And I've been working on my teaching license for four years. I started as a bilingual teacher in Kinder. Then I was bilingual team leader this year, and now I have a position as a resource teacher (interview with Gonzales-Berry, 2005).

Middle-class immigrants often play an important role in helping meet the needs of those who come with less formal education and limited job skills. Like many educated immigrants who had professions or careers in Mexico, Juanita and her husband had to step down a few notches on the social ladder when they arrived in this country. However, the human capital that they did possess, together with their strong will to succeed, allowed them to improve their condition. It is not uncommon for immigrants with significant human capital to assimilate into mainstream culture at a rapid pace. Juanita, however, maintains strong cultural roots even as she moves with ease in mainstream culture. She does not ignore those who do not come from her same socioeconomic background. She is an active advocate for immigrant rights, particularly in the field of education, thereby serving as an effective cultural broker between mainstream and *mexicano* communities.

Immigrant rights march, Salem, OR, 2009. Photo by Gwyn Fisher.

Face to Face: Settlers and Post-IRCA Immigrants

As we have seen, some of the earlier Mexican settlers in Oregon were foreign-born *mexicanos;* many others were Mexican Americans from Texas and other Southwestern states. By the mid-1990s, when increasing numbers of Mexican nationals began arriving in Oregon, the settled communities formed by early *mexicano* immigrants and pioneering Mexican Americans were already home to second- and third- (American-born) generations. Generally, more recent immigrants preferred the areas already settled by *tejanos* and *mexicanos*, but large numbers of them also fanned out across the state to other cities and towns whose residents had had little contact with *mexicanos*. Given the historical presence of *mexicanos* in Oregon, as described in the preceding chapter, Oregon is not a "new destination" for Latin American immigrants in the same sense as are North Carolina, Georgia, or Nevada.[9] However, many cities, towns, and rural areas are experiencing the growing pains associated with the recent arrival of Mexican immigrants. Hence, Oregon can be considered a historic and a new destination. Like Southwestern states, it has been a destination with a long-standing history of Mexican immigration, and those early settlers have engaged for decades in the process of carving out a space for themselves. It is also a destination that includes areas that are experiencing recent immigration as a new phenomenon, thereby having a great deal in common with "new destination" areas such as those in the Southeast and portions of the Midwest.[10] However, regardless of when *mexicanos* have come to Oregon, there are two characteristics that bind them together, their "clustering in a small set of low-wage labor markets and dead-end occupations" (Gouveia et al. 2005, 31), and a history of treatment as the "racialized other."

A number of our interviewees reported hostility on the part of settled *mexicanos* toward more recent arrivals. Others report both conflict and cooperation. Irma, for example, observed:

> It's like everything else. There are groups and individuals that yes, do help new arrivals integrate into society. There are other types of individuals who, by the fact of having been born here or lived here longer, even if their parents are Mexican, do not mix with immigrants. They don't want to speak Spanish, but the majority does value its roots (interview with Gonzales-Berry, 2007).

Recently arrived immigrants have reported being called derogatory terms and being shunned by more established "Hispanics." There undoubtedly are cases of conflict at the group or individual level. However, there are numerous instances in which organizations with substantial "Hispanic" representation are valuable advocates for recent immigrants. The labor union PCUN continues to be a strong advocate for farmworkers, regardless of their country of origin and the length of their presence in Oregon. The union has played an important role in assisting new arrivals maneuver in the local environment. CAUSA, an organization affiliated with PCUN, and whose membership comprises both native-born *mexicanos* and immigrants, is one of the major advocates in the state for immigrant rights. In 2001 CAUSA published a report that documented numerous instances of racism and discrimination against *mexicanos*. These labor and human rights organizations have organized dozens of pro-immigrant demonstrations, and they are staunch defenders of immigrant interests in state politics.

In Eugene, Latino activists are well represented by sons and daughters of *tejano* settlers. In Washington County, the community center established in the 1960s by *mexicano* and *tejano* activists offers English and computer classes for recent immigrants, social services, and sponsors a day-labor

Día de los Muertos *celebration, 2009. Salem, OR. Courtesy of OCIMO.*

pick-up site that has come under attack by nativist groups. *El Hispanic News*, founded in 1985, represents the interests of Latinos in the Northwest regardless of their immigration status or length of residency. Many of the *mexicano* educators and political leaders who emerged during a time of community empowerment in the sixties and seventies are still active today serving immigrants and their children. Thus, settlers and newcomers meet at the site where organized struggle and activism take place to engage in face-to-face conversations, sometimes in conflict but also in unity and common purpose to eventually create a sense of belonging—if not for themselves, certainly for future generations.

---

1. NAFTA is the acronym for North American Free Trade Agreement signed between the United States, Mexico, and Canada in 1993.

2. IRCA was not the only consequence of negative coverage of immigration. Introduction of "English Only" bills in Congress and state legislatures, opposition to bilingual education, and Proposition 187 in California (which sought to deny immigrants public assistance and education) would all unfold in the wake of its passage.

3. Bustamante (1992) points out the glaring contradictions in this piece of legislation, claiming that "the ideology and economy of undocumented migration from Mexico to the United States are reflected in the discrepancies between the objectives and the written text." Employers, for example, were allowed to indicate legal status merely by signing INS form I-9, even if applicants had produced no documents to prove their legal status.

4. 1986 was the same year Mexico joined GATT, placing it squarely in the midst of the globalized economically and politically elite nations.

5. While almost three million individuals were regularized through IRCA, one aspect of this program that is not commonly explained is the way in which many undocumented women were discriminated against in the deployment of the program. Such women either heard from the radio or acquaintances, or were actually told by people administering the program, that if they had received public assistance, they were not eligible for authorization. Having received aid for their children, they did not apply. Others who had received aid applied and were denied amnesty. A class action suit, *Zambrano v. INS*, was filed in California on behalf of women who had been denied authorization or had been discouraged from applying because they had received public assistance for their children who were American citizens and thus entitled to benefits. Chang (2000) affirms that at least four thousand potential applicants based their decision to not apply on the information they received regarding the public-charge provisions of IRCA, even though these provisions did not apply to their specific cases. Chang emphasizes that one consequence of this differential treatment has been the perpetuation of the feminization of poverty among undocumented women.

6. Militarization of the border had already been launched with initiatives such as Operation Hold the Line in El Paso and Operation Gatekeeper in California. The former was a highly successful program introduced in 1993 by Border Patrol Chief Silvestre Reyes, who paid four hundred and fifty Border Patrol agents overtime to patrol a twenty-mile stretch in El Paso. The success of Hold the Line got Reyes elected to Congress and encouraged the adoption of similar programs in other heavily traversed points of entry: Operation Gatekeeper in California, Operation Safeguard in Nogales, Arizona, in 1994, and Operation Rio Grande in East Texas in 1997 (Andreas 1998). In California, economic recession, increasingly ineffective local government, and significant changes in the socio-cultural fabric of the society led nativists and state officials to declare a high-intensity campaign against "illegal immigrants," who were portrayed in the media as criminals who threatened the sovereignty of the nation. Under the auspices of Operation Gatekeeper, this campaign virtually turned into a border war zone (Nevins 2002). Included in these operations were measures that provided for the doubling of Border Patrol agents, the construction of fences, multiplication of equipment such as vehicles, night scopes, and underground sensors, and the deployment of military personnel and National Guard to assist in detection (Andreas 1998). According to one scholar, the inauguration of Operation Gatekeeper resulted in an "increase of 58 percent quarterly in the number of immigrant deaths along the Mexico/ California border" (Burr 2001,15).

7. In 1990, about 45 percent of the country's unauthorized immigrants (1.6 million) lived in California. By 2004, this number had dropped to 24 percent (Passel 2005). Many workers who normally would have gravitated toward California headed to the South, others to the Midwest, and thousands found their way to New York and Pennsylvania (Díaz McConnel 2004; Durand et al. 2005; Millard and Chapa 2004).

8. In 2006, 52 percent of the foreign-born age five and older had limited English proficiency, according to the American Community Survey of the U.S. Census Bureau, tabulated by the Migration Policy Institute (www.migrationinformation.org).

9. Scholars associated with the Russell Sage Foundation have coined the phrase "new destinations" for current research projects exploring immigration to areas that had not previously received large numbers of Latin American, particularly Mexican, immigrants.

10. However, areas such as Chicago and other industrialized cities have had a long presence of *mexicanos*. Their arrival in fact dates back to the early twentieth century. For a study of *mexicanos* in the Chicago area see Farr 2006 and Millard and Chapa 2004.

Testimonio

by Lucio

Lucio was interviewed by San Juana Acosta in Hood River, Oregon, in 2003. Excerpts were taken from that interview and transcribed, translated, and arranged by the authors to form a testimony that sheds light on the life of an educated immigrant who is forced to take a position for which he would be overqualified in his native country—yet he finds reasons to be thankful.

At the age of 16, I went to Mexico City to study. I took a vocational education program then I went to medical school where I graduated as an obstetrician and surgeon. I worked for the ISTE and for the Social Security Department of Health. Finally, I was given an opportunity to open my own practice under the auspices of Social Security. The truth is, I had a very good job. I never intended to come here to stay. I had traveled here to visit, and I liked it because everything is so well organized. It is beautiful and all, but I did not think of coming to work here. In 1998, by sheer luck, a young woman whom I had known when I was 15 presented herself in my office. Shortly after, I began to organize my affairs and a year later joined Felicitas, the love of my life since childhood, here in Oregon. I came legally.

When I first got here I began doing pruning work in an orchard alongside Felicitas. I had no idea what this work was. But I thank God that I never had to struggle. Since I arrived here, I arrived like a little angel. Shortly after, my daughter was born, and I have never had any difficulties. The job I now have was practically given to me. I asked at a local store if they needed a cashier, and they said yes. An American gentleman who managed the store gave me the application and an appointment for an interview. He gave me the job and now I am the manager of the store. I'm not crazy about the job, but one has to work, right? And in comparison to the skills I have, I am not very happy. But in comparison to other jobs I could be doing, I am happy. I don't get benefits. The company is small and my salary—given my administrative responsibilities—is quite low. My English is adequate. I understand most things, but it is difficult for me to speak the language. If I spoke better English, I would have a better job. I am now thinking of changing jobs.

You ask me which country I identify with. My answer is Mexico. The country that sheltered me, trained me, educated me—I always had a government scholarship. I am also loyal to the country that is currently sheltering me.

I have experienced a tremendous change in my life. I suspended my profession. Here things are more difficult. I need to speak the language well in order to develop. I need to go to the university and take courses I never took over there. I feel as if I have sacrificed a lot. But I have never cursed my lot because I have what is most important to me, and that is my daughter and the mother of my daughter.

What do I expect from the future? I see a lovely future because I live with the woman I love and who understands me. And as for my children, I see a lovely future, because we will have given them everything that is positive, and they will not have ill feelings about us, because during the time they were growing we will have shared with them and we will have given them only those things that are positive.

Testimonio

by Mario Magaña

Mario Magaña was interviewed by Gonzales-Berry in 2005 for this testimonio *at Oregon State University, where he is a Professor in the OSU Extension Program. Excerpts were taken from that Spanish-language interview and transcribed, translated, and arranged by the authors.*

One reason why I came was when I got together with my friends, when I was fourteen, fifteen, eighteen years old and they would say, "Let's go eat" or "Let's have a refreshment," I didn't have money to pay for my drink or my supper. So many times I preferred to go home, to hide, because I didn't have money for myself or for a friend. I would just go home. And another reason was when I began to have girlfriends, sometimes one would have a birthday and I didn't have money to buy her a little gift or the like. This is when I began to think that my situation in Mexico was very difficult. I began to think that I was going to have a family tomorrow or the day after and, how was I going to feed my family? How were we going to live? My father gave us a small piece of land, and my children and my brother's children, for we were many, were not going to live off that little piece of land.

And when we planted we were not able to recover our investment at harvest time because seed was very expensive and the harvest was expensive. When we went to sell our harvest, it was worth nothing. All the work that we invested was free because at best we got our expenses but we got nothing for our labor. This is when I began to think that I had to do something about my life. And also I would see those who returned well dressed with new trucks. They still may have owed on them, but they had their new trucks, and I became convinced. A friend told me, "Let's go over. I'll take you to Washington, where I work." So I left. This was in 1983. They got us at the Tijuana border and threw us back. We returned and they threw us back. We kept doing this until we were finally able to cross.

When I arrived here in Washington, I lived with, I believe, we were seven or eight cousins, in a three-bedroom trailer. We slept two or three in one bedroom, others in the living room and like that. There was no problem sleeping. The problem was cooking on only one stove. There were several of us, but there was one or two persons who knew how to cook and the rest of us didn't. Then we did other chores and they cooked. I think that since we are all in reality, we have to assume reality. But some of us don't like to do this kind of work. Unfortunately that is part of what we bring from our culture. I wish that in my home they had taught me to iron, to wash, to cook, and things like that. But they never taught us. Then, when we arrived here, I don't know, perhaps it's cultural. I don't say it's machismo or laziness, but that it is part of our culture. That is how they taught us, and you want to do things that way for the rest of your life. Unfortunately, there are times that you can't continue like that and we have to make changes in our lives.

I was picking apples and I heard on the radio that you could get a GED in Spanish at Washington State University. I climbed down from the ladder, ran to my car, and turned on the radio. I took a pencil and wrote down the phone number of the office in Greenville where I lived. After work I went to the office. It was just about closing time. The woman in charge told me I would have to return on Friday to fill out the forms. On Friday morning I returned instead of going to work. They told me I would have to take a preliminary exam. It took me about two hours. Then they sent it by FAX, and I waited until three or four when they told me I had been accepted. But I had to report the following Saturday, and I would have to stay until Sunday for orientation and begin classes on Monday. I went home to discuss things with my wife. She has always been very supportive. She would remain with our two daughters. One of them had just been born and the other was two. So I went and got my GED.

When I finished my GED, my professor asked me if I wanted to continue my studies at Corvallis. I said to him, "How can I go to the university?" I didn't know English, how to read and write it, and my Spanish was very limited. I read and wrote very little and spoke like those of us from Mexican ranches. Our communication is very humble. He told me it didn't matter what I knew. What mattered was what one could learn. "Just as you've learned everything we taught you here, you can learn English…."

Yes, he was the main key in my career, because unfortunately, we who come from rural areas don't know what we are capable of. We have no learning. We don't know how to evaluate ourselves. So he evaluated me and told me, "You have the capacity. You are very dedicated and responsible. When we tell you to do something, you do the impossible to accomplish it." I guess that was what he saw in me, that I had the ability to do things.

In the beginning it was very difficult because I didn't speak English and I didn't read or write absolutely anything. In the classroom, I understood nothing, and I was very traumatized in the beginning. I would ask myself, "Will I be able to do this?' It was very difficult. I was very desperate because, before coming here, I had my house in Washington. I had two daughters and my wife was pregnant with the third. I would go back and forth on weekends. My wife gave birth in November, and I had to go home to see how the family was doing and help a bit, so I kept going back and forth. I had little time to do my homework because there was so much to do at home. Finally after six months I told my wife, "I've finished two quarters banging my head but I've passed all the classes. If you want, let's move over there." We put the house up for sale and we came to live here in university-owned apartments. They were tiny. From a three-bedroom home to a two-bedroom apartment and tiny rooms at that. We didn't change, but we did begin to adapt. That's what our life was like for five years until I finished my studies. The way I learned was that I would translate almost all my books from English to Spanish. I bought a small dictionary and by the end of the year it looked as if it had been used for twenty years. I couldn't close it from so much use. After two years, I began to learn to read, write, speak, and I could take my own notes and read without having to translate. Something else that helped me is that the third year, I began audio recording all my classes like we're doing now. I would tape my classes. Unfortunately, as in all things, one encounters professors who are a bit racist, or who don't understand the needs of some of their students, and they didn't let me tape. One time in a Biology class, I took a video camera because I thought if I had a video I could watch it after class and I would be able to learn easier. The professor turned off my camera. Those are the things I found hard, when professors didn't understand the needs of their own students. But I did tape my classes and went over the tapes three, four, five times using headphones. When I walked to class, instead of listening to music, I listened to the taped lectures.

I did internships and the last one I did was in Extension. That opened up an opportunity to pursue a Masters degree. When I did my final presentation the professor told me he would like to help me out if I wanted to keep on studying. He asked what I wanted to do after I graduated. I told him I wanted to work with the 4H program helping out the Hispanic community. He told me that would be a great opportunity because there were no professional Latinos in 4H. I would have to get an MA, but he would support me if that's what I wanted to do. I spoke with my wife and told her they were offering me a good opportunity to get an MA, and she told me to continue. She said, "If that's what you want to do, do it for yourself, do it for me. We are accustomed to this student life and one or two more years won't make a difference in our lives." I began my studies that same year.

Yes, everyone helped me, and that's when I began to change my way of thinking about Americans. When I came here I began to see that the majority of Americans I met are lovely persons and up to this point I believe that I owe my career to Americans. I didn't have any support from Latinos or from a single Mexican, neither in the GED, nor in the university, nor in my MA studies. All that time the support came from Americans.

Here I think if I ran across three or four professors who made my life difficult that would be a lot. Instead I ran into fifty or one hundred professors who wanted me to succeed and wanted my life to change. They did even the impossible so I could get ahead.

Testimonio

by José Sandoval

This testimonio *was written by José Sandoval, the second-generation son of immigrant parents from Hood River, Oregon, for a class on immigration taught by Gonzales-Berry at Oregon State University in 2005. His essay is published as written.*

My father began his immigrant pilgrimage into the United States at a very young age, in 1962. He is originally from Aguas Calientes, Zacatecas, and he made his first trip when he was only nineteen years old, right after he spent one year in the Mexican National Guard. He came to the U.S. on the *Bracero* program and spent his first six months in San Luis Rey Valley, where he picked an assortment of fruits and vegetables. When the harvest was over, he moved to Tijuana, Mexico, and stayed with his brother until the new harvest, and then he returned back to the U.S. My dad did this for several years. His travels took him all over California and all the way to Chicago, where he washed dishes. My parents were married in 1969, and my dad settled back down in Zacatecas and started his own little store in his village. Then in 1976, he got fed up with being broke and moved the family to Tijuana, where he became a street vendor. My mom used a fake passport to travel freely into San Diego to visit my aunt and cousins. On August 20th 1976, she crossed over the line to give birth to me, making me a legal citizen of the U.S. That same year my father traveled to Hood River, Oregon, on the advice of his brother- in-law. He began picking fruit for Mr. ———, who encouraged my dad to move the family up north, where he would provide housing and offer my father a supervisor position in the orchards. For nearly thirty years my father has worked on the same land and for the same landowner, and he is currently suffering from painful arthritis in both of his hands due to the miserable working conditions. My parents bought a new house in 1991, and, when we first moved in, we had six acres of strawberry fields that my dad soon got rid of and planted pear and apple trees. To this day he is constantly praised for having one of the best-looking orchards in town.

Growing up in Hood River would prove to be very challenging for our family. My family was one of the first families to stay year round in Hood River, which is a big farmer and logger town. Up until I was in the third grade, there was just one other Mexican kid in my class, and his name was José

Burrito. José and I quickly learned how to fight. We were constantly harassed by a lot of the white kids in our school. I learned to hate the word "Beaner." Eventually more Mexican migrants came along, and I didn't feel so different anymore. Most of my friends consisted of first-generation Mexicans who were here to stay just like me. But I also had many friends whose parents were a part of the transnational migrant circuit, so they would be in school for a year or two, then they would go back to Mexico or other parts of the U.S. for different types of jobs. José Burrito was one of these kids. They were usually gone for about a year or sometimes more. When the kids would return from wherever they were, they always had strange and new stories of gang life in the streets of Los Angeles or their poor living conditions in Mexico. Many times these kids would come back to Hood River, drop out of school, and go to work in the fields with their parents in order to help out their families. They were forced to grow up much faster than the friends they left behind in the public school system. Their families were stuck on the international migrant circuit, maybe forever. Life is different for the first- and second-generation youth from Mexico in a world that they don't understand as being normal, but it is all they know. They are stuck between two worlds, locked in a different type of hyperspace where not everything is black and white but mostly just gray. They are not considered U.S. Americans because they look brown, and, at the other end, they are not considered Mexican because of the sloppy Spanish that they speak. A lot of these first- and second-generation Latino kids have no choice when they lose their native language because they come from a working-class family where both parents often work two jobs and rarely have the opportunities to spend quality time with their loved ones. Kids are now speaking *poquito español* as *bueno* as they can. These kids are now being raised in the public school systems where the first language they learn is English and their very own Mexican language and history will never be taught to them, nor will their parents have time to teach them or help them with their English-speaking homework.

Oftentimes what happens is that the family begins to reshape the original family structure that was once held in Mexico. Although the parents' social mobility is often restricted due to the lack of education and the language barrier, the kids are now given the freedom to make choices, which is something they may not have had in Mexico. In my family, everyone has gone their own directions, and it seems that the only time we get back together is for the holidays. Our family parties used to consist of heavy-drinking uncles and other migrant workers whose real families were missing them somewhere in Mexico. Back then our parties were fun. Now the holidays are boring and quiet; they consist mostly of my parents and siblings. We usually end up watching the little kids run around yelling in English. There is not much talking between the adults.

The fluid stages of migration will continue to flow and evolve with time and space. The numbers will speak for themselves as the Latino Nation in the U.S. is on a steady increase. Negative attitudes from the government and the media about the Latino movement in society only fuel the fire of ambition and determination. If one Mexican successfully crosses the border, it will prove that he or she is strong enough to survive in a country that may not want them. But their chances of making it are great and *por la gracia de Dios*, they will be successful.

Chapter 4

New Migrations: Mexican Workers and Their Families Since the 1990s

Oregon's Latino population grew by 70 percent between the 1980 and 1990 decennial censuses, and by more than 140 percent between the 1990 and 2000 censuses. It went from representing 4 percent of the state's total population to 8 percent in just ten years. This moved Oregon's national ranking among states with large Latino populations from twentieth in 1990 to fourteenth in 2000. Third-, second-, and first-generation Mexicans and their descendants live today in almost every city and small town in Oregon.

Dancehall. Photo by Paulina Hermosillo.

In the places where these new Oregonians settled, young *mexicanos* are already starting their families. In fact, all thirty-three counties in the state except for Gilliam, Sherman, and Wheeler counties have reported births to Hispanic mothers in 2007[1] (Oregon Department of Human Services 2007). "The Mexican presence is well established from Coos Bay to Nyssa, from Medford to Portland, from Milton-Freewater to Astoria," said Nusz and Ricciardi (2003) in an essay about Mexican history and culture. We review in this chapter the unprecedented demographic growth of the Latino population during the 1990s, and also review the type of industries that employ Oregonians of Mexican descent, providing an overview of the places in which they settled, assisted by social networks that helped these new immigrants to find jobs and affordable housing. It occurred while the entire population in the state also grew by 20.4 percent— the twelfth-fastest demographic growth in the nation (Boswell 2004).

A booming "new economy" of electronic products, marketing, and services around the Portland metropolitan area—characterized by the Silicon Forest's[2] technology, investment, and software companies—played a major role in attracting immigrant workers during the 1990s because it created a range of employment opportunities in services and light manufacturing unavailable before to *mexicanos*.

Although small *mexicano* communities were already established in Oregon's rural areas as early as the 1950s and 1960s, the migration stream since the late 1980s has been increasingly composed of family households that "settled-out" permanently in the Willamette Valley, along the Oregon coast, in the Rogue Valley, in the Columbia River Basin, and in the Snake River Valley. New migrant streams evolved as employment opportunities became available in urban areas and many workers moved away from agriculture. The majority are now unlike the solo males or the families who used to engage in patterns of circular migration traveling from Mexico to Oregon for a short time during the harvest season; however a considerable number of *mexicano* men and women are still hired for seasonal agricultural tasks, primarily harvesting berry and vegetable crops in the rural suburbs of Portland, and in agricultural areas across the state. *Mexicano* laborers also work seasonally in forest restoration and management in southern Oregon and the Willamette Valley (Moseley 2006). They are hired seasonally for pruning, weeding, thinning, and planting operations in the orchards of Hood River and the Rogue River Valley, performing tasks that involve intensive hand labor (McCauley et al. 2001).

Our discussion below situates their most recent settlement in different localities, ranging from metropolitan urban and suburban to remotely rural areas, interspersed with small and mid-size towns. These various localities embody Oregon's early farming and extractive economy, characterized by an Old West "go-your-own-way" attitude and by a strong historically rooted conservatism that coexists—sometimes colliding—with the progressive reputation of the new "Silicon suburbs" economy. This economy most resembles the open-minded social landscapes of other metropolitan areas in the nation, although in Oregon urbanites manifest a unique interest in nature preservation and small urban growth (Abbot 2001).

In 2004, the estimated population in the state was about six hundred thousand Mexican nationals, and according to this estimate from the Mexican Consulate of Portland, four hundred and forty thousand of them would have had an undocumented immigration status (Hernández-Coss 2004). By the mid-decade these recent immigrants had already been incorporated into the local economy, but most were only marginally integrated into the civic and social fabric in the places where they lived. Also, Oregonians in various localities responded differently to the settlement of immigrant families. In a region once called "one of the last Caucasian bastions in the United States" (Hardwick and Goworoska 2008), where less than 3 percent of the entire population was classified as non-white in 1970s, many Oregonians welcomed the *mexicanos*, but others despised the presence of these new neighbors. Immigration, as other authors have pointed out, is a kind of mirror that reflects not only the internal and external dynamics of economic development, but also the characteristics of social hierarchies and unresolved social issues in the receiving society.

Immigrant rights march in Salem, OR, 2009. Photo by Gwyn Fisher.

Metropolitan Mexicanos

Immigrants are most concentrated in urban and suburban areas where they provide low-cost, flexible labor to employers. The influx of immigrant workers raised the relative supply of low-education labor in the metropolitan areas located along Oregon's I-5 corridor. Portland, for example, a city with a historically small *mexicano* population, has experienced a very rapid inflow over the past decade. Portland, said Carl Abbot, "has been a white person's city for most of its history (from early territorial laws against African Americans to the KKK in the 1920s, anti-Japanese sentiment in the 1940s, and skinhead violence in the 1980s)" (2001,13). But according to U.S. Census Bureau estimates, by 2005 Mexicans constituted 30.94 percent of the foreign-born population in the Portland-Vancouver-Beaverton, Oregon-Washington metropolitan area, some 77,634 people.

Table 1: Top Ten Foreign-born Populations in Portland-Vancouver-Beaverton, Oregon-Washington Metropolitan Area, 2005

Country of Origin of the Foreign-born	Total Foreign-born	Percent of Foreign-born	Percent of Total
Total Foreign-born population*	250,955		
Mexico	77,634	30.94%	3.76%
Vietnam	17,644		0.86%
Ukraine	12,644	7.03%	0.61%
Korea	11,968	4.77%	0.58%
China, excluding Hong Kong & Taiwan	9,701	3.87%	0.47%
Canada	9,184	3.78%	0.47%
India	7,902	3.15%	0.38%
Russia	7,348	2.93%	0.36%
United Kingdom	7,316	2.92%	0.35%

*Total population: 2,063,277; percentage of foreign-born: 12.16%

Mexicanos reside in long-established multiethnic neighborhoods of North and Northeast Portland. They find employment in the warehouses and light-manufacturing plants of the industrial districts. These areas of the city suffered in the past from unemployment, high crime rates, and poor school performance, though more recent concerns among Mexican and African American residents are gentrification, highway expansion, and pollution (Podobnik 2003). Other *mexicanos* settled near agricultural jobs in the outer suburbs of Portland, such as Hillsboro and Gresham. Descendants of farmworkers who arrived in the 1980s now predominate in the West Hills of Hillsboro and in other neighborhoods (Abbot 2001). In the western suburbs between Hillsboro and Beaverton, Latino-owned businesses and residences border upscale developments like Orenco Station.[3] Also, many *mexicanos* reside in Rockwood, the poorest and most diverse neighborhood of Gresham. Three Rockwood census tracts, for example, have Multnomah County's highest concentration of people who speak limited or no English at home (Boswell 2003). Rockwood is a place where problems such as joblessness and gang violence intersect with the promise of civic participation and activism (Michael et al. 2008).

In the early 1990s, the metropolitan areas of Portland, Salem-Keizer, and Eugene-Springfield were already developing high-tech manufacturing, bio-tech industries, heavy-equipment manufacturing, and health care services. Employers in these areas rapidly reacted to labor market shortages by tapping into a seemingly uninterrupted inflow of reliable and committed *mexicano* workers. The fast pace of Oregon's economic diversification and growth (nearly twice the growth rate of the U.S. economy) had created a shortage of workers in both high-skilled and low-skilled occupations. Businesses reached out for alternative sources of labor, including workers with limited English proficiency. In a process of economic development that has been replicated in other areas of the Pacific Northwest, *mexicanos* were being hired in the metropolitan areas along the I-5 corridor and in cities across the Willamette Valley for a wide range of non-agricultural and non-service-related occupations in a variety of industries (Sweet and Meiksins 2008). Thus Oregon's Silicon Forest made many jobs available to *mexicanos* in the secondary labor market—creating opportunities that otherwise would not have existed for them. Those jobs offered training, better wages, and an environment that was conducive to learning more work-related English (Boswell 2004).

While still working on farms, a number of Mexican laborers moved their families to cities such as Hillsboro, Forest Grove, and Gresham. Other workers left the farms altogether and settled in suburbia, becoming a source of information and assistance to relatives and friends on the farms and back home in Mexico. New immigrants used these social networks to find urban jobs—loading and unloading freight, dry-walling for development contractors, washing dishes in restaurants, making beds in hotels, washing cars, as kitchen aides in nursing homes, working in landscaping and in private home services, circumventing rural employment altogether. For example, McGlade and Dahlstrom (2001) found that many students in Latino families transferring to Portland public schools during the 1990s were coming from agricultural towns such as Boring, Molalla, and Woodburn, while Latino student transfers in the opposite direction were much less common.

Table 2: *Mexicans in Oregon by Place of Birth, Citizenship Status, and Year of Entry, 2005**		
	Total population in Oregon	Mexicans in Oregon
Total population	3,560,109	302,852
Native	3,215,534	155,535
Male	49.2%	49.4%
Female	50.8%	50.6%
Foreign-born	344,575	147,317
Male	52.0%	57.8%
Female	48.0%	42.2%
Naturalized U.S. Citizen	115,660	20,088
Male	48.9%	59.3%
Female	51.1%	40.7%
Not a U.S. Citizen	228,915	127,229
Male	53.5%	57.6%
Female	46.5%	42.4%
Entered in 2000 or later	26.8%	30.2%
Entered in 1990 to 1999	34.9%	41.7%
Entered before 1990	38.3%	28.1%

*Source: 2005 American Community Survey, U.S. Bureau of the Census. Table S0201, Selected Population Profile of the Mexican Population in Oregon.

Oregon's economic boom during the 1990s had created the conditions for *mexicanos* to find relatively better paid year-round employment outside agriculture, which is the lowest paid of all occupations. Yet other *mexicanos*, many of indigenous descent, filled the agricultural jobs vacated by those who had moved to urban areas. The marketability of *mexicano* workers was certainly an effect of already developed hiring networks (the social capital of immigrants) and it was also a consequence of the increasing ability of these workers to interact comfortably with employers in various workplaces. As a result of their parents' previous settlement, in the last fifteen years many second-generation Oregonians of Mexican descent have become fully integrated into the economy of the state, and a sizable portion of second- and third-generation Mexican Americans are gaining incorporation into the middle class. The number of Latino households with incomes greater than $100,000 a year grew more than five times between 1990 and 2000, while those with incomes between $50,000 and $99,999 grew by 359 percent (see Table 3 below). These Mexican Americans in leadership positions continue to work creatively to promote the social and cultural incorporation of all Latinos in Oregon (Kissam 2008).

Table 3: Growth of Annual Income of Latino Households in Oregon, 1990-2000*					
Annual Income Latino Households in Oregon	1990 Total No. Households	1990 % of Total Population	2000 Total No. Households	2000 % Total Population	1990-2000 % of Change
Under $24,999	15,829	58%	18,991	36.8%	20%
$25,000 to $49,999	8,781	32%	19,625	38.0%	123%
$50,000 to $99,999	2,396	9%	11,000	21.3%	359%
$100,000 and over	312	1%	1,973	3.8%	532%
Total	27,318	100%	51,589	100%	89%

*Source: U.S. Bureau of the Census, 1990 and 2000 Decennial Census, adapted from Boswell 2004.

During the last two decades, Oregon businesses became more aware of the growing purchasing power of Mexican households and began targeting the metropolitan Latino market—now called a "hypermarket" by marketing researchers. For example, Spanish-language radio stations sprang into local broadcasting, Spanish-language newspapers and publications continued to expand their distribution, and more Spanish language channels were being offered through cable and satellite television in the Portland, Salem and Eugene metropolitan areas. Also the Mexican Consulate opened an office in Portland with jurisdiction over the whole state, Aeroméxico started direct flights to Mexico from the Portland International Airport, and the Spanish channels Univisión and Telemundo became widely available throughout the Willamette Valley.

Mexicano *Workers' Occupations*

Latinos constituted 10 percent of Oregon's labor force in the mid-2000s. Not surprisingly, over the previous decade the Latino labor force had grown faster than the state's labor force as a whole. According to researchers with the Oregon Department of Employment, from 1990 to 2005 the overall trend in the occupational employment profile of Mexicans in Oregon has been away from agriculture to increasing numbers in almost all other industries and occupations. More *mexicanos* are now employed in service industries (as retail sales representatives, bank tellers, insurance company representatives, and administrative and clerical employees), in health care service-related occupations, in construction, light manufacturing, and material moving and handling, than in agriculture (Turner and Wood 1998; Libby 2007). However, *mexicanos* in urban areas continue to be situated among the working poor, with limited access to jobs beyond the low-wage sector that would offer health insurance. In part because many are of prime working age, Mexican men show high rates of labor force participation and their unemployment rate is close to the rate of the entire Oregon labor force. Mexican women are also augmenting their participation in the labor force (O'Connor 2006).

The most dramatic increase has been Latino employment in the public sector, which rose from 3 percent in 1990 to 7 percent in 2002 (Ferrara 2006). Greater access to government jobs is usually a measure of immigrants' successful economic and social integration. It is also an indication of growing representation of *mexicanos* in positions with the authority to recruit and hire for those jobs (Fernández and Fernández Mateo 2006). Latino participation in the ranks of government jobs is very visible in Salem, the state capital, and it is also visible in the municipal governments of the Portland metropolitan area.

Many of the *mexicanos* who arrived recently in Oregon have the same limited education and English language skills as those who had arrived in previous decades, though they find urban employment desirable and make efforts to continue their education to access more skilled positions in the local labor market. Ignacio Elizarraga is an example of a common trajectory of recent immigrants. Elizarraga left Mexico in 1988, worked as a laborer for a truck company in California, and moved to Oregon in the 1990s. He found employment in construction, formed a family, learned English, earned a GED, and trained in welding at Chemeketa Community College in Salem (Ferrara 2006).

Mexicanos obtain employment in the local labor markets through private staffing agencies and also via chains of word-of-mouth referrals that place jobs within the reach of workers with modest levels of education,

English proficiency, and/or skills. These referrals are very effective, since the ethnicity and nativity of laborers have considerable influence on hiring decisions when employers rely heavily on personal networks of workers to fill vacancies (Waldinger and Lichter 2003). In fact, co-ethnic referrals function in combination with informal transnational networks of *coyotes, raiteros*[4], and *mayordomos* to help balance labor supply and demand for Oregon's construction workers, berry pickers, forest firefighters, dairy-farm employees, and other low-wage workers in local industries (Kissam 2008).

Today, employers who offer entry-level positions in light manufacturing, construction, restaurants, and hotels could hardly operate without these flexible and dependable workers, although not all of them have legal residency or valid work permits. *Mexicanos* are equally well represented in nursing home and elder care, landscaping, house cleaning, auto-repair shops, car-wash businesses, and fast-food restaurants. These workers, for example, filled most of Salem metropolitan area's new construction jobs in recent years, enabling an unprecedented fast growth in the construction sector of this area (O'Connor 2008). However, labor surplus combined with recent economic downturns have increased the supply of unskilled immigrant workers who seek employment in Portland and other metropolitan areas. Although the rate of in-migration to Oregon has slowed among all population groups since 2006, possibly due to increased unemployment and hardship across economic sectors, Latinos—*mexicanos* in particular—continue to be the population group with the largest in-migration rates, contributing to a situation in which the labor supply continues to grow while unemployment rates also increase due to macroeconomic conditions (Opinion Research Northwest 2008). The current imbalance between the supply of workers and the availability of jobs in landscaping and construction, for example, produced organizing opportunities for Latino activists and advocates, who celebrated the opening of the City of Portland's first Center for Day Laborers in the summer of 2008 (Griffin 2008).

Mexican laborers often work non-standard times on evenings and nights, working rotating shifts and during weekends, when many other employees are already home. They are found among those who work the third shifts at the plants or start their work schedule between midnight and 7 a.m. As is true in other areas of the Pacific Northwest, second-generation Mexican Americans are overrepresented among workers who start their work between mid-afternoon and late night. The wages and the occupational prestige of these workers tend to be lower than those of employees who work standard shifts. The non-standard work schedules of *mexicanos* are associated with risks of injuries, health problems, and disruption of family life (Pransky et al.

2002). Men and women who work non-standard schedules are marginalized from their children's school activities, find it difficult to keep medical appointments, and have to rely on informal arrangements to care for their children while they are at work, at times when day-care facilities are not open (Saenz 2008). Our interviewees have told us about having to leave older children in charge of the younger ones when they worked in the night shift and no other adult was present in the home. Isabel, a Mexican woman in her mid-twenties, shared with us her childcare arrangement in the Portland apartment complex where she lives.

> *I prepare tortillas at a Mexican restaurant in downtown. The owners like my tortillas very much ... they say that mine are the best. They serve the tortillas fresh but I also prepare stacks for the next day. I go there in the evening and stay until 11:30 at night. If my husband is not at home when I have to leave, a neighbor in the same apartment building watches over our children. My husband puts them to sleep and he watches TV or sometimes he goes to bed, too. But he wakes up to get me from the restaurant because I'm scared to take the bus so late at night. I go to work in the bus but my husband picks me up. If the children are awake, he bundles them up and brings them in the truck too (interview with Mendoza, 2008).*

More than half of all *mexicanos* in the state work in industries other than agriculture, but still a significant number are farmworkers.[5] Men and women fill these year-round full-time and part-time agricultural jobs. They are also hired seasonally (temporarily) and migrate from employer to employer to work in field agriculture, in nursery and greenhouse operations, in food processing (for example, crop preparation for markets, and in processing plants preparing canned fruits and vegetables, and frozen fruits, fruit juices, and vegetables), and on dairy farms (Larson 2002; Baksys 2006; Parra-Cardona et al. 2006). Approximately 90 percent of the workforce in Oregon's nursery industry is Latino (Mathers 2004). Laborers in this important sector of the state's economy[6] are employed to work with crops raised on open acreage, but they work most with crops grown in covered structures, such as bedding plants, cut flowers, florists' greens, floriculture, flower seed crops, foliage plants, greenhouse vegetables, mushrooms, potted flowering plants, sod, and vegetable seed crops (Larson 2002).

Some eleven thousand farms in Oregon report hiring outside employees for some portion of farm work. Large production, however, is concentrated on about seventeen hundred farms that incur over 75 percent of the costs of hiring workers (Searle 2007, 85). The number of employees on Oregon's farms fluctuates from thirty thousand in winter to ninety thousand during the peak of harvest season (this does not include family members of farmworkers). Many laborers, particularly indigenous men and women from rural areas in Mexico, are experienced farmworkers, but others have learned their agricultural skills on the job.

Women working at a tulip farm in Woodburn, OR, 2009. Photo by Gwyn Fisher.

As they did in the past, *mexicanos* continue to seek agricultural jobs in Oregon because of the wage differentials between the labor markets of Mexico and the United States. Starting in the 1990s, however, Mexico's trade liberalization affected the wages of Mexicans across all occupations. Interestingly, workers in border regions with stronger links to the international economy experienced decreased wage returns per year of schooling when compared to workers in the rest of the country. Several of our interviewees displaced by economic downturn from white collar jobs in northern Mexico have arrived in Oregon with their families in the early 2000s. Chirquiar (2005) analyzed regional wage differentials among Mexican workers and found evidence supporting the effects of economic globalization across different levels of education, but particularly among high-skilled workers residing along the Mexico-U.S. border and also in northern Mexico, who for that reason were more prone to migrate to the United States.

Mexicanos in Oregon also work with forest products, harvesting timber and Christmas trees, and doing reforestation—although these jobs are not considered "agricultural" occupations (Filsinger 2004). In fact, the Mexican workforce undertakes the most laborious tasks in the woods, under the worst working conditions. Researchers who analyze recent developments point to the Latinization of the forestry industry in Oregon (Moseley 2006a; Sarathy 2006).

Table 4: *Mexicans in Oregon by Occupation, 2005**		
	Total population in Oregon	Mexicans in Oregon
Total civilian population employed 16 years and over	1,713,126	129,617
Occupation		
Management, professional, and related occupations	33.3%	10.0%
Service occupations	16.1%	25.5%
Sales and office occupations	25.7%	15.4%
Farming, fishing, and forestry occupations	1.8%	12.6%
Construction, extraction, maintenance and repair	9.8%	13.1%
Production, transportation, and material moving	13.2%	23.5%
Class of worker		
Private wage and salary workers	77.1%	90.3%
Government workers	13.9%	5.8%
Self-employed workers in own not incorporated business	8.7%	3.7%

*Source: 2005 American Community Survey, U.S. Bureau of the Census. Table S0201, Selected Population Profile of the Mexican Population in Oregon.

Many Mexican farmworkers and their families are intrastate migrants, traveling only within the state of Oregon, moving from one farming community to another, though other farmworkers come from outside the state to work in Oregon (interstate migrants). Some of these latter farmworkers and their families are part of the western migratory flow that supplies temporary farm labor in western and southwestern states. Others come to Oregon on a seasonal basis, either from the states of Washington or California, or directly from Mexico. Yet Mexican laborers continue to be hired by Oregon employers who use visa programs (H-2A and H-2B) created by the Immigration Reform and Control Act (IRCA) of 1986 to contract temporary foreign labor. These federal guest worker programs were intended to help agricultural employers find seasonal laborers. Employers are certified to hire foreign guest workers on a limited basis after they have demonstrated a shortage of domestic employees. Approximately one hundred H-2A guest workers worked in Oregon's agriculture in 2002 (Filsinger 2004). Commenting on the characteristics of the state's year-round, migratory, and seasonal agricultural workforce, John Aguirre (executive director of the Oregon Association of Nurseries, a non-profit trade association), said "Those who make bumper-sticker statements against immigrants show a lack of understanding of how business in Oregon works" (Peters 2007).

The occupational structure of Oregon's workforce is quite similar to that of the rest of the nation in most industries, but the state has more workers employed in farming, fishing, and forestry than the national average. *Mexicanos* are overrepresented in these occupations (nearly 12 percent of Hispanic workers are employed in farming, fishing, and forestry while only 1.7 percent of Oregon's total employment is in these occupations). The employment profile of *mexicanos* in Oregon also differs from that of other Oregonians in that a higher proportion of Mexicans are employed in service industries, production, transportation, and material handling. *Mexicano* farmworkers are most concentrated in the agricultural industries of Malheur, Morrow, Hood River, and Marion counties (O'Connor 2006).

Generally *mexicanos* in Oregon receive the lowest return for their skills compared to other population groups in the local labor market (Aguilera et al. 2008). In part, this is because many of the foreign-born arrive with less than a ninth-grade education, limited English proficiency, and/or an undocumented immigration status.[7] The 2008 Oregon Population Survey, for example, reported that Latinos continue to be the population group with the least education in the state (Oregon Progress Board 2009). The Oregon Farmers Association estimated that about half of the state dairy industry's workers are undocumented, and these workers are essential to the functioning of the industry. "If they were forced to leave," said Jim Krahn, executive director of the Oregon Farmers Association, interviewed by Melissa Navas (2008), "it would be hard to replace the jobs that machines couldn't do, such as caring for cows." Undocumented status also seriously limits the opportunities for skilled workers to advance beyond entry-level employment. In our interviews, we often encountered highly educated *mexicanos* employed in low-skill jobs due to lack of valid work permits. Scholars refer to this well-known occurrence as "brain waste" (Mattoo et al. 2005; Batalova and Fix 2008).

Table 5: *Selected Demographics, Educational Attainment, and Language Spoken at Home of Mexicans in Oregon, 2005**		
	Total population in Oregon	Mexicans in Oregon
Total population	3,560,109	302,852
Sex		
Male	49.4%	53.5%
Female	50.6%	46.5%
Age		
Median age (years)	37.0	24.2
Children under 5 years	6.3%	12.3%
Adults 75 years and over	6.2%	0.7%
Live in family households	63.8%	80.3%
Average household size	2.5	3.7
Educational Attainment		
Population 25 years and over with less than high school diploma	17.5%	51.5%
Speak a language other than English at home		
Population 5 years and over	13.9%	77.7%

*Source: 2005 American Community Survey, U.S. Bureau of the Census. Table S0201, Selected Population Profile of the Mexican Population in Oregon.

Mexicanos who work in economic sectors that employ large numbers of low-skilled immigrant laborers generally have worse working conditions than those employed in high-skilled occupations and government jobs, where Mexican immigrants are less well represented (Catanzarite and Aguilera 2002). If they work for labor contractors, *mexicanos* are paid lower wages than other workers. Such is the case of indigenous farmworkers working in labor-intensive crops, who are also often subjected to disrespect and discrimination based on their unique languages and cultures (Farquhar et al. 2008a). Indigenous farmworkers from Mexico and Guatemala provide approximately 40 percent of Oregon's farm labor according to estimates by researchers at Portland State University and the Oregon Law Center. These researchers identified twelve native languages on Oregon's farms, with the majority of indigenous laborers originating from the Mexican states of Oaxaca and Guerrero (Farquhar et al. 2008b). Nonetheless, Ramón Ramírez, who heads PCUN, the farmworkers' union, estimates that as many as 60 percent of all Mexican workers in Oregon's agriculture are indigenous (Frazier 2006).

Recent Immigrants in Older Mexicano Communities

As we described in previous chapters, some of Oregon's older and best-known *mexicano* communities are located in distinct agricultural regions, such as the irrigated areas of semi-arid north central and eastern Oregon, Hood River, Odell, Mosier, The Dalles, and the Willamette Valley. Researchers speculate that earlier *mexicano* immigrants from Southwestern states chose to settle in dry irrigated lands that resembled their native environments. Oregonians of Mexican descent in these older communities are employed in a variety of positions: they work in government jobs and in urban occupations, on dairy

Danza de los Diablitos *de San Mateo Tunuchi,* Guelaguetza *celebration, Salem, OR, 2009. Courtesy of OCIMO, permission Justo Rodríguez.*

farms, in fisheries, and in ranching activities with livestock. These workers operate equipment associated with farming, and drive trucks transporting agricultural products. The presence of these workers and their families is evident in school districts of Eastern Oregon, such as Milton-Freewater Unified School District 7 (Umatilla County), Nyssa School District 26, and Ontario School District 9C (Malheur County), in which slightly more than half of all students are now Latino. In the following sections we elaborate on the arrival of the newest immigrants in communities where other *mexicanos* had settled before, establishing tight-knit second- and third- generation social networks that many times helped the newcomers, but other times hampered their desire to integrate and succeed.

Laborers in the Orchards, Ranches, and Farms
of Eastern and Central Oregon

The Snake River and the Columbia River mark the route defined first by the Oregon Trail, then the Northern Pacific Railroad, and later by the Interstate Highway. The Columbia-Snake River system links the dry-farming and ranching hinterlands to metropolitan areas in the Pacific Northwest. *Mexicano* communities in north-central and eastern Oregon are located in the non-irrigated land east of the Cascades used for cattle and sheep grazing, while wheat, barley, hay, sugar beets, potatoes, peppermint, asparagus, onions, and grapes account for much of the crop-land acreage. This region is so distinctive that a group of residents recently floated the idea of making of Eastern Oregon its own state, stretching from east of the Cascade Mountains to the Idaho border (Wright 2008).

Also in Eastern Oregon are the orchards of Hood River (Hood River County), and the farms around Boardman (Morrow County) and Milton-Freewater and Hermiston (Umatilla County) in the Columbia River Basin. Today, community leaders say that about eight thousand *mexicanos* are settled on both sides of the Mid-Columbia River (in both Oregon and Washington). This number is twice as high from February to October, when migrant and seasonal farm laborers work in this region (McCauley et al. 2001). The demographic, economic, and socio-cultural impacts of their presence have been immense, particularly in public schools and churches of different denominations. In the 2008-2009 academic year[8], for example, the Hood River County School District enrolled 1,730 Latino students, which amounts to 43.5 percent of the total student population (the large majority of Latino students are *mexicanos*). In some elementary schools of this district, such as Mid Valley Elementary, Latino enrollment now accounts for 66.1 percent of the total. In Jefferson County, the second generation is very visible in public schools. In the 2008-2009 academic year, one third (33.9 percent) of the student body of the Jefferson County School District 509J is Latino— roughly the other two-thirds are either white or Native American. In a town like Metolius (total population 634), where *mexicano* families began to settle in the 1950s, by 2008-2009 more than 50 percent of the students in the town's elementary school are Hispanic. Their parents are Oregonians of Mexican descent who work on farms to hoe, irrigate, and harvest crops, and are also employed in the potato sheds and in mills converting scrap wood from lumber operations.

Similarly, a quarter of the population in Culver (total population 802) was Mexican and 24.8 percent spoke Spanish at home in 2007. Economic hardship and unemployment may have discouraged the settlement of new immigrants, but there is a resilient core of *mexicano* settlers in Culver. Jack Ickler, a retired farmer from Culver interviewed by Lauren Duke (2008), said that he used to have eight to ten highly skilled Mexican laborers who worked for him on a seasonal basis, and some of these hard workers could have been undocumented. "They are the only ones that want to work," Ickler said. "People don't like to do farm work.... Even if you paid $15 an hour and they could work at the soda fountain for $10, they would do that." In Madras (total population 6,070), where *mexicanos* account for more than 35 percent of the population, these workers are employed in potato and onion sheds processing, sorting, cleaning, and storing crops. Explaining that he needed to hire workers quickly and on a short-term basis for his onion fields, Madras farmer Gary Harris said in an interview with Duke (2008), "In Madras we don't have year-round work, we have a seasonal harvest peak for employees.... Our major emphasis is on harvest crews, [who are] here for a short time." The demographic and social landscape of the student population in the Madras school district is unusual: one third is Native American (many students are from the Confederated Tribes of Warm Springs), one third is Latino (mostly *mexicano*), and another third is composed of Oregonians of European descent. However, in this locality *mexicanos* are still striving to open-up opportunities for civic representation.

Mexicans in Eastern and Central Oregon also work in manufacturing, construction, and service jobs in cities and small towns. In recent years, some have experienced job losses due to closure and relocation of food-processing plants, such as the closure of J.R. Simplot potato-processing plant in Hermiston (Umatilla County), and the 2005 closure of Amalgamated Sugar, a sugar-processing plant in Nyssa, a town located two miles from the Oregon Trail's Snake River crossing in Malheur County. Diego Castellanoz, a city councilor, school board member, and former mayor of Nyssa, was employed for twenty-eight years at Amalgamated Sugar until the plant closed. "I began working there right out of high school, I've basically grown up there," said Castellanoz to interviewers with the Oregon's Stories Project. "I also have three other brothers that worked at Amalgamated Sugar" (Geoghegan and Koch 2006). Castellanoz' sister, Genoveva, a *curandera* healer born in Guanajuato, Mexico, immigrated with her husband Teodoro to the Snake River Valley in 1938. She has worked as a farm laborer, teacher, and traditional artist, in addition to rearing nine children (Salas 2006). Genoveva Castellanoz is known for her creation of *coronas* (wax and paper flower crowns used for baptisms, weddings, and *quinceañeras*[9]) and received an award from the National Endowment of the Arts in 1987 in recognition of her accomplishments (Mulcahy 2005).[10] Nyssa was already a "minority-majority" town in 2000.[11] Mexicano residents publicly celebrate their traditions, such as *Cinco de Mayo*, a national holiday in Mexico, with dances and musical performances. They also support a well-attended soccer league.

A common concern among Oregonians of Mexican descent in these well-established communities is to create opportunities for participation in local civic activities and to open up avenues for representation in local government, and on the governing boards of social service agencies and not-for-profit organizations. Such is the case of *mexicanos* in Boardman, where the population is equally divided between Latinos (50.1 percent) and non-Hispanic whites (49.9 percent), and where Latino residents have expressed their interest in having representation on the city council (Weber et al. 2007). Issues of civic representation and social and cultural integration are likely to surface also in other Eastern Oregon towns with a well-established *mexicano* presence.

From Orchards to Forest Work to Service Jobs in the Rogue Valley

Mexicano men and women performed temporary work in the fruit farms of the Rogue Valley well before entrepreneurial labor contractors and their

all-Mexican male crews were able to obtain timber harvesting and reforestation contracts with the U.S. Forest Service as part of a set-aside program that reserves federal contracts for small, disadvantaged, and minority-owned businesses (Moseley 2006; Sarathy 2006, 2008). When the Northwest Forest Plan of 1994 shifted forest work to ecosystem-management activities—a plan that resulted in a severe decline of logging on federal lands—*mexicano* crews of *pineros* (tree-planters) were quick to move into this manually intensive work, including hand-thinning dense underbrush, piling and burning brush, and planting trees.

Today, *mexicano* workers dominate the forest management

Jinete Charro, Salem, OR. Photo by Paulina Hermosillo.

workforce particularly on public lands in southern Oregon, in the Willamette Valley, and in other parts of the state (Moseley 2006). In the Rogue Valley, these farmworkers and forest workers are sustained by long-term, settled communities, with their own *tiendas* (grocery stores), restaurants, check-cashing and money-sending services, churches (both Catholic and Evangelical congregations), soccer leagues, community health centers, English as a second language classes, a Latino Chamber of Commerce, and a Hispanic Interagency Committee. In 1990, Latinos constituted approximately 4 percent of the total population of Jackson County, and 5 percent of the population in the Rogue Valley. By 2000, the proportion of Latino residents was 7 percent in Jackson County and about 10 percent in the Rogue Valley (Sarathy 2006). In 1990, 768 households were headed by someone of Latino origin or descent in the Rogue Valley, while the corresponding figure in the year 2000 was 2,016, an increase of more than 160 percent. Almost 44 percent of Latino households were owner occupied—a clear indication of a trend toward long-term settlement of *mexicanos* in the area.

Recent immigrants have settled in the cities of Medford, Central Point, White City, Talent, Phoenix, and Eagle Point in and around the Medford-Ashland metropolitan area. This area has not been immune to occasional anti-immigrant sentiment. In April 2009, a white supremacist group based in Phoenix that denies the Holocaust, wants Mexican illegal immigrants deported, and demands legal protections to prevent extinction of the white race set out to distribute about three thousand white pride fliers at parking lots "from Eagle Point to south Medford" (Burke 2009a; Specht 2009). Community members in Phoenix gathered to express their opposition to the ideology of this particular small group of neo-Nazis (Specht 2009). Also a coalition of Rogue Valley peace and human-rights organizations that came together in 2008 to speak out against hate after a KKK symbol was burned into the lawn of an interracial couple in west Medford has developed strategies to counter the hateful messages of the Oregon unit of the National Socialist Movement based in Phoenix (Burke 2009b).

Agricultural Intensification in the Willamette Valley

The majority of the *mexicanos* who arrived in Oregon in the last fifteen years, particularly those of indigenous descent, found employment in the Willamette Valley—the most densely populated and agriculturally productive region in the state. Well-known *mexicano* communities were already established in Woodburn and in neighboring Independence and McMinnville. By the 1990s the city of Woodburn was being portrayed as

Oregon's Little Mexico. The *mexicano* settlement grew to transform this city into the state's first "minority-majority" municipality, where more than half of the population is Latino (Stephen 2007; Nelson and Hiemstra 2008).

Farmworkers find employment in the Willamette Valley because this valley offers a unique environment for specialty crops and seed production due to its climate.[12] Seed production, organic farms, vineyards, orchards, tree nurseries, ornamental-plant and greenhouse businesses that thrive in the Willamette Valley all require year-round labor input and strenuous seasonal manual labor. Geographer Michael McGlade (2002) has argued that local growers and agricultural companies have been able to intensify agricultural production in this unique environment thanks to a large extent to availability of Mexican labor, combined with support from transportation, and value-added vegetable and seed-cleaning and processing infrastructure. Referring to the farmworkers who provide labor in the Willamette Valley, Dan McGrath, an agriculture professor at Oregon State University interviewed by Bates and Wilson (2005), said, "We had a need and they filled it."

Availability of adequate labor is critical to Oregon's crop production. Tree fruits, berries, nurseries, vineyards, and many other specialty crops require labor rates much higher than traditional farm production and much of the work has to be done by hand by trained employees, many of them hired seasonally. However, growers' concerns with the cost and availability of farm labor have led to increased mechanization.[13] A few specialty crops, such as strawberries, broccoli, and cauliflower, have nearly disappeared from Oregon and Washington due to growers' preoccupation with labor cost and accessibility, and are now produced in California and Mexico instead (Searle 2007).

In 2008 we interviewed Esteban, a father of two in his early thirties. He was born and raised in northern Mexico and had never worked in agriculture before arriving in Oregon. We reproduce his *testimonio* separately. Esteban explained his migration experience and the nature of the work at an organic farm in the Southern Willamette Valley. Esteban's story hints at the personal and cultural changes that occur after long-term adaptation to a new place. We also interviewed recent immigrants who are currently employed on organic farms and at tree nurseries in the Willamette Valley. Our interviewees talked about the rigors of their jobs and the mistreatment they are subjected to, particularly those hired to fill seasonal labor shortages. They mentioned the discrimination that indigenous immigrants experience from their employers and from other non-indigenous Mexican co-workers.[14] Mistreatment notwithstanding, recent immigrants appreciate their jobs and want to keep them to support their families, although young men and women who are parents of school-age children feel trapped by long and demanding work schedules—a feeling that is more acute among those who learned farm work after arriving in Oregon. They regret missing their children's daily activities, and lament that they cannot spend more time with their families as the children grow and adjust to become Oregonians of Mexican descent. "When you ask the children," interviewees say, "they don't want to go back to Mexico. The children like it here." Although recent immigrants value the future opportunities that their new lives in the United States may still offer them, the adults are always longing for extended family and friends in their hometowns, and the youth who were brought to the United States during childhood or adolescence often have fond memories about their previous lives in Mexico.

Agricultural intensification in irrigated valleys near large urban labor markets generally attracts more workers than agricultural production in other less labor-intensive areas. Since the 1980s, agricultural intensification has caused a dramatic increase in the number of migrant and seasonal workers employed in the Willamette Valley, with spill-over effects on other areas (McGlade 2002). There was also a spill over of *mexicano* workers to adjacent urban areas. As their social networks matured, new arrivals began to fill jobs in the cities, which offered more housing choices, schools, shopping, and urban amenities. Nonetheless, the need for affordable housing in rural areas became so acute that in 1991 a coalition of organizations in Woodburn established the Farmworker Housing Development Corporation (FHDC). Since then FHDC has built two state-subsidized housing projects for agricultural workers within Woodburn city limits (Nelson 2007).

McGlade (2002) suggested that *mexicano* settlement in urban areas located at less than a one-hour drive from labor-intensive agriculture would grow faster than that in urban areas located further than seventy miles from the core of agricultural intensification. In the Portland and Salem metropolitan areas, for example, the Mexican population more than quintupled from 1980 to 2000. It grew substantially, although to a lesser extent, around the Medford-Ashland metropolitan area in southern Oregon (Hardwick and Goworowska 2008).

Mariana, a woman in her late twenties, arrived in Oregon in 2002. Her move, accompanied by her husband and their daughter, was possible because of the strength of their family networks. Upon arrival, Mariana's husband found employment in reforestation in the southern Willamette Valley, and she started a successful house-cleaning business in Monroe. These *mexicano* parents soon became economically integrated into the small town where they settled, and had another child. Through time, they began to view their former life in Mexico from a different perspective, questioning and evaluating the characteristics of Mexican society. Today they are more concerned about their older daughter's undocumented immigration status than about their own unauthorized status. Mariana said:

> *I'm from Monterrey, Nuevo León, which is an industrial city. My sister encouraged me to come to Oregon with my husband and our daughter, who then was five years old. My sister is married to a man from Oaxaca, and they decided to move to the southern Willamette Valley because his family is here. As soon as my sister arrived in Oregon, she started calling me and my husband to join them. We arrived in Portland on December 24th, 2002, directly from Monterrey. We entered the country with tourist visas and overstayed. At the beginning, we stayed with my sister. It was difficult because my husband was working all day at a tree nursery and we didn't see one another much. I started to do private house cleaning. Then I got pregnant. Our son was born here; he is three now. When I think of it, we didn't come to the United States out of economic need, but moved by our ambition. We didn't lack much in Mexico, but wished for something even better. At that time I was a secretary in Monterrey, and my husband was a business associate for a large company. We owned a house that was built by the government, and we had a car. Now I have my own house-cleaning business in Monroe and my husband is employed at a small farm. To make things easier, we rent an apartment at walking distance from our daughter's school. In the morning, a Mexican neighbor takes care of my son in the apartment complex, and I walk my daughter to school. She has breakfast there, and I pick her up when I come back from work. Whenever I can, I attend English classes at night. With our work, we have been able to save some money. We bought two cars, a truck for my husband and a smaller car for me. We also bought a small lot of land in Mexico. We would like to go back, but we sure value what we have here. In four years we have been able to achieve what we could not have achieved in ten years in our own country. One gets used to living in the United States; the children like it here, too. Our daughter is doing very well in school. But what makes me really sad is that my daughter doesn't know that she has an undocumented immigration status. We haven't mentioned this to her; I worry about it because I know that she doesn't have the same rights as my son has (interview with Mendoza, 2008).*

Mexicans in the Willamette Valley "come here for one reason, to work," said Edgardo Rodríguez, a long-time employee at a Christmas tree nursery near Monroe, interviewed by Susan Palmer (2006). The kind of employment these workers find allows for the settlement of families, which explains the growth in school enrollment of Latino students across the valley. *Mexicano* families contribute to the revitalization of aging Oregon communities and offset population decline in rural areas and small towns. Some immigrant entrepreneurs have opened restaurants and *tiendas* that cater to the ethnic community. Our interviewees said that wherever you see a Mexican family restaurant on the main street and a Catholic Church with weekly Spanish mass, it means that there is a growing *mexicano* community in town. These new Oregonians patronize local businesses, rejuvenate the affordable-housing market, revitalize city parks, and provide needed tax revenue. At the same time, increased visibility of the foreign-born in towns, in the schools, health clinics, and at churches, could cause friction with long-term residents "in a society that is still not cured from its racist afflictions" (Waldinger et al. 2007).

Nursery and ornamental-plant jobs are a step up from orchards and other agricultural work because of their year-round schedules. We interviewed a number of young women who are employed in ornamental-plant nurseries and greenhouses in the southern Willamette Valley. In keeping with their cultural values, when these women start a family or have a second child most would like to remain at home and take care of their children, but none of them is able to because they would not be able to sustain their household with their husbands' low-wage income in forestry or agriculture. Young immigrant parents in Oregon's small towns rely on the support of extended family members or on informal childcare arrangements to continue their participation in the labor force. Estela, a woman in her early twenties, was born in Oaxaca. She had a two-month old baby girl at that time and was personally struggling with the idea of going back to work.

> *I have worked for more than two years at this ornamental plant nursery located at a ten-minute drive from here. Many other mexicanos work there. We work under a covered structure; we don't have to go out to the field. The nursery owner is a European woman; she is actually from Europe. She likes me because I understand Spanish and English and can get along with the workers. The owner asked me to supervise the other women and gave me a raise. I know how to do the job, and some employees come in only for the peak season and don't care much about the quality of their work. During the peak of production—in spring and late summer—we are at the nursery many hours a day and I never know when I'll be*

able to come home. We stay until late at night until all the plants [that are included] in the orders are shipped out. When I got this job, we moved to a small apartment one block from the elementary school that our older daughter attends; before we had been living with my brother-in-law and his family in a larger apartment on the other side of town. My husband does tree planting for a contractor and he gets moved around a lot. When the nursery owner started to pay me a little more, we bought another truck. That's the one I drive. My husband drives an older truck. We also bought a computer for our daughter. She is very smart and likes to play games on the computer and watch TV. Then we had our second child. I wanted to stay at home with both girls because I don't see them much and my husband doesn't see them much either. The baby is so happy when my husband is around! She loves him very much. But the owner of the nursery wants me to go back to work because she cannot deal with the other workers. My mother offered to care for the baby while my older daughter is in school, and she would pick the older one up after school. I would really want to be with them but I know that we cannot afford it (interview with Mendoza, 2008).

Estela accepted the support of her mother and went back to work at the nursery. A few months later she had an accident at the workplace. Her medical treatment was covered by the employer's health insurance. After she recuperated from her injury, Estela felt obligated to remain loyal to the grower and continued to work at the nursery. *Mexicanos* have the highest fatality rate and relative risk of work-related injuries among all workers ages sixteen and older in the United States (American Federation of Labor & Congress of Industrial Organizations 2005). Mexican men and women are at greater risk of being injured and killed on the job than native-born workers partly because they are likely to be employed in high-risk occupations or work dangerous jobs in the unregulated "informal" economy. These workers may have not received occupational-safety training in a language that they understand, and may fear reporting workplace injuries. Many immigrants are not aware of their legal rights to safety and health on the job, and also to workers' compensation if they are injured (Pransky et al. 2002; Moseley 2006). As another interviewee put it, "[W]e are always a workplace injury away from disability."

The story of Graciela, a woman in her late thirties who was recuperating from a workplace injury, illustrates the type of linguistic and cultural barriers encountered by immigrant workers. Graciela and her family moved to Junction City from northern California about six years ago. With the support of a friend from his hometown, Graciela's husband found employment at a large manufacturing company of recreational vehicles. Graciela toiled in town doing private home cleaning, and also took a temporary job at a fast-food restaurant because she wanted to avoid agricultural employment altogether, until she landed a job at the same manufacturing company where her husband is employed. She was content with her job until a heavy piece of equipment fell on her. Graciela described her feelings about a slow healing process from her back injury, the pressures from her employer to go back to work, and her desire to keep up with their teenage children's demands for consumption. Graciela said:

> I don't feel well yet; I have headaches, my back hurts, I can barely walk, but the doctor says that I'm fine, that I should go back to work. I have been seeing this doctor more than four times. My husband takes me to this clinic in Eugene. They have an interpreter in the clinic because many workers don't understand English, and I understand even less when I get nervous. My older brother who lives in the state of Washington came to Oregon the last time I had to see the doctor, and accompanied me to the medical visit. He knows how to handle these things. He told the doctor that I won't be able to go back to do the same type of work that I was doing before, but this doctor insisted that the health insurance company has already done all they can do for me. I have [immigration] papers; my husband got papers, too, when his father was doing farm work in California; but working in the fields is hard. We both prefer to work in a factory or a warehouse; we don't want to go back to do agriculture. And besides, I wouldn't be able to bend over now. Our children are in high school, they like it in this town, they have friends, and they ask for more things now. I want to give them what they want but I need a job to do that. If they don't hire me back I'll try to get hired at one of the nurseries [near town]; they always need help in the warehouses, and I can get a ride with other Mexicans who work there (interview with Mendoza, 2008).

Availability of an adequate supply of labor is critical to maintain the success of Oregon's industries that employ immigrant workers, but a large part of the immigrant workforce might face sanctions or other legal actions if federal legislation applying the "no match" rule, requiring employers to fire workers whose social security numbers did not match those in the agency's database, were implemented consistently. In the summer of 2008, a coalition of Oregon employer groups released a commissioned study on the potential economic impacts on the state, which estimated that the local economy would lose 173,500 jobs or 7.7 percent of the Oregon workforce if some 97,500 undocumented workers were to leave the state because of enforcement of immigration rules (Jaeger 2008).

We interviewed workers employed seasonally and also year-round at seed companies in the southern Willamette Valley. Seasonal workers endure much harder working conditions in the fields, whereas year-round employees work indoors in warehouses. They are generally more satisfied with their jobs than forestry workers, tree planters, or farmworkers. Those in managerial positions often receive housing from the company; nevertheless few would be able to support a family and remit money to their parents in Mexico without a contribution from the part-time or full-time salaries of their spouses. Rodolfo, for example, explained to us the type of work he does at a seed warehouse and talked about his yearning for his hometown in Oaxaca.

I'm from Santiago Apóstol, a town of about five thousand in Oaxaca. Most people in my town got the migration fever. I did too. When I finished high school in 1997 I decided to come to Oregon. I made the decision by myself. I got interested by listening to other people's conversations. I said to myself: "I'm going to take a look at that." I have two brothers and two sisters living here in the southern Willamette Valley. My older brother was the first one to migrate. He went to California in 1987 and then moved to Oregon with his family. He brought the other siblings. Now he's trying to bring my parents too. First I worked in the fields in Harrisburg and lived with my brother, but I went back to Santiago Apóstol in 2002 because I missed the place. There is more money in the town now and more services are available. Other people [who were not originally from there] moved in and started small business. The town is growing, there are more opportunities than before, but people emigrate anyway. Down there, you pay rent and electricity once a year; here I pay every month.

I decided to come back to Oregon and I got married here. My wife is from the same town. We have a daughter who is two. My wife completed the GED and she works part-time at a hotel during the weekends, so I can take care of our daughter while she is at work. I don't forget my parents; I send them US $70 per month. I work at a seed company here in the southern Willamette Valley. My brother is a manager for this company and he recommended me for the job. At the warehouse where I work, we fill out orders. We mix three or four types of seeds to prepare a blend. For example, we mix 10 percent of this type and 5 percent of another type. Different types of seeds are kept in bags of 20,000 lbs. and 44,000 lbs. The seeds are placed in a *mixer, then they go to another container, and those seeds (already mixed) are bagged. Each bag has the product number, a reference number, and a card with the percentage of each type of seed blended in the product. These bags weight 55 lbs. I use the forklift to make piles of forty bags. We have grass seeds, seeds for turfs, others to feed cows. About half of the production goes to the domestic market and half is for export. The company does business with Japan, Korea, Russia, Colombia, Mexico, Argentina, Brazil, and Ecuador. The company also sells vegetable seeds: onion, radish, lettuce, kale, and canola seeds to produce ethanol.*

I work with three other employees: an American and a Mexican to fill out the orders and put the bags in containers, and another American who drives the truck to bring the seeds back and forth to other warehouses. We have annual safety meetings; the owners post notices, explain to us new regulations. We have OSHA authorization; the inspectors could come anytime to verify that we comply. I work mostly indoors in the warehouse but sometimes the grass grows uneven and we are sent to the fields to cut the flowers. At the end of summer, between August and October, we have more work and the company owners hire temporary workers. The company owners contract with farmers to grow plants with their seeds, care for them, cut them, and take them to a seed-cleaning plant. When we bag vegetable seeds, we need to pay attention not to mix them with grass seeds. Then I pile the bags with vegetable seeds into containers [if they are for export] or in trailers [if they are sold in the domestic market]. We also fill out orders in paper and plastic bags that require much more care (interview with Mendoza, 2008).

Along Highway 99 there are many family-owned seed companies, in Junction City, Harrisburg, Tangent, Corvallis, and other places. Farmers around Salem plant vegetables for the seed companies. These companies contract with farmers all the way up to the state of Washington. The farmers and the companies employ Mexican laborers who work in the fields from 6:00 am to 7:00-8:00 pm, because American workers don't like to do that type of farm work.

Throughout the Willamette Valley and across the state, *mexicanos* provide labor that is equally essential to large and small agricultural operations, particularly in labor-intensive agricultural locations near metropolitan areas. Workers in these rural locations are likely to face many of the same challenges that confront low-wage workers living in other more isolated places, yet they differ in their levels of experience and occupational distribution. Their employers say that losing these *mexicano* workers would be devastating to the agricultural industry. "We have not been particularly successful at finding huge numbers of people that are willing to roll up from the public to work on farms," said Barry Bushue, president of the Oregon Farm Bureau, in an interview with Ed Johnson (2008); "these are skilled positions.... You can't just remove one group of people from the farm and replace them with someone off the street."

Currently, *mexicano* farmworkers are also almost irreplaceable in the Willamette Valley and elsewhere in the state where growers and ranchers use contingent labor during production peaks. Part-time or contingent labor arrangements enable employers in agriculture and also forestry industries to maintain the same activities but with little employment security and worker benefits. Employers are well aware of their dependence on these low-wage immigrant workers and worry about the outcomes of federal immigration legislation. There is an unspoken mutual agreement between employers and workers to keep the best workers—regardless of their immigration status—and also to hire as many other workers as are needed each season.

Nevertheless, reliable immigrant workers usually come with families and want to settle.

The Families of Mexicano Workers

Two strong indicators of the settlement of families in Oregon are the increase in the number of births to Mexican mothers and in the number of students of Mexican origin or descent in public schools. Today, slightly over 20 percent of all births in Oregon are to Hispanic mothers, who are mostly *mexicanas* (Oregon Department of Human Services 2007); some of these mothers are young women giving birth to their first child and others are mothers who already have more than two or three children. Because the families are settled in different regions, these births occur unevenly throughout the state. For example, only one Hispanic mother gave birth in Gilliam County between 2005 and 2007, but more children were born to Hispanic mothers in Malheur and Jefferson counties during the same period than to white non-Hispanic mothers (Oregon Department of Human Services 2008). Similarly, the number of Latino students enrolled in Oregon's public schools varies among school districts in different counties, although it has generally increased from under 5 percent in 1990 to 15 percent in 2005 (Oregon University System Brief 2009). One in every six students in the Oregon's public school system is Latino (Carter 2007), that is 17.2 percent of all students in 2008-2009. Some school districts have more Latino students than others; for example, 70 percent of the student population in the elementary schools of Gresham (Multnomah County) and in the labor-intensive agricultural area of Woodburn (Marion County) is Latino.

These children who attend public schools—the youngest are usually American born, and some of the older children may be foreign born—soon adapt to their new social environments. Most second-generation Mexican American youth would like to remain in the Oregon places where they live. Compared to their parents, these one-and-a-half and second generation *mexicanos* seem to integrate much more rapidly into life and circumstances in the United States. Through time, the internal dynamics of families get adjusted, and the relations between immigrant parents and their children undergo cultural changes that would have been inconceivable in the Mexican tight-knit communities where many parents have been socialized. However, the successful integration of adults in the workplace and the achievement of students in the schools do not come easily for members of immigrant families. Many parents continue to face challenges because they have skills that mismatch their jobs, have limited English language proficiency, or have an undocumented immigration status; and many children in immigrant households continue to experience achievement gaps in schools. Latino students have the lowest high-school graduation rate among all population groups in Oregon (63.7 percent in 2006-2007, as reported by the Oregon Department of Education). The dropout rate [15] of Latino students in the state (currently at 7.9 percent) has improved substantially since the mid-1990s, when it had reached 18 percent, but is still a matter of concern.

Mexicano family households not only include more small children than those in the overall population, but are also generally larger.[16] Because immigrants are young (the median age for Latinos in Oregon in 2000 was 22.8, and for all Oregonians it was 36.3), they are expected to have children. Children now being born to Mexican parents can be expected to begin having children of their own in about twenty years. At that point, even with a continued influx of the foreign-born, the largest component of Oregon's Mexican-origin population would be U.S. born.

Moreover the households of farmworkers often include family members who are non-farmworkers, and small children and youth younger than eighteen. The earnings and income levels of these households are low relative to Oregon's overall population. For example, the average income of farmworker households in a convenience sample of 106 Mexican families analyzed by Dodge-Vera and Patton-Lopez (2008) in Linn and Benton counties was $26,700. Following 2008 federal poverty guidelines, which set the gross yearly income for a family of five at $24,800, almost half of these families were living in poverty and experiencing food insecurity (Grussing

2007). The families in this sample had resided in Oregon about nine years on average. They traveled on average twenty-five minutes (from five to one hundred and twenty minutes) to the grocery store, which indicates the rural isolation in which some of them lived (Dodge-Vera and Patton-Lopez 2008).

Nonetheless many farmworkers and other recent immigrant workers employed in low-wage jobs send part of their earnings to support family members in Mexico. *Mexicanos*, particularly those who have arrived in Oregon most recently, send money to their parents, to their spouses and children, or to other relatives, to pay for education, small investments, and basic necessities; their remittances also build new houses or pay for additions to older buildings, and contribute to community projects in their home towns. Researchers found evidence that migrants send more remittances when they have more family members in Mexico and fewer in the United States, when they own land or real estate in Mexico, and when they plan on returning soon to their communities of origin (McCoy et al. 2007). Fairchild and Simpson (2004) analyzed data for 2,495 Mexican male heads of households who engaged in circular migration during the 1990s to work in agriculture in the Pacific Northwest. They sent home more remittances than farmworkers in other regions of the United States. In 1995, for example, the average monthly remittance of Mexican farmworkers in the Pacific Northwest was $363.91.

Farm workers playing cards in camp, Woodburn, OR. Photo by Paulina Hermosillo.

The flows of remittances are parallel to long-established migration patterns between Mexico and the United States. Transfers of funds provide evidence of continuing social connections between workers and their communities of origin. Migrants send home money, along with food, letters, photos, and other goods, using a variety of channels—informal hand-delivery, formal courier services, *paqueterías* contracted at ethnic stores, and formal fund-transfer systems such as Orlandi Valuta, Western Union, or MoneyGram. Many migrants who had been prevented from accessing formal financial institutions due to lack of acceptable documented identification have been able to transfer funds by using Matrícula Consular identification cards issued by the Mexican Consulate in Portland. In 2004, Mexican nationals who were living in the Portland's Mexican Consular jurisdiction—which includes the whole state of Oregon—sent remittances to recipients in the following Mexican states: 1) Michoacán, 2) Oaxaca, 3) Jalisco, 4) Guerrero, 5) Guanajuato, 6) Veracruz, 7) Puebla, 8) Distrito Federal, 9) Estado de México, and 10) Hidalgo (listed by value of money sent) (Hernández-Coss 2004).

Since 2006, the value of remittances sent through both formal and informal channels from Oregon to Mexico has diminished considerably. For example, Juana Ayala Pastor, interviewed by Sara Miller Llana (2008) in the village of Emiliano Zapata in Michoacán, said that her son, who works on farms in Oregon, now sends her money only sporadically. "His money was our only source of hope," said Ayala Pastor. The $500 that she received each month has been reduced to an occasional $200 because he could not find a job for six months. There were other signs of economic downturn in the Oregon economy. The number of Latino students receiving free meals at public school and visiting school health clinics increased noticeably in Lane County. Maxine Proskurowski, a longtime Eugene School District nurse who manages the school-based health clinics, said in an interview with Anne Williams (2008), "I always feel I know the barometer of what is going on, and all these families who have done really well—some of them came here as immigrants, legal immigrants, and they bought their homes and had jobs—and they are coming totally panicked. Their hours have either been drastically cut back or they've lost their jobs." Mexican workers in Oregon and elsewhere in the nation experienced job loss and cuts in overtime and in regular hours. Those working "bad" or marginal jobs characterized by low wages, dangerous working conditions, no benefits, and contingent labor arrangements have experienced the most lay-offs. Some of our interviewees started to talk about returning to their communities of origin, but others said that it would be equally hard for them or even more difficult to find a job back in their home towns because the economies of Mexico and the United States are intrinsically connected.

1. Less than 3 percent of the population in Gilliam County was Latino in 2007, while the Latino population accounted for more than 6 percent in Sherman and Wheeler counties. Data on Oregon's resident births by ethnicity, race, and country of residence of the mother are found in the Oregon Department of Human Services' Vital Statistics reports. Other demographic data are found on the Web site of the U.S. Bureau of the Census.

2. The term Silicon Forest refers to all technology companies in Oregon and more specifically to the cluster of high-tech companies located in the industrial corridor of the Portland metropolitan area, between Beaverton and Hillsboro.

3. Some residents in Orenco Station, an affluent and ethnically homogeneous community have expressed exclusionary attitudes with respect to littering, parking, and safety issues caused by non-residents in public parks (Podobnik 2003).

4. Workers without transportation pay a *raitero* for a ride to get to work and back home.

5. A farmworker is any person who works for pay in the production and harvesting of agricultural commodities (crops and horticultural specialties), dairying, and raising livestock (Filsinger 2004).

6. According to the Oregon Agricultural Statistics Service, in 2007 greenhouse and nursery products became the first agricultural commodity in the state to generate more than $1 billion in value. Oregon produces 15 percent of U.S. nursery crops, and it ranks as the nation's top producer of shade trees, coniferous evergreens, and Christmas trees. The state ranks second among states in production of deciduous flowering trees and broadleaf evergreens. Three-quarters of nursery products are shipped to nationwide and global customers.

7. Ayre (2006), a researcher with the Oregon Department of Employment, estimated that undocumented immigrants comprised 3.6 to 4.8 percent of employed Oregon residents in 2005—that is, between 63,000 and 83,200 workers.

8. All data on school enrollment by ethnicity of the students is available from the Oregon Department of Education at http://www.ode.state.or.us/sfda/reports/r0067Select2.asp

9. *Quinceañera* is a celebration in which a fifteen-year-old girl is symbolically ushered into adulthood. This celebration originally had, and continues to have, a religious connotation, since the Catholic Mass remains central to this event.

10. In 2002, her work also inspired a community project by Oregon AHEC (Area Health Education Centers) to explore the role of folk medicine in health access, and to bridge the gap between allopathic providers and traditional healers.

11. In 2000, 57 percent of the total population was Latino, mostly Mexican, and 39 percent was white.

12. Although the total annual rainfall in this valley is more than 40 inches, it rarely rains during July and August—which makes it ideal not only for specialty crops but also for grass-seed production. Seeds can grow without irrigation, and are dried in the fields with little risk of rain.

13. The cost of farm labor on production is impacted by minimum-wage indexing tied to the Consumer Price Index for inflation in Portland. According to the growers, Oregon's wage is among the highest in the nation (Searle 2007).

14. This "double discrimination" may push indigenous workers into the most labor-intensive and worst housing conditions, argue Farquhar et al. (2008b).

15. The Oregon Department of Education defines a "dropout" as a student in grades 9-12 who withdraws from school without receiving a high school diploma, GED, modified diploma, or transferring to another school.

16. In 2000, Latino families in Oregon averaged four persons per family compared with three persons per family for the entire population.

Testimonio

by Esteban

This testimonio *is composed from excerpts of an interview conducted by Mendoza in 2008 in Esteban's home in Harrisburg, which he shares with his wife and two children. Esteban agreed to be interviewed late at night, while his children were in bed and his wife was baby-sitting for a Mexican neighbor who works the night shift at a fast food restaurant in town. The interview was conducted in Spanish, and excerpts were selected, transcribed, translated and arranged by the authors.*

When I arrived in Oregon, I spent one month looking for work. Some days I would go with my brother-in-law to a construction site to help out with tiling or something, but I didn't have full-time employment. I had already resigned from my job in Mexico and my former boss lent me some money to buy airline tickets for me and my family. I dreamed that soon after arriving here I would find a job without delay. On the first week someone helped me to get a license and lent me the equipment to gather wild mushrooms. They left me alone and I tried but I got lost in the forest, couldn't do it. The only forest that I had seen in my life had been on TV. I was fat; I had never used a shovel before. I knew that here in Oregon I wouldn't be working eight hours at an office desk but never anticipated that it would be so difficult. Then a cousin of my brother-in-law took me with him to plant pine trees on a mountainside. Those crews always need workers for that type of job. I got used to planting. I worked as a tree planter for three years (I was on the side of the mountain every day, even Sunday). We worked ten months and rested in October and November.

One day I learned that the owner of an organic farm here in the Willamette Valley was looking for workers. I went with a group of people from Oaxaca. They are of indigenous descent, they are short, and they are discriminated just for that. The owner of this farm saw that I was taller and looked different and asked me: "Where you are from?" I answered that I'm Mexican, but the patron replied: "You are not like them." The other men who were in the same group said that I could work in the fields too and the patron sent us to clean the vegetable beds. At the beginning I didn't know how to do it. My companions from Oaxaca had been working in the fields since they were five years old, but I had only worked in factories before. Somehow I learned to do it. In organic farms, the farmer doesn't use pesticides. We had to take the weeds out by hand. This farmer grows tomatoes, corn, garlic, watermelons, melons, leeks, carrots, and artichokes. When we started working there, the owner had one tractor in partnership with a neighbor, and he employed three older Oaxacans to work on a small field. These three did the same job as six other workers would have done it. He hired me and five other Oaxacans to work in his fields. Now the patron has six different fields and employs thirty workers. We work up to sixteen hours per day, and you cannot say "I'm in pain" or "I have stomachache." You cannot miss a day of work because there are three or four immigrants waiting to take that same job. We start at 5:30 am and we go on until 2:00 pm without a break, then we have lunch and continue until the job it's done. The first manager was Hispanic. He made us work very hard just to please the grower. There are no laws to protect you in the fields. You have no rights, only the right to remain silent. We get called names in English and we have to endure mistreatment.

I get paid $10 per hour, but before I was paid $7.50 an hour. It was a fixed monthly salary, no matter how many hours you spent working in the fields each day. But there was a problem. Many workers left because the grower treated them poorly; then a guy came to the farm—I think he was with PCUN or with another organization. After that, the patron raised our hourly wage. He is beginning to understand that we are people, not animals, and now he treats us better. He gives us some incentives, listens to us, he is more flexible now. If one sees something that's not done well we can tell the patron, and it gets corrected. He takes better care of the employees. He even prepared a Christmas party for the workers. I am in charge of a crew and drive a tractor. The patron gave me paid vacations this year, for the first time in five years. I feel that my job is more secure. Even if I have to work many hours a day and almost never see my children awake I feel that I can't leave this job now. Although I would like to get a GED and apply for another type of job, I feel that I cannot leave this farm now. There are some workers who come seasonally and they don't care much about how they are treated. These temporary workers are all men; they come to the valley for eight months, ten months and leave. Some are from Guatemala. I'm always thinking about the rest of my family back in Mexico and I miss them. My family lives in a city located at a two-hour drive from the border. There are American factories there. With my wife, we are always talking about what to do—either we stay here and forget about Mexico or we go back there. My father-in-law is a carpenter. I have invested in his business, bought him some tools. He says that we need to return, that there are more jobs in the city now, but I see that it's still very hard to live in Mexico. When you move to the United States, you start looking at things in your own country under a different light and you view your co-nationals from another point of view. You realize how damaging the drug traffic is. Traffickers get people killed and they are never charged for their crimes, indigenous peoples are always fighting for their rights, and politicians never stop lying for their own benefit.

Chapter 5

The Changing Faces of Migration: Immigration, Gender, and Family Dynamics

Mexican immigrants are much more likely to settle permanently in Oregon today than they were in the past, at least in part because the most recent immigrant influx includes an increased number of women (Fry 2006). The arrival of women, who are more likely to stay, has a significant impact on immigrant communities because women have a major role in the formation of families, raising children, and building social networks. Mexican immigrant women are generally young (younger than foreign-born Jamaican, Filipino, Indian, and Chinese women studied by Zhou 2003). Three-fourths of Mexican women arrive with less than a high-school education, and they are more likely to be employed in farming and other unskilled labor-intensive occupations than most other foreign-born women who arrived during the 1990s (Zhou 2003).[1]

After passage of IRCA in 1986, we saw a marked increase in the number of women and children—undocumented and documented—coming to join their husbands and fathers, and subsequently to settle in the United States; we are also seeing a rise in the number of single women immigrants. In fact, IRCA has been marked by scholars as a decisive moment in the subsequent feminization of Mexican immigration (Massey et al. 2002), particularly undocumented immigration.

Other factors have contributed to this trend. In Mexico, rising levels of education across the country[2] but decreasing numbers of available jobs propelled not just men but also women into the U.S. migrant stream (Salinas 2007). In the post-NAFTA years, the displacement of agricultural households by multinational agricultural enterprises has forced both males and females in Mexico to become wage earners in a labor market that is already stressed. Labor restructuring and employment patterns in the United States have also contributed to the enticement of female workers from Mexico (Bacon 2008). As more American women enter the labor market, they are in need of caretakers for their children and immigrant women step in to fill this role. Today, Mexican men and women employed as farmworkers in the U.S. have completed about seven grades of schooling, are on average thirty-three years old, have two children, and earn an annual household income of about $20,000 to $22,000 (Carroll et al. 2005). The expansion of service jobs, particularly in hospitality, health caretaking, and janitorial services has also enticed *mexicanas*, particularly at a time when the U.S. population is experiencing an imbalance in the number of available new workers as compared to older, retiring workers (Myers 2007). While macro-forces such as those cited above account in large measure for increasing migratory flows of workers to the United States, immigration scholars have also examined how micro-level decisions made at the household level act as an "adaptive strategy responsive to changing internal characteristics of households as well as to external structural conditions," thus integrating micro- and macro-factors in the analysis of migratory flows (Crummett 1993, 153). Crummett argues, however, that micro and macro forces affect males and females differently. Hondagneu-Sotelo likewise affirms, "[M]igration is gendered. Women and men do not share the same experiences with migration, and their gender relations—patterns of separation, conflict, and cooperation—produce distinct migration patterns" (1994, 192). A gendered migration not only reshapes settlement but also redefines gender roles and family relations. Many Mexican women find themselves immersed in conflicting obligations, as they struggle to function simultaneously as wage workers, wives, and mothers —while they renegotiate gender hierarchies in their new homes (Zhou 2003).

Gendered Mexicano *Migration*

It is an accepted axiom that gender roles are learned, that humans are socialized to enact gender roles ascribed by a masculine/feminine binary construct. But gender roles are also contested and subverted in our everyday lives, and it is important also to understand how structural factors affect gender behaviors. When examining gender in Latino communities, there has been a tendency in the past to view Latinos as a monolithic pan-ethnic group in which gender-role behaviors are determined by "traditional" cultural moorings that are invariably linked to the patriarchal ideal of male dominance and female subordination. While it is true that such a perspective yields stereotypes that are consistently belied by a plurality of gender relations and impacted by structural and social formations such as class, education, generation, and race/ethnicity, cultural ideals frequently produce shared ideologies related to how social relations "ought" to function. These ideals then are held up as models of desired social behavior to which a great deal of lip service is paid, but which in fact are consistently resisted and transgressed (Hondagneu-Sotelo 2004). It is also the case that social conditions and material realities engender real-life experiences that fly in the face of cultural "ideals" as they relate to gender. When women are forced to become wage earners in order to support their families, the ideal that mothers belong at home is of necessity set aside. When birth-control practices are available for women, it becomes possible to reconsider, though not without a great deal of conflict and doubt amongst faithful Catholic women, the religious and cultural mandate of "bearing all the children God sends."

There is no doubt that migration has contributed to gender transitions within *mexicano* families and couple relations. For example, when women are left behind by partners who migrate to *el norte*, they frequently take on the obligations normally reserved for males in Mexico. Women may take over work associated with sustenance farming, including purchasing seeds, actual physical labor, and selling in the marketplace. Women left behind in the cities may become participants in the urban labor force, actively interacting in the public sphere, and certainly both rural and urban women become intensely involved in the decision-making process as it relates to family dynamics while fathers are absent. The net result of these changes is greater autonomy for women and opportunities for "greater gender egalitarianism" (Hondagneu-Sotelo 1994, 193). Under these conditions, "new forms of gender relations and subjectivities surface, and ultimately challenge previous ideals of what it means to be a woman" (Boehan 2004, 13). Men who leave mothers or wives at home, on the other hand, find themselves having to engage in social reproductive work such as cooking, laundry, and housekeeping normally reserved for women. In this sense, migration itself is a process that expands the parameters of cultural ideals as they pertain to the enactment of gender roles (Hondagneu-Sotelo 2004).

It is not uncommon to attribute changes in gender-role performance to the changes inherent in migration from a rural to an urban environment—in the case of many *mexicanos*, from a communal existence in rural Mexico to the postindustrial space of a self-reliant and individualistic nation in which a strong feminist movement has subverted the patriarchal patterns of pre-industrial societies—or to feminist notions regarding the strictures attached to gender roles. Hirsch (2003) critiques this latter assumption, demonstrating through her research on two agrarian communities in Mexico that traditional gender roles have been transformed even in rural Mexico, but not necessarily as the result of migration or feminist tenets. The ideal of masculinity as the site of familial power and of control over subjected females has given way to what she terms "companionate" marriage. Rather than restricting women to the private space of the home while males wander freely in public spaces in the company of other males, many Mexican men, she argues, are more likely to spend time with their families and to take their wives out on public outings. Women may have more freedom to leave the home without their husband's permission, and they may collude with their daughters in creating apertures of freedom for the younger generation previously not accessible

Washing and ironing clothes, ca. 1942. Oregon State University Archives.

to them. The rigid patriarchal code of honor, sustained through the ideal of female virtue, has given way in rural villages to more open dating patterns, and the practice of chaperoned courtship is contested by young couples who may consummate physical relations openly as a way to force consensual unions—sanctioned and non-sanctioned—on the couple's, rather than the community's, terms. Hirsch argues that these changes, which are encapsulated in the phrase *Ya no somos como nuestras madres* (We are no longer like our mothers), are the result of the desire of rural *mexicanos* to avoid the stigma of "backwardness." It is the desire to be seen as modern that compels males to shun the *machista* label and young women to be less concerned with *el qué dirán* (what will people say) should they not follow the cultural mandate of female virtue and chastity, the cornerstone of familial honor. This desire to be modern is inculcated by access to modern urban lifestyles, which reach rural communities through television, movies, popular music, and returning migrants from urban centers and from *el norte*. Thus, when males or females venture north, they already bring with them ideas regarding gender relations that differ considerably from those that were the norm several decades ago. Their experiences in the United States will very likely continue to encourage change in gender relations and familial roles, particularly if women become wage earners. Perilla concurs with this assessment, but she adds a caveat: "Because of economic realities at times, because of direct confrontation with majority values at times, the roles and expectations for males and females in Latino communities appear to be undergoing important changes. Whereas these changes may increase gender-role flexibility, they may also affect the stabilizing influence of traditional gender roles on the family" (1999, 114).

In her study of two sending communities in rural Mexico, Crummett (1993) found that decisions to migrate are generally made in unison among middle-class families and, because they have the financial resources, families may migrate as a nuclear unit. Families with few economic resources, however, are more apt to engage in chain migration, with men migrating first, followed by members of the family, perhaps over a period of time. Males in poorer households are more apt simply to decide on their own to migrate without taking into account their spouse's opinion. Women, on the other hand, may have to consult with husbands and/or other members of the immediate and extended family before arriving at a decision to migrate. Scholars have noted that women depend more on *coyotes* than males (Donato and Patterson 2004). Their crossing is frequently arranged with professional guides by a spouse or by parents as a way of protecting their womenfolk. Moreover, those crossing with paid guides are less likely to be apprehended. A recent study by Cornelius et al. (2008) revealed that 100 percent of their subjects who crossed with guides were successful in reaching the United States. The exception to this pattern is found among older women who have crossed the border more than once before, who may rely on personal knowledge rather than on paid guides (Donato and Patterson 2004).

Starting in the early 1990s, when Mexican workers were discouraged by tougher sanctions and more dangerous crossing conditions from making their usual treks home to spend time with their families, many women began to resent being left behind for longer periods of time. What women had been doing while their husbands lived in *el norte* played no small role in the creation of this resentment. Aysa and Massey (2004) found that urban women especially tend to join the labor force once their husbands leave, thus increasing considerably their autonomy. Rural women are less likely to do so, as tradition encourages them to stay home and guarantees support and protection from the extended family. The family, in fact, is used to control women left at home. According to Boehan (2004), spouses often ask family members, or perhaps friends, to report on the behavior of wives left behind. If the report is unfavorable, they may refuse to send them money or even threaten to abandon them. However, women in rural settings take on responsibilities previously held by their husbands, including a greater role in decision making and family control. There is no doubt that the experiences of separation, of taking on new responsibilities, and of increasing autonomy give women a sense of empowerment that motivates them to demand that their husbands allow them to join them in the United States. Rosalía, who we interviewed for this project in 2006, reported that after seventeen years of remaining in Mexico while her husband worked in the United States, she reached a point where she was no longer willing to stay behind. "It was very difficult for me being alone, with all the responsibility for the children. He was home only for a month or month and a half twice a year. I told him he had better make arrangements to take us. I was seeing that lots of men in the village easily arranged papers for their families, so I insisted he do the same" (interview with Gonzales-Berry, 2008). Her husband finally gave in to her demands and, because he was here legally and had a stable job with decent wages, he was able to apply for visas for the entire family. Carmen reported to us that when she was left in her village by her husband, who journeyed to Alaska, she was seen as "fair game" by males in her village because she had no male to protect her. She finally got fed up with being treated in this way, and when she came to Oregon on a two-week visa to visit her parents, who were working here, she announced to her husband that she was not returning to her village. He protested, but as she was intransigent in her demands, he gradually acquiesced and allowed her to stay (interview with Gonzales-Berry, 2008).

While women have spoken openly about the burden of migration on families who remain behind and, like Rosalía and Carmen, insisted at some point on joining their husbands, men have said little about the emotional impact of familial separation. This is not surprising given that the ideal of masculinity exhorts men to *aguantar* [endure] misfortune, suffering, injustice, etc. One transgression of this unwritten code is found in the documentary *Romántico* (2005). In this gripping portrayal of the struggles of two immigrant males trying to make a living as musicians in San Francisco, one of the men, who for years has engaged in circular migration, sheds tears as he speaks of the pain of leaving family behind and of the impact of this lifestyle on his health.

There are other cases in which, fearing that their husbands would not approve of their plans to head north, women resolve on their own to take the risk, seeking support from parents, friends, or women already in the United States. Hondagneu-Sotelo, for example, found that women in a California barrio that she studied "circumvented reliance on male-dominated networks by appealing to the assistance of immigrant women already established in the United States. And as more women migrated and settled in the U.S., women's social-network ties emerged and widened" (1994, 188). Numerous women have reported presenting themselves at their husband's door much to the surprise, and sometimes chagrin, of the uninformed mate. The latter is especially true in cases in which an uninformed mate is found living with another woman.

The migration of single women, which notably has increased in the past two decades, may also occur within the constraints of the household model. Alvarez and Broder reported in the *New York Times* that "a growing number of single women ... are coming not to join husbands, but to find jobs, send money home and escape a bleak future in Mexico. They come to find work in the booming underground economy, through a vast network of friends and relatives already employed here as maids, cooks, kitchen helpers, factory workers and baby sitters" (January 10, 2006). And Ibarra observes that "*Mexicanas* persuade parents, husbands or lovers to support their migration; they seek financial help or build up their savings through employment, and they make connections and undertake negotiations with different people (relatives, friends, acquaintances, and ex-employers in the Unites States) who can help them once they are on the other side" (2003, 269).

In our interviews, we spoke with four unattached women who migrated to Oregon. The first was only fifteen when the decision was made by the family to let her come to California. Intending to protect their daughter, Celina's parents arranged with an acquaintance in California to help her get across the border. In return, Celina would keep house for her. However, the family contact did not meet her in Tijuana. Fortunately, the people she had traveled with to the border were, in her words, "good people." One woman said to her, "They don't want to take responsibility for you, but how can I leave you here? I will take you with us. And some day if you remember us that is fine, if not that's okay too. The important thing is to not leave you here, because you know how the border is" (interview with Gonzales-Berry, 2007). This Good Samaritan was, of course, referring to the physical danger women face on the migration journey. Ibarra (2003) speaks directly of these dangers: "Human rights organizations also regularly document 'abuses' of power at the hands of the border patrol, including sexual violations, beatings, and shootings. Additionally, thieves, drug smugglers, and vigilantes, as well as *coyotes* themselves, prey on vulnerable people who often carry the money they need to cross the border" (272).

Paula was young and single when she decided to come north. She was motivated to leave Mexico because, *Eramos muchos y había poco* (We were many and there was little). Her case bears witness to the conditions Crummett (1993) found among poor families in Oaxaca, where "young single girls overwhelmingly comprise the rural-urban migrant stream. According to Young, economic conditions force daughters rather than sons to leave the household for two main reasons. First the division of labor within the household placed the burden of agricultural production on men. Second and more important, many of the economic activities carried out by mothers and their daughters—the making of food and clothing and preparation of products for sale on the local market—were being undercut by more efficiently produced manufactured goods" (154). In Paula's story, it is apparent that economic conditions in her village in Zacatecas and the lack of opportunities for young rural women prompted her departure. But Paula also had an independent and adventurous streak about her, bringing her story more in line with the male immigrant migration narrative which posits migration as a rite of passage. When an uncle told her he was coming over, Paula boldly announced that she was coming with him. Her family did not discourage her; in fact, her father borrowed money for her journey. Paula recalls, "I didn't know a thing. I simply said, 'I'm going.' It was sort of, 'Let's see what happens. I'll go see what it's like over there, I'll work, and I'll help my parents' " (interview with Gonzales-Berry, 2007). A local *coyote* charged her $400—this was in 1994, just before the militarization of the border and the attendant rise in crossing fees. He easily crossed Paula and others at Tijuana and delivered them to El Monte, California. Paula, being the independent spirit that she is, did not depend on networks; instead, she hit the sidewalk on her own to look for a job. She was hired that same day at a car wash.

After she spent a couple of years in California, where she met and married a young man from Guadalajara, Paula and her husband moved to Oregon, where he had a brother and sister. She was happy to leave California because "it is very expensive and not a good place to learn English. Here you have to learn it." Paula recalls that they had luck when they arrived here. Her husband's sister referred them to a family who was looking for a couple to care for their child and the offer included a place to live. They worked there for five years. Paula liked the job but realized she was not going to learn English; instead, the child was learning Spanish. When the child entered school, the job ended. However, their boss helped her find another job. She now cleans houses and her husband works for a gas company. The couple is pleased that their son is receiving a good education, and they are already talking about starting up a college fund for him. Paula speaks forcefully about the importance of an egalitarian relationship, a position she has arrived at by virtue of having migrated and becoming a wage earner. "In Mexico you have to ask permission for everything, because the husband is the boss. Here there is more equality. If he works and I work and we both get home at the same time, it's 'Let's both make dinner. You're hungry. I'm hungry.' If the husband comes home and sits around waiting for his wife to fix dinner, what time will they eat? It has to be about equality. I have a sister in Mexico who says her husband won't let her work. I tell her, well don't ask for his permission." While Paula appreciates the quality of her life here, she does not for a day forget the conditions in which her family lives in Mexico. "I came from having nothing to having a lot. This makes me feel bad, because my parents don't have much. My son's doing well, but I wonder how my sisters' daughters are doing. Who would have dreamed in Mexico, of owning a car?" She and her sister regularly send home boxes—the size of a refrigerator—packed with goods. The carrier, an acquaintance who has a business taking and bringing goods to and from Mexico, charges them $150 for the service.

Paula's enduring transnational connections to her family in Mexico offer psychosocial benefits which, according to Viruell-Fuentes (2006), are central to the experience of immigrant women; however, these benefits represent an added burden to the already demanding and challenging experiences that govern their lives:

> *Transnational exchanges offer first-generation women an alternative space of belonging and a space from which to draw resources to live their lives in the United States. In this respect, transnationalism may be considered a liberatory practice; however, these transnational exchanges consisted mainly of women's gendered work. As the narratives analyzed below show, family needs in Mexico often required that immigrant women in the United States extend their care-taking roles across borders. So although women could derive psychosocial resources from these exchanges, they also bore the brunt of the emotional toil that maintaining these relationships entailed (353).*

Given Paula's ambition, her self-assuredness, and her positive outlook, we were surprised to learn that she does not have legal status and were also impressed that she expresses no fear regarding her vulnerable position. "I'm a 'wetback', " she declared; "in fact, I'm two times a wetback" (when she visited her family in Mexico she once again crossed without papers). She feels certain that the U.S. government will not give Mexicans amnesty. "There are too many of us here. But who knows, there might be a miracle. I believe in miracles!"

Nina, who is also single, had been expelled by economic need from her village in Michoacán long before she came to the U.S (interview with Gonzales-Berry, 2007). She had already been on her own for ten years working as a domestic in Guadalajara when she finally decided to head north. She had a sister and three brothers in Oregon and wanted very much to join them. But she would not dare make the journey without a visa. After ten years of rejected visa applications, she accepted that she would never fulfill her dream. Then, one day, an aunt and her two children returned to Mexico for a visit. They encouraged Nina to join them on their return journey, and she took the plunge. The cousin, who was a legal resident, was able to cross Nina without incident.

Nina is now working at two jobs: one in the kitchen of a fast-food chain restaurant and the second at a dry cleaner. She is fortunate to live with her sister and brother-in-law, who both have legal status, have good jobs, and own their home—they have been here eighteen years. Nina realizes that her options are limited because of her undocumented status and because she does not speak English. Regarding the latter, she says, "I know it is necessary to advance here, and I would like to learn it, but it just doesn't sink in. I'm too old to learn." Age, of course, is a factor in acquiring a second language, but also important is the opportunity to interact with speakers of English. It is truly a conundrum. How can she learn the language if she can't interact with members of the host culture, and how can she interact with English speakers if she doesn't speak the language? We repeatedly found this to be the case among our subjects. Many immigrant women do not access the support available due to limited English proficiency, unfamiliarity with the culture, and sometimes self-imposed social isolation. Nina, however, sees herself as a sojourner. She appreciates life in this country, particularly the bounty, and the fact that there are more men than women. In Mexican villages there are many single women and few eligible males; they have followed their star to *el norte*. She nonetheless looks forward to returning home where she insists, "There, I have more freedom and mobility."

The story of Malena, who also came without a partner, is different from that of other single women whom we interviewed in that she was the mother of four children (interview with Gonzales-Berry, 2007). Unable to support her family with the small yield of her parcel of land in Oaxaca, Malena, who had been abandoned by her husband when her eldest child was six, decided that her only hope lay in coming north. Her son had left a few years before at the tender age of thirteen, after Malena sold one of her coffee plants to finance his journey. He promised to send her money to fix her house. He sent her $350 the first year, then turned to drugs and alcohol and the remittances ceased. Meantime, Malena kept burning and plowing her field, sowing, harvesting, and carrying the load to market on her back—"men's work," she said. One day a labor recruiter came to her village; he was looking for people to work in Florida. Seeing a light at the end of the tunnel, she left two of her children with their paternal grandparents and headed north with her thirteen-year-old daughter. During the five-day journey through Mexico, accompanied by a large group of people, she was forced to keep her eye constantly on her daughter, as the *coyote* had made it very clear that she had attracted his attention. One night he tried to separate the mother and daughter, and Malena used her wits to put him off, telling him he had better not try anything because she was traveling with her husband, who would protect them. The *coyote* demanded she point out her husband. Instinctively, she pointed at a fellow traveler, who fortunately backed up her story. That night, when they stopped to sleep, the *coyote* forced her to lie next to her "husband." "Fortunately," she said, "he was an honorable man, and he didn't try anything. If it weren't for him I am sure my daughter, and I as well, would have been raped." After crossing without incident in Arizona, the recruiter abandoned them at a "safe home"—these structures, which are an integral part of the smuggling enterprise, are little more than holding pens and the treatment of migrants held there is akin to the treatment of animals. The travelers had just placed their clothes in the washer when the border patrol stormed the house and took them away with only the clothes on their backs. They were forced to return to Mexico. At the border they found another *coyote*, who delivered them to another safe house, but demanded money to take them further. By this time, Malena had spent the last of the 800 pesos she had brought along for food. She called a woman she knew in Oregon, who told her times were hard, and it would take her a while to collect the money. Malena's experience mirrors that of women in Ibarra's study who waited to connect with their network until they had crossed the border. "This type of waiting strategy," affirms Ibarra, "is a gamble that does not always work, and some women end up homeless, sleeping under freeway underpasses, and gratefully taking the first live-in domestic job that becomes available" (2003, 271). Malena's tactic indeed was a risky one, and she and her daughter ended up spending thirty days locked up in the safe house in Arizona before her female network connection was able to wire her the money required by the *coyote* to deliver them to Oregon. Those thirty days were filled with deprivation, filthy arrangements, and abuse. By the time she was able to leave, she was a psychological wreck.

Life in Corvallis has not been easy for Malena. Her lack of education—she attended school for only two years—and of skills made it very difficult to find work. When she first arrived she got sporadic work in the fields. She then got a job cleaning rooms in a motel. Eventually, she was able to bring the children who had remained behind, but all except the young daughter she brought with her have turned to marginal behaviors. She is currently living in a small trailer with a *mexicano* companion who has papers and works in a nursery. She no longer works because she has an infant with Down syndrome who requires her full attention. What her companion makes is insufficient to make ends meet, and she frequently has to resort to local food and clothing banks. She sees no hope for improving her life, but has hopes for her daughter who shortly after arriving here wanted to drop out of school and work in the fields with her mother. Malena took her to the fields and after a few days, asked her, "Is this what you want to do with your life?" Her daughter changed her mind. Despite the grim outlook, returning to Mexico is out of the question for Malena. There simply are no prospects for her there. Furthermore, in the United States her native-born child will have health care all of his life; here she has access to state-supported care, something that would be out of the question in her homeland.

Married women who migrate to join spouses probably have it easier than single women, for generally their husbands already have jobs and have made living arrangements for their families. They can also serve as brokers, helping their wives navigate the new environment, at least to the extent that they are able to do so. When wives are brought over legally, the accommodation process is generally easier. Wives with legal status are frequently able to obtain a job and the double salary eases the transition. Rosalía and her children, as discussed above, came legally. Financing the entire family's trip and arranging the visas had been a costly affair, and Rosalía was eager to begin working. Initially she got a job where her husband had worked since 1980 on a Christmas tree farm, then in a nursery. She was thrilled when a man she met at her children's school told her about a job at an international electronic firm, where she cleans bathrooms. She doesn't much care for this kind of work, but she is thankful to be working indoors. Rosalía is ambivalent about working; on the one hand she feels she would be bored if she just stayed at home; on the other she bemoans the limited communication she now has with her children, because she works from 5:00 p.m. until 1:00 a.m. This work schedule means that her husband must do much of the child rearing and household duties.

Having lived alone or bunked with other males for so many years in the United States prepared Rosalía's husband for his new responsibilities. While the family lives comfortably, they live in extreme isolation, and Rosalía feels that her options for mobility are limited. They have few social contacts with either the host culture or other immigrants and, aside from attending Mass on Sundays and an occasional outing to a shopping mall, their lives are circumscribed to school, work, and their home. Their isolation raises questions about this family's ability—at least the ability of the first generation—to integrate themselves into the host culture. Their situation is a pattern we saw over and over among low-wage workers: limited mobility, lack of English, extreme isolation. When the family has an undocumented immigration status, the outlook is even more dismal. Perhaps the children, having legal status, will succeed in moving through the public education system, thus expanding their prospects for integration, and for moving beyond their parents' social class. In weighing the benefits against the sacrifices inherent in immigration, Rosalía becomes teary eyed as she talks about the pain of separation from her parents. But she is quick to add, "We're far from home but we're together. We're together, but we miss our homeland."

Nina's assessment that she would have more freedom and mobility in Mexico differs markedly from the majority of women who migrate. In her article on gendered memory, Luin Goldring (1996) discusses the differing ways in which men and women remember their rural places of origin, and how these memories affect their resolve to return to Mexico or remain in the United States. Goldring concludes that descriptions and representations of rural landscapes are gendered and affect "practices of return migration, family politics, and investment in migrants' places of origin" (305). We found a qualitative correlation between Goldring's findings and the attitudes of our interviewees in this regard. Women by and large felt that they had more freedom in the United States and they repeatedly stressed their appreciation for the comforts that life in the United States offers. The perception of greater freedom among working women is linked to their ability to make decisions related to finances and the fact that they are able to spend money as they wish, without asking for permission from their husbands. For women who, like Malena, recall the heavy labor required to subsist in Mexico, life here is seen as easier. They appreciate things like hot water, and washers and dryers. Though they may recall their villages as peaceful rural landscapes where there was more conviviality, they do not idealize village life when it comes to their actual responsibilities (Goldring 1996).

As we saw in Paula's case, patriarchal constraints—such as having to ask men for permission—are more relaxed here. Women are also acutely aware of the fact that their children's identities, particularly of those born here, are tied to the host culture, and they seem to accept that it would be difficult to relocate them to Mexico. Goldring (1996) observes that men, on the other hand, particularly if they own land, a home, or a business in Mexico, are aware of the fact that in their rural communities they had a gendered identity that commanded status and respect. This is especially true if they have legal status in the U.S., for this is equated with greater power in Mexico (Boehan 2004). It is also a fact that when immigrants return home to visit, they are able to demonstrate materially the fruits of their labor—new automobiles, new clothes, appliances purchased for their mothers, or improvements made to homes in the village—thereby raising their status in the eyes of locals. Men, especially, relish the elevated status their migrant status brings them in their local villages (Martínez 2001). It is also true that in Mexico men have more opportunities for gathering socially with their peers in public spaces than they do in the United States. When Mexican men congregate in a public space in the United States—say a street corner, or a public park where they are accustomed to acting out their masculinity—a squad car is sure to materialize (Hondagneu-Sotelo, 1994). Many males we interviewed lamented the fact that here they cannot play their music loud, drink in public, or whistle when they see a beautiful woman passing by. Nonetheless, because in so many villages, migration is "a test of masculinity" (Boehan 2004), males paradoxically endure their loss of freedom and diminished sense of masculinity in order to prove to those back home and to their peers that indeed they are *hombres fuertes* (strong men).

In terms of gender relations, almost all of the men we spoke to reported sharing responsibilities and decision making with their wives. We believe that this is a consequence of a changed social environment, and an effect of the more assertive attitudes gradually assumed by their wives and children. But, their desires to appear modern aside, as Hirsch (2003) postulates, some males are still conscious of their privileged patriarchal status. One of our interviewees, for example, stated: "We make decisions together, but I am the head of the family" (interview with S.J. Acosta). When this individual was asked how he felt about women working outside the home, he responded: "Well, to my way of thinking they should work, contribute, so they can be aware of the sacrifices we make and so they value things more and become thriftier." His attitudes appear governed not so much by a spirit of egalitarianism but by the desire to have his spouse understand the weight of male responsibility. The majority of our interviewees felt that it was acceptable for women to work if the additional wages were needed. Eligio offered the following opinion on this topic: "Well, both things are good. Both things are good because here, if one does not have the help of his wife, you can't get ahead. But, clearly, it is much nicer if she is able to stay home. But because of the many expenses one has here, both have to work" (interview with S.J. Acosta, 2003).

The caveat, when necessary, suggests that male immigrants feel very strongly about their socially ascribed responsibility to support their families. And both men and women believe that the wife's counter-responsibility is to care for the home and family, a value that according to Hondagneu-Sotelo is viewed as "achievements and privileges, not as sources of subordination" (1994, 156). This arrangement allows women to see themselves as collaborators in a strategy that ensures the common good of the family, rather than as victims, and their commitment to this value is extraordinarily powerful, as we shall see below.

Jesús, in a tone that betrays a certain level of self-mockery, rails against the changes that women undergo in the United States: "Here the damned old lady wants to do what she damn pleases. You can't tell her anything because she talks back or calls the police. She just wants to do what she damn pleases.

I think well maybe we bring that thing, the way we are in Mexico, not because we want to be macho, but because in Mexico it's a whole other story and you just want to have control. And here, it's another story; women are just more liberated. They want to do as they damned please" (interview with S.J. Acosta, 2003). At the same time, and revealing not just a little ambivalence, Jesús positions himself as a "new man," criticizing his compatriots' attitudes toward working women: "Like lots of us—and I've heard this on the radio— lots of guys feel belittled if their wife earns more than them. Bullshit. If my wife earns a million dollars, bring it on. Let her work. And if she doesn't work, that's fine too, she can stay home."

If Jesús' self-assessment betrays just a bit of youthful bravado, Manuel's humble comments on the topic of gender roles within the family reflect a measure of wisdom gained from many years of experience living in a heterosexual relationship: "We've been married twenty-eight years. Until now life has a lot of, how can I say it, not turns, but it has taught us a lot. We've had a lot of falls, but I don't get discouraged or let them get discouraged. Before I didn't think that way. I was ignorant. As I've seen more things, I've begun to see that my wife is equal. I think she has equal rights. That's how I see it" (interview with S.J. Acosta, 2003).

When asked if they desired to stay or return to Mexico, almost all our male interviewees said they want to return. Goldring (1996) attributes this desire to the fact that in their rural villages, Mexico represents a place where "men can be men either through work or leisure activities, while the United States remains the place of work, proletarian and spatial discipline, and diminished male authority" (318). Men also miss the companionship and trusted relationships they have with male friends in their hometowns. Pedro's words sum up this perspective "[What I miss is] moving around freely like a Mexican. They say this is a free country, but you have to give up many things." For Pedro (interview with S.J. Acosta, 2003), the United States clearly represents a space in which Mexicans must give up behavior patterns that they associate with masculinity and privilege, also a place where first-generation men are usually isolated from other men and constrained to the household and an occasional soccer game. Women, on the other hand, said it would be nice to reunite with their parents or extended family but, aside from that, they prefer to remain in the United States. Nina's preference for life in Mexico must be assessed in the context of her unique situation. She has no family to anchor her to the United States and, as an older single woman who had migrated from her village to a city in Mexico, she did not have to come to the United States in order to achieve independence; without English or driving skills, she cannot really attain a greater level of independence in the United States than that which she already had in Mexico.[3]

Reasserting Mexicano *Masculinity*

While immigration is gendered and at the same time creates conditions propitious for gender-role transformations and the emergence of new gender subjectivities, immigrant males may seek ways to reassert traditional masculinity. Perilla holds that because power is linked to resources, a male head of household "may have resources for prevailing in his own family but not over his boss at his job. This lack of social power at work may lead him to become very authoritarian in his relationship with his partner at home" (1999, 119-20). Seeking to exert control of his immediate environment, he may revert to female and family domination through physical violence. Undocumented immigrant women are particularly vulnerable in such conditions (Hancock 2007). Clifford et al. point out that "a foreign-born woman in an abusive situation faces an entangled entrapment: she may be isolated from public contact because she is not in the paid labor force, she faces language and cultural barriers, may not be very familiar with the law and her rights or with community resources. She may not trust the police. Whether or not she is in the paid labor force, she may fear deportation or the loss of her children if she reports her situation. The threat of deportation, in fact, is a common one that abusers use to keep women from leaving" (2005, 7). Undocumented *mexicanas*, who are truly bereft of resources, see no recourse but to endure abuse and violence; the ensuing trauma, as Perilla observes, "leaves [women] shocked and paralyzed, unable to make decisions and act rationally" (1999, 124).

Marisol, a woman born and raised in an indigenous Purépecha village in Michoacán, found herself in such a situation when she migrated with her son's father. After becoming pregnant in her home village, she discovered he was already married. Filled with shame, and subjected to village gossip, she felt she had no choice but to follow him to the United States with her newborn son—one of twins that survived a very difficult birth. In Hermiston, Oregon, she found that her mate was more than a previously married man. He was jealous and abusive. The beatings she could bear, but being locked up daily in the R.V. that served as their home was "like living in hell" (interview with Gonzales-Berry, 2007). He kept the refrigerator stocked with beer, but did not bother to buy food. Yet he beat her for not preparing his meals, and he also beat the child.

One day after he broke a chair on her back, she found the strength to react. Protecting the child in one arm, she hit him over the head with an iron skillet and knocked him out. In snow to her thighs she stumbled through the dark until she reached the apartment of a friend, but her friend refused to give her shelter. She was afraid of Marisol's mate. Marisol struggled to reach the home of another acquaintance, who did take her in. She treated her frozen feet, warmed and fed her and the child and gave them a place to sleep. Early the next morning they were awakened to pounding on the door, and Marisol was forced to return to her prison. After this incident, the friend took Marisol milk, tortillas, and beans and delivered the goods through a window. She was in, Marisol's words, "her angel of mercy."

Her abuser did let her out of the house to go to work; she had a couple of clients whose homes she cleaned and she also helped her partner clean some offices. She never saw her earnings, which he pocketed and used for beer and drugs. Finally, when her child enrolled in Head Start, Marisol sought help. She was taken to a shelter for victims of domestic violence in Pendleton; she could have gone to one closer to "home" in Milton-Freewater, but she insisted on being taken as far away as possible. While at the shelter, she met Matías, who stopped by to do volunteer translation for the Spanish-speaking women at the shelter. They became friends, and he gave her advice and support. Her former mate, who by then had been given a good beating and warned by Marisol's brothers to stay away from her, left the region. In time, she and Matías married. They have created strong family bonds for their sons—Marisol's eldest, who is now in high school, and a twelve-year-old born to her and Matías. Marisol's final words in her interview revealed that a lot of healing has taken place over the years: "I am not ashamed of my life. I have taken ownership of my experiences and I have been able to free myself from them. The Lord has been good to me."

We do not know how many women have endured similar experiences. Many community and social service organizations, however, are mindful of this at-risk population, and it is important that they educate immigrant women regarding the fact that domestic violence is one area in which undocumented women are protected against deportation. Under the stipulations of the Violence Against Women Act, they may, in fact, petition for legal status in the United States without relying on abusive spouses, parents, or children who are U.S. citizens or legal permanent residents to sponsor applications (Orloff 2003).

Women's Work

Gender is not a category that can be studied in isolation. Class, ethnicity, and legal status (as we have seen above) are more often than not intertwined in the experiences of immigrant women. The intersection of class and gender is especially evident in the case of women who engage in domestic work. Gonzales-Berry interviewed Norma, Tina, and Carmen in Norma's home one fall evening in 2008. All three women have been in Corvallis for almost twenty years, and all three have legal status. Norma and Carmen are older;

they each have raised three children in Oregon. Tina is younger, with two children still in elementary school. Their friendship has been melded by their shared work experience and also by the companionship they share through their activities at their church. The three women engaged in an animated discussion regarding their lives in Oregon, the differences between Mexican and American cultures, and their experiences as domestic workers.

Tina is the only one of the three women to have engaged in agricultural work when she first arrived in Oregon. Both she and her husband struggled for seven years to make a go of their lives on their paltry salaries as farmworkers. After becoming increasingly unhappy with the exploitation and the psychological abuse heaped on them by their boss—his constant yelling not only kept them in line, but it intimidated them and kept them paralyzed in fear—they left this job. It was then that Tina began to do housework, taking over some of Carmen's clients. Tina does not see herself doing this kind of work all her life: "It is convenient for the moment, but it is not fulfilling work. When I was young in Mexico, I was studying journalism, and I wanted to become a war correspondent. I never imagined myself doing housework. This is the lowest kind of work one can do in Mexico." Her working mates, recognizing and supporting her intelligence and her drive, assure her that she will go on to do great things in the future--that is, after her children are grown.

Norma's first job was running a day-care center in her home. She did this when her children were very young and this allowed her to care for them while earning some money by taking in six additional children. When all her daughters were in school she turned to cleaning houses. Her husband started out as a field hand, earned a Masters Degree and currently works as a professor in Oregon State University Extension services. Norma acknowledges that her husband earns enough to provide for the needs of the family, but she adds, "I like to spend, so that is why I do this work."

Carmen credits her husband, who works for a contractor, with pushing her to become independent. "When I first arrived here, he told me, 'You need to learn to drive. I don't want you begging people for a ride. I want you be able to fend for yourself.' " He gave her two driving lessons and then she was on her own. For several years, Carmen didn't work. She holds tight to the belief that women's primary job is to rear their children, and she was not willing to leave them to take a job. However, once they entered school, she went to work with her husband, cleaning up the dust and grime his work left behind. A professor who had hired him to remodel his kitchen liked Carmen's work and asked—not Carmen, but her husband—if she could do housework for him. Carmen's husband said, "Yes, but you are going to have to pay her more than you pay me," which was $15 an hour. The two men agreed on $20 an hour and Carmen took the job. Later, the professor taught her how to negotiate her salary and she sought additional positions.

These three women have studied English at different times, and they all drive. They see themselves as modern women, and as proof, they talk enthusiastically of their involvement in their children's education. Carmen recalls how she attended all the field trips taken by her children's classes, often driving her own car to transport children, and always encouraging other immigrant parents to get involved. She takes pride in having served her community in a variety of ways, including teaching women to drive, taking people to medical appointments, and serving as interpreter. Norma is proud of the fact that her constant support helped her daughter receive a Gates Scholarship for her university studies. Tina, Carmen, and Norma like their lives here because they are able to maintain a higher standard of living than they would have had in Mexico. Carmen and Norma also acknowledge that had they not come to the United States, they would have never taken a salaried job outside the home.

Life in the United States, however, did not offer these *mexicanas* the luxury of staying true to their traditional cultural values. Here, their husband's salaries were enough to get by, but in order to truly "get ahead," they had to find a job. So why did they choose domestic work? For these women, the answer is simple: domestic work is the only kind of job that allows them to both earn some money and carry out the responsibility of rearing their children as is culturally expected. Domestic work offers plenty of additional advantages. It allows them to be away from home only during the hours that their children are in school. Because they are able to work out flexible schedules—none of them works full time for any single employer—they are able to pick up their children after school and spend the rest of the day with them. This makes what in their own villages would be frowned upon as the lowliest of jobs a desirable enterprise in their current context. They tout the fact that they are their own bosses; they set the pace of their work; and their bosses generally do not hang around to manage their progress. They stress that they establish their parameters from the beginning, and they know exactly what needs to be done. If their employers want them to take on extra duties, like doing laundry, making beds, or doing dishes, they leave a note, and employers can expect to pay an additional amount—an added bonus is that they do not pay taxes on their income.[4]

All the women we interviewed for this project who do private house cleaning in different towns of the Willamette Valley have reported that their employers treat them with respect and frequently go out of their way to be kind with small gestures like leaving coffee and rolls, CDs for their listening pleasure, aromatic candles burning. When asked if they could recall times when they had been mistreated, Carmen was quick to respond: "Very few times. But when it does happen, I leave that position. I don't need to be abused or humiliated." She cited an example of how she deals with problems. "One day *la señora* told me I hadn't cleaned the floor in the dog area. I had, but she had let the dog in afterwards and he messed up the floor. I told her I had mopped it, but she insisted I hadn't. I told her, 'If you want me to clean it again, just tell me and I will, but don't say that I didn't clean it when I know that I did.' " She cleaned the floor, but never returned to that client. In another case, she recalled that an elderly woman left one hundred dollars on a table. The second time, she left two hundred, and the following week three hundred. Carmen humored her: "Ma'am, you had better put that money away. Or don't you need it? If you don't, you can give it to me. I could sure use it." That was the last time this employer tried to tempt her by leaving money lying around. Norma and Tina relished Carmen's stories, and their approving comments suggested that, like Carmen, they do not tolerate unfavorable working conditions. They were quick to point out that people in Corvallis have a high level of education, and they attribute the good treatment they receive from their employers to this fact. "Sometimes," Carmen observed, "when they come from other places— Texas and California—they aren't as pleasant." But rarely have they felt the sting of racism or discrimination from their employers.

Leading scholars of female migration have observed that as women in the United States have penetrated the white-collar and professional job market, but the quality of childcare centers has remained underdeveloped, the demand for immigrant women to carry on the child/elder care and domestic service previously carried out by stay-at-home wives has increased (Chang 2000; Hondagneu-Sotelo 2002). Immigrant women's labor, particularly housekeeping and taking care of children, the infirm, and the elderly, "makes possible the maintenance and reproduction of the American labor force at virtually no cost to the U.S. government. At the same time, this labor is extracted in such a way as to make immigrant women's sustenance of their own families nearly impossible" (Chang 2000). We were surprised to find that very few of the women who employed our interviewees were career women. Most were stay-at-home housewives, some with, and some without, children, and some were elderly women. Our interviewees had a good deal to say about the latter cases. Norma, for example, observed, "In Mexico you would never allow an elder to live alone. They would live with a son or a daughter. Here they are frequently abandoned. It is very sad to see these older women living by themselves, hardly ever seeing their children. Their houses are small, and they don't really need a lot of cleaning. So working for them is more about companionship." Carmen added, "The elderly can be more cranky and demanding, but you can't help but feel sorry for them, living alone like they do." When we asked why they thought their other clients relied on them to clean their houses when they were not employed, our interviewees offered a number of opinions, including: these *señoras* have their hands full with their children (several of the women were under thirty and cared for their infant children); they have the financial means to hire housekeepers; they don't like to do this kind of work, especially cleaning bathrooms; they prefer to devote their time to their hobbies and creative activities. The difference in socio-economic class between the immigrant women and their employers is evident, but it does not necessarily relate to freeing middle-class women so they can pursue careers, but rather so they can pursue a privileged lifestyle made possible by their socioeconomic status. Such arrangements, however, do allow immigrant women to care for their own families for they can arrange their work schedules in such a way that it does not interfere with raising their own children. In fact, *mexicanas* believe it enhances their ability to care for their own families; as Norma observed, "Doing this kind of work means we can buy extra things for the kids. We can, for example, pay the rent for a musical instrument, something that would be out of the question without my wages."

We do recognize, of course, that for many women who do not have partners or social networks to rely on and who are forced to leave their children with relatives in their country of origin and to become domestic live-ins in this country, Hondagneu-Sotelo's and Chang's observations are indeed germane. Some immigrant women view domestic work as an advantageous situation, allowing them to exert agency and a certain amount of control over their lives. The wages they earn give them a sense of independence and achievement. At the same time, they are able to fulfill their culturally prescribed gender roles, and this plays no small part in giving meaning and satisfaction to their lives. What we found, then, is that domestic work is one of those fields that circumscribes traditional gender roles and at the same time offers women a degree of freedom and autonomy. They are, of course, burdened with the phenomenon of the "double day," perhaps in a more pernicious way than most working women, in that the double duty—on the job and at home—involves the same kind of low-status work.

Changing Family Dynamics

The structure of immigrant families is socially dynamic. These families are affected by factors that go beyond those affecting non-immigrant families. In addition to class, education, religion, size of family and so forth, immigrant families must contend with changes related to the forced encounter of diverse cultural ways of being in the world. Just as there exist diverse family experiences within mainstream culture, there is no single model for discussing *mexicano* families. There are, for example, families composed of male and female parents; single female parents; extended families living together; same-gender parents; and older siblings acting as parents. In addition, within a single family, different members may have a different immigration status; some may be second generation, others first or one-and-a-half (children born in Mexico and brought to the United States); some will be citizens, others legal residents or naturalized citizens, and others may have an undocumented immigration status. These conditions, according to Hancock (2007), create hierarchies of privilege and foment inequality within the family:

> *Children who have the sniffles may be taken right away to the doctor, while others are taken only if they are very ill, depending on who has legal status and Medicaid coverage. These circumstances create additional stressors for low-income undocumented immigrant mothers who are socialized to emphasize the importance of collective well-being of their families but who have to treat their children differently, depending on their children's citizenship status. (181)*

Moreover, in today's political and economic environment, traditional families are being torn apart by inadequate immigration policies in the United States, by repressive political policies in Mexico (vis-à-vis indigenous people in Oaxaca), and by the creation, through neo-liberal economic practices, of an international workforce that is increasingly becoming feminized.

Yet despite their heterogeneity, there may be some commonalities among *mexicano* families influenced by learned cultural values and patterns (Perilla 1999). Diversity within families notwithstanding, the literature repeatedly points to the centrality of the family in the lives of *mexicanos*, referred to as familism, a value that places the collective interests of the family above the interests of any one individual member and stresses the duties and responsibilities of each family member to others within the family unit. Each member of the family has his or her role to play in helping sustain and maintain family unity. For children, this frequently means doing chores, running errands, and caring for younger siblings, and like all members of the family, they must accept their position within ranked authority based, for example, on gender, age, experience, knowledge, education, and social status. To not abide by one's position within this familial order is to transgress the tenets of *respeto* (respect). Familism and *respeto* are often mentioned as protective qualities that help *mexicano* families overcome the challenges of adapting to the new culture (Perreira et al. 2006). *Respeto* is earned by knowing and carrying out one's role within the family and by adhering to principles of courtesy and decorum (Perreira et al. 2006). The primacy of family applies not only to meeting basic physical and emotional needs, but also extends to the social realm. Parties, holidays, and celebrations include all family members. Children accompany parents to weddings, wakes, dances, public meetings. Families, in other words, work, worship, and play together, and children and youths are not separated from adults to the same degree they are in mainstream culture in the United States (Quiñones-Mayo and Dempsey 2005). The American practice of young people spending the night at each others' homes is quite foreign to immigrant parents, as is the idea of sending children off to camp.

Quinceañera, *Independence, OR. Photo by Paulina Hermosillo.*

Immigrant families face many challenges as they attempt to navigate their lives in a new environment. To begin with, adult immigrants lose their social standing, their social support networks, and the familiar social roles to which they were accustomed in their communities of origin (Perreira et al. 2006). In the new setting, parents are challenged not just by the new—a foreign and unknown culture and society—but also by the fact that all they learned in their home countries in terms of parenting and family socialization may no longer work; or their ways of parenting may be frowned upon or even discouraged. According to the tenets of patriarchy in which familial honor is attached to female virtue, male children have more freedom than female children, who are deemed in need of vigilance and protection. Physical punishment may be used as a means of disciplining children. And the axiom "it takes a village to raise a child" has a great deal of validity to many immigrants, particularly those from rural villages, where if a son or daughter transgresses social codes in public, parents are sure to hear about it from neighbors or other acquaintances. According to Quiñones-Mayo and Dempsey, in this country,

> parents are expected to control an adolescent whose behavior already may be out of control, while being told that the traditional ways of discipline are considered abusive. Or for a parent, already frustrated from trying to understand the adolescent's behavior, the school's request and the child welfare laws may only add more frustration. The focus group noted how, in contrast, the school in their country acted as a surrogate parent by imposing discipline, becoming part of the extended family, where every family member, including distant ones, would have a role. (2005, 655)

In addition, social tenets such as *el qué dirán* (what will people say) and *chisme* (gossip) serve as socialization mechanisms and social constraints not just for children, but for adults as well (Hirsch 2003). There are also the contributions of extended family and kinship networks to the process of child rearing and socialization. All of these patterns may become ineffectual in a society that values individualism, independence, choice, and role experimentation. While all that is familiar diminishes for immigrant parents, the new concomitantly asserts itself with unrelenting force. And it is precisely children who bring home the new, especially adolescent children who are learning American ways of being at school, from mainstream media, from their peers, from popular culture, ways that may be at odds with the expectations of their parents.

Adolescence is a time of change, of erratic behavior, of experimentation and rebellion. It is also a time when peer pressure may override parental guidance. Caught between these influences and their desire for freedom from the demands of their parents to act in ways that would be culturally appropriate in their country of origin, immigrant adolescents may find it difficult to strike a balance (Quiñones-Mayo and Dempsey 2005). If they feel ashamed of their status as immigrants or see their parents as "old-fashioned," they may engage in rebellious behaviors such as lying and sneaking about. The disconnect between immigrant parents and their teenage children can also create rigidity in parents as they attempt to stave off the changes that are occurring to their children (Perreira 2006). Parental rigidity, in turn, may encourage rebellion in adolescents. Martinez et al. note that the frustration associated with the gaps between cultural values may lead non-acculturated parents "to reduce support, communication and monitoring with their teens. Unfortunately, this response greatly increases the susceptibility of their children to negative peer influences and the genesis of problem behaviors" (2008, 6).

The experience of Edith, one of our Mexican-born interviewees, and her father is instructive, as it relates to this disconnect between parental and youth values. Edith and her father were trapped in a cycle of rigidity and rebellion. The more the father tried to impress upon his daughter traditional values, particularly as they relate to appropriate female behavior, the more resentful and rebellious she became. She resorted to lying to her parents and, when she was in college, eventually moved in with her boyfriend. Family ties, however, continued to be extremely important to her, and as her guilt increased she finally decided to confess to her mother that she was living with her boyfriend. Her mother immediately reported this breach of family honor to the father, who virtually disowned Edith and refused to attend her wedding. Gradually Edith became more receptive to her father's point of view: he had made tremendous sacrifices in order to improve the lives of his children, but was not able to understand the new ways because they were so far removed from his own value system. He, in fact, saw her behavior as a betrayal of all that he held dear. As her need to punish her father diminished, the rupture was healed.

The youth in immigrant families act as culture brokers, serving as the primary link between their parents and the host culture, particularly when parents have little social capital. In this sense, it is children who socialize the parents rather than other way around. It is not uncommon, for example, for children to have to interpret for their parents and they may be called on to do so at school, in medical situations, in business transactions, and even in situations involving the law (Duran 2003; Valdés1996). We heard of instances in which children have been asked to interpret by police officers called in response to domestic violence. Interpreting puts children in a position of authority vis-à-vis their parents and creates a situation of infantilization for the latter, creating conflict and tension between the generations. Children may feel guilt and fear regarding their role as interpreters. Francisco, for example, told us how by the age of ten he was serving as the primary interpreter for his family (interview with Gonzales-Berry, 2003). He frequently missed school because he had to accompany his parents to the doctor, to the gas company, to stores and offices of various sorts. He confessed that at night he could not sleep because he was afraid he had made some terrible mistake in the interpreting process, and that the police would come to take his parents away. As cultural brokers, immigrant children often carry responsibilities for which they are not psychologically equipped.

If parents attempt to regain their position as the adults in the family, children may threaten to or, in fact, call the police. Pedro, when asked if he thought children were raised differently in the United States, responded: "Oh, yes, very different. Here their ways are very liberal. Over there we are accustomed to controlling your family, as we say, to discipline it in a certain way. And here, if you discipline them, right away the government is down your neck. And, no, they don't allow you to ... And soon your children are out of control" (interview with S.J. Acosta, 2003). Rosalía, another Mexican-born interviewee, was also very perturbed when she addressed the issue of raising children in the United States: "It is very hard to control your kids here. They say they will call the police. What happens is that friends have a lot to do with this. They tell kids that parents can't touch them here, and if they do, they can call the police. The young influence each other" (interview with Gonzales-Berry, 2007). Jesús attributes the loss of parental control to the more laissez faire approach to child rearing that he perceived in the United States:

> *What can I say? Here children grow up with the ideas of this country. Here you can't yell at them, you can't spank them, because they call the police. Then they teach children to be rebels. For example, I have never told my child anything about the police. Perhaps her mother told her. But when I say something to my daughter—she's barely four years old—she starts in with that, telling me not to yell at her or not to dare spank her. From what I've seen, everything is more liberal here. Once children reach the age of legal adulthood, they do what they please. They don't listen to their parents. And in Mexico, it's totally different. Really, over there the family is more united; there's more love. Truly, that's how I see it (interview with S.J. Acosta, 2003).*

This information regarding the illegality of Mexican child-rearing practices in the United States circulates freely among young people and they often do not take the time to reflect on the consequences of their actions should they call the police. We were told of one case in which an immigrant male physically punished his stepdaughter for behavior that he found inappropriate. The girl called the police, who called the federal Immigration and Customs Enforcement Agency when they discovered the stepfather did not have legal documents. He was deported, leaving the family to fend for itself.

There are, of course, parents who are not intimidated by their children's threats to call the police. Carmen (interviewed in 2008) described to us how she handled similar situations. "When our sons said to me 'I will call the police,' my husband and I replied, 'Go ahead.'" They understood that officials will side with parents if they have not hurt their children. This is something Carmen has tried to explain to other parents. "Don't let your children blackmail you, and don't be afraid of the police if you haven't done anything wrong," she tells them. Carmen dreads the day that her twenty-three- and eighteen-year-old sons will leave home, yet she acknowledges that eventually they will. Knowing that his mother holds on to the Mexican custom that children remain at home until they marry, her twenty-three-year-old uses this knowledge on occasion to manipulate her. When he threatens to leave, she tells him, "Just let me know when, and I will help you pack your bags, and I'll even bake you a cake." She is a wise woman who refuses to be intimidated by her children. But many parents do not recognize manipulation tactics, and they end up feeling torn between their traditional beliefs and their children's new cultural values.

In feminist theory, the family is viewed as a site of the reproduction of inequalities, the site in which historically men have controlled and subjugated women. But for immigrants, the family is also a space that offers solace and protection from the hostilities, discrimination, and social segregation that the family may encounter in the host culture (Perreira et al. 2006). Hondagneu-Sotelo, argues that "occupational exploitation and racism in the public sphere had more often made the family a source of refuge" (2004, 155). Thus, whatever the dynamics are within any given family, we must not forget the crucial role that the family plays in providing a safe harbor and in insuring survival in the difficult conditions that immigrants face. This, then, is why to many immigrants, *la familia* has priority above all else, and all members of the family must make sacrifices for the common good. We have seen cases in which parents, but especially women—and especially mothers who are raising children alone—give up their personal needs and dreams for their children; and children likewise must put aside their desires for freedom in order to help out at home. Older children are often called upon to make greater sacrifices. In these cases, it is the younger children who benefit from the sacrifices of older siblings (Gonzales-Berry et al. 2006-2007).

The challenges are indeed pressing and may at times appear overwhelming to both parents and children of immigrant families. However, we cannot lose sight of the fact that immigrant families do exert agency as they navigate their new surroundings, and they seek and find ways to adapt, to accommodate, and to reshape their environment in such a way as to ensure collective survival and the development of bicultural identities, a topic we will address in greater depth in Chapter 6.

1. Only Chinese immigrant women are similarly represented in laborer and production occupations (Zhou 2003).

2. In the last decade or so the number of years of education has risen to six years for many people in rural areas of Mexico, and to nine for urban dwellers. For years, people in rural areas had reported three years of education.

3. We found a reaction similar to Nina's in our interview with Loyola. She recalled her rural village with tenderness and nostalgia, wishing that she were still there. Because Loyola came here as a widow and has remained single over the years, she may not be aware of the struggle related to gender-role transformations among couples and the sense of freedom that married women associate with life in the United States.

4. Carmen reported paying taxes because she and her husband wanted to buy a house. In order to do so they need to build their credit rating and show that they were earning a sufficient amount of money in order to obtain a mortgage loan. Researchers have studied the strategies used by immigrants to access homeownership. Ray et al. (2004) analyzed Mexican immigrants' homeownership in the Portland metropolitan area.

Testimonio

by Loyola

This testimonio *is composed from excerpts of an interview conducted by Gonzales-Berry in 2004 in Loyola's home in Woodburn which she shares with her two children, both of whom were away at college. Loyola was not working at the time because of a chronic illness, and she relied on her children for support. The interview was conducted in Spanish, and excerpts were selected, transcribed, translated, and arranged by the authors.*

I lived in a small village with my family. I married quite young—at sixteen—and I had my two children. By the time I was twenty, I was already alone, because my husband died that year. I had to work to support my children, and I worked for eight years in Mexico... .

My brother came over and it was he who invited me, as he saw that I was in great need. He saw that I was alone and had no money, not even enough to come over. So he gave me money to make the journey. It was difficult knowing that you are going to another country where you don't know anyone, but I had no choice because of my children. The preparations were mainly mental, because you have to think positively. You have to think that you are going to another country to work. That's how I gave myself courage, but mostly it was my children. They had always gone to school—to kinder, then to grade school—and I thought it was best for them. I thought, no matter where we are in the world, they had to study. They didn't have a father and they were my sole responsibility. I didn't want them to drop out in order to work, and I was also aware of the fact that they were intelligent and they did well in school. I believed it was best for them if they could go on studying.

The trip was long and tiring because we came by bus. When I arrived in the United States, I was shocked because I expected something very different. We arrived in November, when the leaves are falling and there's water and mud. My brother lived in what they call cabins, little wood houses, without heat or any conveniences. They only had a stove, two bunk beds; that's all. When I saw that, I felt very sad. I expected more. I thought something good awaited me here. I was frustrated, but I was here. With all the mud and leaves and rain, things I didn't expect, I gradually became depressed. In Mexico one gets up early. There is sunshine and warmth. It's quite lovely and one has a home, and a family, and a village... .

My brother got me a job where he worked on a mink ranch. They killed the animals there, thousands of those little animals. They skinned them and dried the pelts. And since I knew how to work on a sewing machine, they gave me a sewing job. I would sew torn pelts. They would stuff them like teddy bears and sell them in San Francisco, Los Angeles, and different places. I worked there about three years, just sewing and sewing, and they paid me twenty-five cents per piece. I would have to work late into the night, and I became ill. When I got sick, the boss fired me. Then he took my cabin and told me I had to leave. He gave me three days. I turned to my church for help, and started fending for myself.

My children had to adapt to many things in school. They came fairly advanced in their studies, but when they arrived here they put them in a low level and later [they] were placed in special education with children who were retarded. This set them back. Fortunately there are always conscientious teachers, and they placed them in another grade and helped my children get ahead. We have to be strong in order to face all situations, and I believe we have been prepared to do this. All I ever did here was work for my children. There are many who send money home to Mexico to build a house, buy some land, or for other necessities because that's what they come for. I came with another goal. All my money was for them, so they could study. That was my only goal. And we're still working on this. I'm still struggling so my children can finish their studies. It's getting easier now that we've been at it for fifteen years. The strength, I've drawn it from my children. Many parents think that when their children are grown they need to leave school and work to help out, but I think differently. I think my children have to be different, and that's why I don't get worn out. I keep struggling, although sometimes I feel cheated, not by my children but by the system. They are good and intelligent. I have brought them up well, but they still encounter obstacles. I don't understand why there are those who won't let them get ahead, who wish to impede their progress and destroy them. This hurts me because I know they are intelligent and their whole life they have studied hard. I think there are people in positions who decide who gets to pursue a career and who doesn't. Some move along even though they are not intelligent. I don't know if this happens because they have money, or they are just destined to be wealthy. Yes, those who have get ahead. I want my children to be mentally healthy, and if they are not able to complete their careers, I tell them, that is fine. We all did our best and I am happy knowing that the knowledge they have acquired, no one can take it from them, even those who attempt to humiliate them and impede their success.

My children are strong; I think they got that from me. Because we are strong, we are going to get ahead. What is sad is that there is so much work and so few possibilities for getting ahead. It's as if the sky falls on you. Nonetheless, people go on; one job, two jobs, three at a time. I believe all our people are so strong. They are so brave to do what they do. Every day, the same routine. But God has given them strength to do their work, and even if they are poorly paid, they manage to pay the rent, buy food, pay their bills, buy insurance. The money comes and it goes. I think we are in a bad situation, yet we think that we will have a good future by coming here. Yet we are no better off than we were in Mexico.

Testimonio

by María Damaris

This testimonio *is composed from excerpts of an hour-long interview conducted at the offices of PCUN where María was working at the time, after having worked as a labor organizer in Portland. She had divorced her American husband and married a Mexican immigrant. Speaking mainly in English, María occasionally slipped into Spanish. The excerpts were transcribed, selected, and arranged by the authors.*

I was nine when my parents divorced. That was a big challenge for me, my sister, and my brother, who were growing up together with my parents. My mom went on her own. She started working very hard, and my dad started drinking more and more. So, I come from a so-called dysfunctional family. But just facing all the challenges of growing up without a father helped me a lot to take more responsibilities. I just had to do everything from helping my mom carry the water two blocks to our home to helping my siblings. If we were on the bus and someone would touch my sister's butt, I would be the one defending her and facing men.

My mother, she works at the University of Michoacán, which is called La Universidad Michoacana de San Nicolas de Hidalgo, which is the government public university. She started working as a cook there. Then she worked her way up. We always were involved in rallies and marches. My mom used to always take us to the rallies, so I've been in that environment since I was very young. I understood the sense of justice and I understood that when people or the government try to take something away from you, you have to fight back. And there's no choice, because if you don't fight back then you lose the little things. That's what my mother taught me, and I'm very grateful for that.

It just happened that a *gabacho*—he was of Irish descent—a Spanish student, came to my home town. Actually we met in a place called Patzcuaro in Michoacán, and we fell in love. Everything happened so quick. It was a big shock for my family. But it was good. I needed to take a break from my family problems. My mom was having some hard times with my stepfather, and I had been working too hard. I was working so hard helping my family. I was the main breadwinner at that time in the family. So it was very harsh. At the age of twenty-one, on January first of 1994, I married _____. We flew back to Eugene, Oregon. And while I was trying to adjust to the cultural shock of being in a little town like Eugene, Oregon, with—oh, I don't know—95 percent white people, the Zapatistas rose up and they were saying, "*Basta* [enough]" and "We are all Indians." This had a major impact on me, because I always grew up defending the rights of women and indigenous people, but I did not really understand the roots of the problems we have in Mexico and the bigger challenges we had, like classism and the impact of colonialism, and trying to understand why some people in my culture were very sexist, and understanding that sexism is everywhere. So when Marcos started saying, "We all are Indians," I started questioning myself. Who was I? My identity? I think it was a great start. I think I started with the right foot in this country, because of the Zapatistas. Otherwise I think I could have lost myself in the American culture.

I was working in Eugene, Oregon, as a community organizer, teaching English to Latino parents, and teaching Spanish to English-speaking teachers. Teaching Spanish through music to white kids. That's the work I did in Eugene. I also worked with the government, with the Lane County government as a Healthy Start assessment and caseworker. Then I worked with Catholic Charities Community. Then I thought it was not enough to be a community organizer. I wanted bigger challenges. My partner had finished his undergraduate studies, so we were ready to move to California to work in the labor movement. He went to work with AFL-CIO, which is one of the most progressive unions. And I went to work with the Janitors' Union. I said, "If I am going to sacrifice my life, sacrifice maternity, sacrifice my marriage, it has to be for my people."

Testimonio

by Marco Antonio Chávez

This testimonio *is composed from excerpts of an interview conducted by José Otáñez in English in 2003 in Corvallis, where Marco Antonio was a student at Oregon State University. After his graduation Marco Antonio attended Bowling Green University where he received his Masters degree in Ethnic Studies before moving on to take a job in admissions at Ohio State University. The excerpts were transcribed, selected, and arranged by the authors.*

My mother arranged for our crossing. She had a friend in Hillsboro who told her to come on over. This friend's husband crossed us and some other men and their families. Crossing over seemed easy to me. We arrived in Nogales where we stayed in a run-down hotel for a few days. Suddenly, one night, they told us we were going to cross. The man explained to us what was going to happen. We all crossed at night. Mother told us wait in this parking lot. I had no idea what she went to do. While we were waiting we saw some patrolmen—border patrol or whatever. And in the distance I could see a McDonalds, but at that time I had no idea what it was. But I thought it was lovely. We waited there in the open parking lot by the fence. When she returned, she said "Okay, we're going to cross." By then the patrols had left. The fence had a hole covered by some fencing. I lifted it and she passed with my small brother. Then she held it while I passed with Juanito. That made me feel really proud, because I liked to carry my little brothers. We walked a few blocks until we saw a pickup where we had agreed to meet. We got in the truck and we laid down. Then the others arrived, and we took off. I remember that it started to rain and I saw a rainbow. I thought it was fabulous. It was the first rainbow I ever saw and it was in the south.

When we got to Hillsboro, we stayed with my mother's friend for three weeks in her apartment. Her friend had five kids and we always fought with them. What could my mom do? There we were while she worked in the fields.... .

As for family, my mother's brother is here. He started coming in '98. He comes and goes from Mexico City where he has a *combi* (collective taxi) business. He comes and goes. Then he brought my two cousins, his two sons. One of them just left. He just came to learn English because he is studying tourism. The other is working here because there was no space for him in the university, so he is here. My cousin, my uncle, my aunt, my grandmother. She comes every now and then, just enough to earn her social security. The truth is they are all here because of my mother, because she came and became a resident. Then she made her kids residents and she became a citizen. She is trying to get residency for her brother and his sons. In California, my grandma's brother lives there with his kids. My grandma's sister lives in Farmington, New Mexico, with her sons and grandchildren. They come and go to and from Pátzcuaro, Michoacán, in Mexico... .

I think if we were in Mexico my brothers wouldn't be such rebels, they wouldn't complain so much. They would obey Mother more. The same goes for me. When I was growing up, I was very rebellious. I would sneak out through the window and go with my friends. One time my mother called the cops. They brought me home and she gave me a good slap. The cop didn't do a thing! Here I think parents are useless. I don't mean useless, but they have less authority to raise their kids the way they want. Not that the way they want is good or bad. But, for example, here they have no choice but to go [to] work. In Mexico, you still have the possibility of the mother staying home, right? Here things change; the roles of each family member changes. The mother has to work outside the home. The father by force has to work. So while the parents are at work, the kids, well, you know. So parents have less control over their kids... . In Mexico, for example, if the parents weren't around, someone would be there, an uncle, an older cousin. But not here. Here, you can't depend on anyone. If there is a compatriot here, people fight amongst themselves. Because we do fight as compatriots. In Mexico we help each other more... .

I don't feel that I belong. Well, now my community is here in this apartment building. At least a third of the people here are people of color, that is, *mexicanos*, Africans, Chinese, or whatever. And, in a sense, I do fit here, because we can relate to each other as immigrants or as people of color from this country. But at the same time, I don't consider myself part of this city, or of this country, because I don't feel that I have the same values as Anglos. I have noticed that lots of people who immigrate adopt Anglo values. I think that is so they can survive better. I recognize that I have done the same to a certain point. But in some things, no way. Instead, I reject things. Things like Anglos having to move from home at eighteen. Things like that, I reject. Or that if you marry you can't live with your family. I reject that also. Or that at a certain age you don't have to obey your parents. I reject that. Following popular culture rather than what your parents say. No way. I recognize that I am actively rejecting this culture. It's something subliminal if not superliminal. It's something I do deliberately, consciously. I think that is why I don't belong.

Chapter 6

One-and-a-Half Generation Mexicano Youth: Their Journey to Bicultural Integration[1]

In the previous chapter we explored the numerous challenges immigrant families face in adapting to their new environment. The pressure on children to learn new cultural values and ways of being are often at odds with those of parents who do not speak English and who have limited contacts with members and institutions of the host culture. These parents raise bicultural children in a new land, separated from familiar cultural contexts, networks, and support (Mendoza 2009). In this chapter we discuss the successful process of integration of one-and-a-half-generation youths who have achieved a positive identity formation in Oregon supported by strong family bonds.

Much of the literature on this topic highlights the negative consequences of the acculturation gap between parents and their children, pointing out how youth caught in this dilemma frequently end up dropping out of school or engaging in harmful behaviors, including membership in gangs, the use of drugs and alcohol, and sexual activity that leads to teenage pregnancy (Partida 1996). The familial stresses associated with parenthood and migration notwithstanding, examples abound of families who also manage to maintain "healthy family dynamics despite experiencing stress and socioeconomic disadvantages" (Smokowski et al. 2008).

Defining Generations and Models of Incorporation

In migration studies, the second generation is generally defined as the native-born children of at least one foreign-born parent. Recent scholarship, however, broadens this definition to accommodate changes in migration patterns affected by family reunification and the emergence of a highly mobile transnational labor force created by globalization. After passage of the Immigration and Reform Control Act, which went into effect in 1987, we have witnessed an exponential increase in the migration of entire families to *el norte*. These families brought with them young children who, though born in Mexico, would have experienced a socialization process similar to those of siblings born in the United States. Hence migration scholars now tend to classify immigrant children younger than five years, along with those born in the United States, as part of the second generation.

As there are important differences in the socialization of these children and those who migrate at a later age, the term one-and-a-half generation has been coined to identify foreign-born children who were brought to the United States after the age of five up through adolescence. Sons and daughters brought after the age of eighteen, who go directly into the workforce (without attending school in the U.S.), are counted as part of the first generation. Scholars agree that these distinct cohorts will have different experiences in their psychological developmental stages, in their socialization processes within the family, in their orientation toward their homeland, and in their experiences of accommodation to the new host culture (Portes and Zhou 1993; Rumbaut 1994; Portes and Rumbaut 2001).

Early migration theory posited a linear theory—"straight-line assimilation theory"—of incorporation of immigrants into their new country (Gordon 1964). Under this model of social membership and national belonging, immigration was viewed as a fairly transparent series of stages: uprooting from the place of origin, settlement in the new nation, eventual integration or incorporation of the uprooted immigrant (Rumbaut 1994; López and Stanton-Salazar 2001). Incorporation demanded a shedding of skins, so to speak, the relegation of the culture of origin to memory. This process has been conceptualized as an incremental process which—while not without discomfort—includes a sense of alienation among the first generation, and is generally complete by the time the second generation matures, with the third generation becoming full-fledged members of what once was the host country of immigrant ancestors. This model was intimately linked to ideologies of nation building and does not take into account the diverse nature of social formations in the United States:

> *The traditional analysis that focuses on acculturation as measured by language change, cultural identity, and social relations simply reproduced frameworks tied to a national ideology of monoculturalism and assimilation which is the analogue of the ideological conviction of nationalism. Such traditional approaches fail to consider the bidirectionality of cultural processes, the creation of localized and regional cultural and linguistic forms, the emergence of multidimensional social identities based on class, intermarriage, and binationalism, and the development of localized scripts and localities in the midst of institutional and national repressive policies, actions, and megascripts (Vélez-Ibáñez et al. 2002, 23).*

This model has been conceived to describe the experiences of European immigrants during a period of intense industrialization; however, social, economic, and political changes in the post-industrial era have engendered distinct patterns of incorporation and identity development. Furthermore, given that race historically has played an important role in determining social status in the United States, *mestizo* and *mulato* immigrants from Latin America tend to face discrimination in education, the labor market, and social domains that may trump any human capital they might have (López and Stanton-Salazar 2001). These conditions contribute to diverse integration patterns, belying the linear theory of assimilation.

Immigration scholars examining the lives of children of immigrants have begun to explore how "new" ethnic minorities resist hegemonic notions of assimilation, often creating new identities and images of themselves (Portes and Zhou 1993; Rumbaut 1994; Zhou 1997; Perlmann 2002). Portes and Rumbaut (1996, 2001) postulated that three major factors affect the ways in which immigrants are incorporated economically and politically into a host society. The amount of human capital possessed by the first generation is certainly germane to the ability of the second generation to integrate itself into mainstream society in the United States. But beyond the educational level, job skills, wealth, and knowledge of English of the first generation, contextual factors are also important. Among them, the reception by the host government and the host society are of major importance. The position of the receiving government can be one of exclusion—that is, of denying legal status to immigrants. It may also grant passive acceptance, such as the granting of legal status under the provisions of the 1986 Immigration and Reform Act. Or a government may offer active encouragement, as in the case, for example, of political refugees, who are offered not only legal status but also government assistance to help facilitate their relocation. In addition to these contextual factors, Portes and Rumbaut (2001) point to family composition as a crucial factor in determining the kind of incorporation that the one-and-a-half generation will undergo as they grow and attempt to make their way in U.S. society: children from intact families will likely have greater success.

Portes and Rumbaut (2001) have linked the factors cited above to three different types of acculturation experienced by immigrants in their incorporation into U.S. society. *Dissonant acculturation* refers to circumstances in which children of immigrant parents with low human capital acculturate at a more rapid rate then their parents, frequently abandoning the home culture and distancing themselves from their parents. It is also likely that these youths will take on an adversarial stance vis-à-vis mainstream culture, identify with counter cultures, and ultimately face irregular employment and poverty. *Consonant acculturation* takes place when both parents and children acculturate at an even pace, experiencing the gradual abandonment of the home culture and language and finally

Chicano Cultural Center, Oregon State University, 1977. Oregon State University Archives.

assimilating into mainstream culture. This pattern is most apt to occur when parents possess higher levels of human capital. *Selective acculturation* occurs when the learning process of the first and second generations is embedded in a strong co-ethnic community whose large size and institutional diversity slow down the cultural shift and promote partial retention of the language and norms of the first generation. Unlike dissonant acculturation, which results in role reversal—children helping parents navigate in the host culture—this mode does not undermine parental authority.

An additional contextual factor relates to the presence and position of communities of co-ethnics. If compatriots already are present in the receiving society, they may be in a position to help newer immigrants find housing and jobs.

This kind of social capital often facilitates incorporation, but it can also have a negative effect; if co-ethnics are already embedded in structurally segregated low-wage occupations, newer immigrants with considerable human capital may be channeled into these same occupations as well. This certainly has been the case in Oregon where, historically speaking, *mexicanos* have been channeled into farm, nursery, tree-planting, logging, and service industries. More recently, new segmented spaces have opened up in other industries.

In today's restructured economy, jobs are segmented into communications and technology positions requiring high levels of education and jobs in the service sector requiring little education. In this kind of labor economy the children of immigrants, if they are to get jobs that will differentiate their social status from that of parents with low human capital, must overcome the education gap in one generation. Children of European immigrants were often been able to secure well-paid jobs in production and manufacturing despite low levels of education—to a large extent because those manufacturing jobs were available. Bridging the education gap was not as crucial for the latter as it is for immigrants today (Portes and Rumbaut 2001).

The Unique Situation of the One-and-a-Half Generation

Rumbaut (1991, 1994) analyzes the situation of those children who are born abroad, whose education begins in the home country but who come of age and complete their education in the United States. The experiences of these children, as we have seen, are distinct from those of younger children whose identities are not yet well defined when the family migrates. Adolescence is a moment of crossing, an important identity-forming threshold. In addition to the physical and psychological changes involved in crossing this threshold, the individual's sense of identity is also expanding to include a national consciousness. While attending school in their native land, the children of immigrants are constructing their identities as members not only of a family, but of broader social groups, and also as members of a particular national space (e.g., learning the national anthem, reciting the pledge of allegiance). Given the extreme physical and turbulent psychological changes involved in crossing the adolescence threshold in a new country, the process may be likened to a trauma not unlike that experienced by adult migrants as they move from a familiar and secure geo-social and political space to a foreign and frequently hostile environment. Rumbaut remarks, "The literature on migration and mental health has repeatedly observed that long-distance journeys entail stressful life events, at points of both exit and destination, which severely test the emotional resilience of migrants" (1991, 56).

The simultaneous crossing of a psychological-development border and a national border is a distressing event that may be experienced by adolescent migrants as a double crisis. However, the one-and-a-half and the second generations will share a similar socializing process experienced through American schooling.

One-and-a-Half Generation Youth in Oregon

The information in this section was collated from interviews with twelve one-and-a-half generation students enrolled at Oregon State University. All of them self-identify as *mexicanos*. All these youth were born between 1974 and 1982, came to the United States prior to or at early adolescence,[2] and arrived in the United States between 1988 and 1991. They were part of a family migration north spurred by the legalization of a parent who had been working in the fields of Oregon as an undocumented farmworker prior to IRCA. As children, the interviewees had attended elementary or middle school in Mexico. They enrolled in public schools as soon as their families moved to Oregon. We found that the life stories of these twelve *mexicanos*— who didn't know one another before enrolling at Oregon State University— are surprisingly similar in terms of their border-crossing experiences, their insertion into the public school system of Oregon, their experiences of discrimination, their construction of identity, their experiences getting into and being in college, and their aspirations for the future. We attribute the shared nature of their experiences to the fact that, as members of the one-and-a-half generation, they had already been schooled in Mexico prior to coming to the United States; they had been socialized in that country, and that socialization included the beginning of the formation of a national consciousness; their identity as Mexican nationals impinged on their integration in the host culture.

The Families Migrate North

As we have seen in previous chapters, the decision to emigrate is not arrived at willy-nilly, nor are emigrants merely responding to extreme conditions of poverty in Mexico as is frequently assumed. Global labor flows between nations are prompted in part by social and economic transformations that occur as a result of capital penetration and free markets in poor nations. Workers from regions undergoing rapid economic development often find themselves displaced from traditional ways of earning a living, and move to self-insure, acquire capital, and/or substitute for a lack of credit at home by selling their labor abroad (Massey et al. 2002). Moreover, the segmented labor market that has become standard fare in the globalized economy of rich nations creates a demand for this low-wage labor pool in developed countries.

The young people interviewed for this chapter[3] were uncertain about what exactly had motivated their parents to immigrate to Oregon—as Pablo said: "To tell you the truth, I don't really know why we came up here."

Since they were seven to fifteen years old at the time, these children did not participate in their parents' decision to move north. However, given the opportunity to choose, the teenagers would have preferred to stay in Mexico. In the interviews, they said that the move was to join a father or mother, in the hope of improving the family's life chances. Common explanations are that their parents wanted to earn more money, own a home, and give their children a good education.

Before they decided to migrate to Oregon, the parents of the interviewees were low-wage workers in manufacturing, construction, and the service sector in Mexico. Most of the mothers were homemakers or earned an income in the informal economy. All but two parents had less than a ninth-grade education—one father had completed high school in Mexico, while one mother had no schooling.

Nostalgic Recollections and the Search for Opportunities

At the time of migration, most of these youths lived in large, intact families with both parents at home, though two households were headed by single mothers. They have siblings who migrated north with them. They all had fond memories of their childhood in Mexico. They share a common perception that they had a good life in the neighborhoods where they lived, surrounded by friends and extended family. Ricardo explained, "My life in Mexico was a happy one. I had a very happy childhood, with lots of freedom. Because it was healthy it has helped me remain sane and focused, with good examples. I don't remember being poor because we always had enough to eat and we were loved."

Susana had a similar experience: "I had a lot of fun in elementary school in Mexico. I was involved in dance, in poetry. It was really hard for me to leave because I was to be *escolta de la bandera* (escorting the national flag) in sixth grade. I missed my friends. My mom tells me that I never saw how poor we were."

María's recollections are similar, but she pays special attention to the connection between her happiness and the presence of extended family: "My life in Mexico was lots of fun. I never felt that we lacked anything. I didn't understand that my parents may have been having financial problems. My cousins lived across the street and we played together. They lived with their grandmother, my uncle's mother, and I integrated myself into that family."

Carmen, who also valued kinship ties, was particularly saddened by the loss of extended family:

> *My life was more pleasant than the life we have here. I thought it would be better in the United States, but when I remember, I realize*

*that it was better over there. I went to school, I had friends, my
teachers treated me well, I got recognition for my good grades, I had
my family close by, my grandparents, my cousins. I was free to go
wherever I wanted and didn't have to worry about anything. It was
better in Mexico. Here I don't feel free, I don't have [extended] family.*

Initially most interviewees did not think that the move would be permanent,
since their parents often talked about going back to Mexico. Their parents
may have headed north intending to follow the decades-long pattern of
circular migration rather than with settlement in mind. These families really
didn't have much concrete knowledge about life in the United States, or else
they had unreal expectations. They were, however, certain about one thing:
the availability of increased opportunities, particularly in the education
domain, as Alicia explained: "My parents decided to come to have a better
life than we had in Mexico, less economic limitations and better education
for us." She added: "I didn't know anything about the United States, besides
that you come to work and that this is the dream land." Luis knew that in
the north people spoke a different language and the president was Ronald
Reagan. "I thought that just for coming here we would become rich," said
Ricardo.

That education for their children was an important motivating factor for
her parents is apparent in Marta's recollection: "My father was already here
[in Oregon] and he saw how easy it was to go to school here, while my mom
was struggling to send my two older brothers to high school in Mexico. My
dad told my mom that she needed to bring the kids to Oregon so they could
finish high school here. My parents thought that they would have a better life
and could own a house." She added: "I knew nothing about *el norte* before we
came, only that it had snow, they grew cherries, and spoke English."

These youth and their parents knew very little about the language, the
society, and the culture of the host country. But they did carry in their
imaginations visions of modernity and of a pristine environment. Roberto,
for example, observed: "My parents knew that the U.S. was more modern,
had big freeways, green spaces, and playgrounds for kids."

Social Networks

While structural conditions in large measure create migratory flows from
developing to wealthy nations, as we have seen in previous chapters, social
networks play an important role there in initiating and sustaining those flows.

The most important network relationships are based on kinship,
friendship, and *paisanaje*, which are reinforced through regular interaction

in voluntary associations. In moving to a strange and often hostile land, migrants naturally draw upon these familiar bonds to share the hazards and hardships of life in exile, and those left behind rely on the same ties to mitigate the loneliness and anxiety of having a loved one far away. As migration continues, however, these well-known social connections acquire new meanings and functions. They are transformed into a set of social relationships whose content and meaning are defined within the migrant context. Over time, shared understandings develop about what it means to be a friend, relative, or *paisano* with a community of migrants. Eventually these understandings crystallize into a set of interrelationships that define the migrant network (Massey et al. 1987, 140).

In fact, social networks become such an effective catalyst for migration that host countries actually have experienced a decrease in the need for labor recruitment. In the same way that migration saves the host country the costs connected with reproducing a labor force, migrant networks absorb labor-recruitment costs that otherwise would be borne by employers (Waldinger and Lichter 2003).

The parents of the interviewees had family and friends in Oregon who helped them to find a job and enroll their children in school. Interestingly, all the fathers and the two single mothers who headed these households had spent time as farmworkers in of Oregon before they decided to bring their families north. Some parents had engaged in circular migration before making the decision to finally settle in rural Oregon, supporting the observation that "[o]nce a migrant has left and returned, he or she is very likely to make another U.S. trip, setting off another cycle of crossing, arriving, working, remitting, and returning" (Massey et al. 2002, 64). Two of the interviewees are grandchildren of former *bracero* workers. This comes as no surprise given that the *Bracero* Program gave thousands of workers valuable knowledge of and experience in the United States, thus creating a robust cache of social capital for future generations.

The networks that attracted and retained these immigrant families in small towns in Oregon were formed by brothers, sisters, friends, and co-nationals who created enclaves throughout the agricultural regions of the state. These relatives and friends remained in touch with one another throughout the years. For example, Marta explained: "My father came to Oregon in 1985. He had most of his family already here (two sisters with their own families). My dad worked in Oregon for a while, and visited us back in Mexico about once a year. He sent money to my mom, and letters with photos in the snow and with the cherries. When he visited us in Mexico, my dad came in a truck, and bought toys and clothes for us."

In Susana's words,

My father's sister had been in Oregon for about ten years and kept calling my dad to come and join her family. My dad came for two years, worked in the fields and sent money to my mom. Then he went back to Mexico for about one year, but couldn't find a good job. My brothers were in high school and there was not enough money, so my father returned to Oregon and my parents decided that we would all go there. We are seven children now, six born in Mexico and one in Oregon.

The breadwinners in each household (ten fathers and two mothers) did not have work permits when they first arrived in Oregon to do farm work. However, they were able to obtain permanent residency through IRCA and eventually, with the support of social networks, they brought their families to join them. Recalling this situation, María said: "My dad had been here before and he was able to legalize his situation through the amnesty program. My mom couldn't bear her loneliness in Mexico and she brought us here, too."

Crossing the Border

Between 1988 and 1991, most of these Mexican youths crossed the international border into the United States without immigration documents. One interviewee whose mother had become a permanent resident entered the country with a tourist visa. In their recollections, two of our informants said that immigration officers let their fathers cross with their families even though the wives and children did not have documents. Marta was one of them: "My father came in a truck to pick us up. He had permanent residency in the U.S. since 1989 but we didn't." This experience points to the rather casual attitude that the border patrol was known to display prior to the nineties (Nevins 2002).

Another youth crossed the border into the United States guided by smugglers, along with his siblings and other families. He informed us:

A friend of my mother's was going to come to Portland as an illegal and we came with them. We crossed with some smugglers in Tijuana, we hid, and we traveled for a good while along a lengthy road. The other group that accompanied us was grabbed by the border patrol. The smugglers settled us in an apartment in Los Angeles for two or three days. There was little food. The Oaxaqueños who were with us had to wait for their relatives to pay the smugglers to bring them to Portland. We arrived in Portland with them one night and had to sleep in the bus station. My father picked us up at the Greyhound and we went to the ranch where he worked. The boss gave him a trailer for us [to live in].

José's journey was very similar: "My mother knew someone who was coming and we crossed with her. We crossed the line running at Tijuana and they picked us up in Los Angeles. The *coyotes* kept us four days in a room without windows until the wee hours. There were eight of us. My mother's kinfolk brought us to Portland and my father then picked us up."

Regarding his own crossing, Luis reported: "One day my mother told me we were coming to the U.S. with my little brothers. I was about to turn eight. We arrived in Nogales. The husband of a friend of my mother's crossed us and some other families. A pickup took us to Los Angeles and from there to Hillsboro. My mother went to work in the fields."

In a study on immigrant women, Andrews et al. (2002) describe the crossing of fifteen women from Mexico to the state of Washington, and the settlement of these women's families in the Pacific Northwest. So similar are their journeys to those of our subjects that these women could well have been the mothers of our interviewees, except that the *mexicano* families who migrated to Washington used more *coyotes* than those in our study, partly because they crossed after 1994. When our subjects crossed, the border had not yet been militarized by programs such as Operation Gatekeeper. Thus, crossing was not yet so dangerous as to force women to depend on *coyotes*.

Settling in Rural Oregon

Before these youth and their siblings arrived in rural Oregon with their mothers, their fathers were already working in the fields, tending crops such as strawberries, cherries, and asparagus. Some had broken away from the fields and were working in tree nurseries and dairy farms.

Initially, the wives and older children helped with the farm work. Susana recalls her family's story:

We arrived in a small village called Amityville. My father worked in a dairy farm milking cows. Then my mother began to work with him and she began to draw a salary. Later we moved to another village, in the same area.

My dad worked in The Dalles picking cherries and apples. He would take us to pick cherries too. In the fall he went to pick apples and pears in Hood River and we went too. We had to stay in the cabin and help out. We only did that for one year because my parents realized that they were going nowhere that way. My dad started working in a mill company and he's still there ten years after. My dad is a forklift operator. He was able to get my brothers to work with him too. My mother has worked at restaurants, hotels, a cannery, and at McDonald's for five years. Now she's working at a hotel.

The interviewees reported that they found the new environment unfamiliar. For example, María said: "I wasn't used to living on a farm because I came from Mexico City." Pedro felt particularly alienated in his new living conditions. He notes: "What I didn't like at first in Oregon was the rain and cold and living with a Christian family because I was a Catholic and couldn't adapt. At first I rejected English because I did not feel comfortable in the United States. I felt that my life had changed here. Everything caved in. In Mexico I ran about and had many friends, and here I was shut in without seeing anyone." Ricardo remorsefully compares his life in Oregon with life in Mexico. He tells us, "When I arrived I didn't like it because of lack of freedom and the cold. Everything was cloudy, sad, lonely, and dark. We lived by a mountain, and several months passed before summer returned. It was a drastic change because in Mexico it was warm, we bathed in the river, and when my friends had to tend the cows, I got to play with them in the hills." The trauma of migration seeps through their narratives as they link climatic changes with the emotions of loss and sadness they were feeling as a result of the dramatic change in their lives.

After obtaining permanent residency in the late 1980s, some parents found employment in manufacturing, in construction, in restaurants and hotels, substantiating Cornelius' (1990) claim that IRCA freed immigrant workers to take jobs beyond agriculture. José said: "My dad used to work in a dairy farm and my mom wasn't employed. Now my dad and my mom work in a factory."

Carmen's mother worked in a nursery and she picked berries in the fields. "Now [that she has permanent residency status] she does all kinds of work. She works in a cannery, sometimes she goes to the fields and, when there is work, in an electronic company." The experiences of Carmen's mother reveal that by settling in a rural area, she can always fall back on field work when jobs are scarce in other sectors.

Schooling in Oregon

All these youths were enrolled in school as soon as they arrived in Oregon. They had attended school in Mexico before—some were in grade school, others in middle or high school. Since they were all monolingual Spanish speakers, these youngsters were initially placed in English as second language classes. The ESL classes were part of the Migrant Education Program (MEP), which has been in existence in Oregon since the 1960s. The youths in our study spoke highly of opportunities afforded to them by the MEP, particularly the field trips and the Migrant Institute of Leadership camps.

For most, it took over one year to learn sufficient English to be able to switch to some monolingual English courses, but Ricardo told us, "We arrived in March and in two weeks I started school. My sister and I were the only Mexicans in that school. The students were all Anglos. They were polite, but nothing more. In another class there was a son of Mexicans who didn't speak Spanish. They put us both in ESL. We would go to another classroom and a Texan teacher taught us English. The first ESL teacher I had was very good and in six months I could speak English. I finished elementary school two years later." Ricardo added: "In school they put us in a cold room with another teacher who taught us English. Afterwards another teacher came who taught us another subject. There was also a bilingual student who came to translate." Despite the fact that these young people learned English, they were often kept in ESL classes until high school. This was María's experience: "We arrived in Oregon in March, during spring break, and I entered the fifth grade in school. They placed me in the Migrant Education Program and also in summer school. I took ESL all those years until high school." Susana, however, had a very different experience. She recalls: "I was in sixth grade in Mexico. In Oregon I went to school in January and they put me in a classroom with a teacher that I couldn't understand. He only took me there when they were doing math, the rest of the time I was in the library watching videos or TV, things like *Sesame Street* and the *Bill Cosby Show*. That's how I started to learn English. At recess nobody would talk to me, I felt that I couldn't relate to anybody." In Luis's case, school counselors pushed him to learn English. "They believed that if I learned English everything would fall in place for me." This is a philosophy that underlies most ESL programs. Yet in so many cases, students who have mastered English are still dropping out from school. This led one researcher to examine the issue of "when English isn't enough" (Valdés 1996).

The lack of English skills at a time when the need to develop peer relations and friendships is paramount to young people was an alienating experience for our subjects, reminding us of Rumbaut's premise that the one-an-a-half generation is uniquely traumatized by migration. Their sense of alienation and frustration vis-à-vis the language question was further exacerbated by the fact that they were immersed in a society that constructs race in a manner different from that experienced in their homeland. Enrique vividly sums up his experience:

> *I went to predominantly white schools. People had a difficult time trying to understand who I was and relating to me. I had a tough time trying to explain myself. The first couple of years in Oregon*

*were tough, not knowing a word of English. I felt that the kids in
elementary school didn't like me simply because I was Mexican. It
was a culture shock trying to adapt and not having friends; the whole
moving away from home to a new environment. I had to put up with
people laughing at me because I couldn't pronounce words properly.
The school didn't have the resources to provide an environment where
I was actually helped with my differences. These are obstacles that I
found but grew stronger because of them.*

Carmen likewise talks about her sense of alienation, and she is able to
succinctly pinpoint its cause when she says, "In school everything was
strange. I felt that people stared at me as if I were not from here. In Mexico
we all looked the same. Yes, one might be darker or lighter skinned, yea.
But here a great deal is made of skin color. Also, I had a hard time learning
English." Perhaps because he was born in Los Angeles but raised in Tijuana,
Paco was not prepared for the kind of discrimination he experienced. With
time he was able to develop a mature response to racism: "When I came over
here, I didn't figure that people were going to dislike me that much for being
different. Even though they treated me like shit, I still told them that I was
Mexican because I grew up in Tijuana, and was born in Los Angeles. Now
if they tell me something racist I don't laugh. I think that they are ignorant
because they are judging without really understanding me."

In the eyes of our interviewees, discrimination extended beyond the
immediate peer group to include school personnel. Although, as Marta
said, they had some inspiring teachers who treated them the same as other
students, most youngsters in our sample experienced what they perceived
as disinterest from school personnel. As Alicia said, "Mexican students
suffer from language barriers and discrimination from teachers." Susana's
experience with indifference became pronounced in high school: "I wasn't
aware of discrimination until high school. My mom always talked about it,
but discrimination didn't hit me until then. My counselors in high school
didn't encourage me to go to college. I would skip classes and wouldn't get in
trouble. They didn't care." Carmen adds more details to this often repeated
story: "My counselors never placed me in chemistry or biology as they did
students who were headed to college. They let them take those classes, but
when they gave me my schedule for the following semester those classes
were nowhere to be seen. I didn't know I could request them. I was satisfied
with what they gave me."

Alicia believes, as her observation highlights, that beyond a simple lack of
interest, discrimination was the direct result of racism. "In high school, they
would put some students in wood shop classes and the other white students
would take classes to prepare for college. A lot of Mexican students were

never taken out of ESL, even when they could do well in regular classes. Some teachers treated me good because I guess they liked me. Some treated me bad probably because I was Mexican. They thought I was inferior to the white kids, that I didn't have the capacities that they have." Luis provided a glimpse of the effects that racism has on a child: "In school they let you know that the culture here is superior, so you start feeling bad about your identity. When I was in fourth grade, I was embarrassed to speak Spanish." José was also deeply affected by racism, but he was able to overcome its negative emotional effects: "I sensed that whites feel superior. It doesn't bother me now because I know it's not true."

Reaction to Perceived Discrimination

Some of these youths reacted to perceived discrimination by trying to assimilate and "acting white," which Alicia defines as acting like Americans by people who feel embarrassed of who they are and where they come from. These youths wanted to dress with the same styles as their classmates. They participated in school sports and listened to their peers' music. However, through time, these strategies left them unsatisfied, and they went back to socializing with other *mexicanos*, listening to Latino music, and enjoying Mexican food.

Enrique was especially articulate regarding his experiences with perceived racism and his coping strategies. He says,

> I remember the first two or three years, I faced a lot of discrimination and hostility from people because I'm Mexican. There was a time when I really tried to assimilate, tried to hang out with white kids. The kids that were born here used to get different treatment than me. I tried to "act white" so I could blend in better, so I could be seen as one of them and not as a Mexican. But then I realized that that was not the way to go and nowadays I don't care. I grew more mature and got more educated.

He added,

> I remember hearing my parents and other people talking about racism and how white people didn't like us because we are brown and Mexican. Every time I felt that people didn't like me or treated me bad, I always thought that it was racism, that they were being discriminatory because I was Mexican. You have to prove yourself everyday. Just because I'm Mexican doesn't mean that you are better than me because you are white. If you are better than me it's because you are better than me, not because you are white.

The effects of discrimination can be wearing according to Carmen: "In school I always feel that I have to prove myself to my teachers. I have to make an extra effort to get the same grade or even a lower grade. I always have to spend a lot of personal energy in order to not lose control when I am being treated badly, and this is true of all Mexicans."

The testimony of our interviewees strongly suggests that racism and discrimination in the public schools either push students out of school or create a glass ceiling that makes college almost inaccessible to them. In Juan's words, "In school we could talk to teachers but they didn't believe in us. The only teacher that supported me was my ESL teacher, but I didn't believe her because none of my peers were going to college, so I just worried about finishing high school. In high school I didn't learn things that would help me find a job, just English."

Family Support

Despite the repeated narrative of lack of institutional support, all of our informants eventually made their way to Oregon State University, received degrees, and have successfully integrated themselves into Oregon communities. Crucial to their achievements has been the unwavering support of parents, siblings, and extended family. If there were intergenerational acculturation conflicts in their lives, as amply documented in immigrant family studies, these young people certainly did not dwell on them. José's statement speaks to his parent's backing: "My parents lived for us. They had jobs that paid very little but what they earned was for us. 'We are doing this for you guys,' my parents used to tell us." Alicia also talked about parental support and the values they passed on to her: "My parents always supported me. They told me to be an honest person, be respectful, to appreciate everything that I have, and not to take things for granted." In these youthful memories, parents helped with homework and made themselves available, although they did not get involved in school activities—in part because of job schedules, and also because these parents would not know how to participate. They, nonetheless, stood behind their children. "My mother supported me as much as she could," said Carmen. "She found me skirts for dances, helped me find the paperwork that I needed."

We did find one instance that pointed to intergenerational conflict. In this case, Marta referred to her parents as being "severe." Despite the numerous restrictions she faced, Marta was able to attain some significant accomplishments, and she is proud of the fact that she did so without realizing her parents' greatest fear. While not devaluing her achievements, her parents were particularly pleased that getting a college degree did not undermine their familial values: "My parents didn't let me go out with friends; I couldn't spend the night or play at somebody's home. They were very strict. My parents changed when I was in high school because I noticed that they were overprotective." She added:

> *My parents told me to go to school and get married with a Christian, not to go away with a boyfriend. If you do that, my dad said, I'm not going to recognize you anymore; you would be dead to me. You have to have a Christian wedding in white, be a good wife, and have children. I'm proud that I didn't go with my boyfriends. All my girlfriends from high school dropped out and now have children, and are living with their boyfriends. My parents are proud that I graduated from high school and I'm in college, but they are proudest because I didn't go out with a boyfriend.*

Family support notwithstanding, it was not always easy to stay in high school and complete a diploma. Several of our informants talked about older siblings who dropped out of high school because of what they describe as lack of incentive and encouragement from the teachers. Juan gave an account of an older brother who had a family of his own and was trapped in low-wage jobs because he didn't finish high school: "My brother regrets that he didn't continue his education in college, but now he has two children and it's a little late. He didn't understand what he was missing when he dropped out of school."

If one takes into account the role of human capital as an important factor in the integration of immigrants in their new host cultures, as Portes and Rumbaut (2001) have postulated, it makes sense that older children, especially those who are actually counted as part of the first generation, will have experiences more akin to those of their parents. The fact that they are already at the threshold of adulthood and have formed their identities in Mexico may have made it difficult for them to adapt to the socializing process of public schooling. Given the cultural tenets of familism, older children are sure to feel the burden of responsibility to a greater degree than younger siblings (Partida 1996; López and Stanton-Salazar 2001). The limited human capital of the parents may act as a pressure point on older children, pushing them to enter the workforce in order to help sustain the rest of the family. Thus, they leave school and, like their parents, enter the low-wage labor sector. However, as they acquire new skills and have broader experiences maneuvering in the real world, they bring additional human capital and, of course, wages into the home. They are then able to direct this human capital, particularly in terms of advice and moral support, toward the advancement of younger members of the family. Marta sums this process up when she says, "My brothers didn't go to college so I could go." The decisions of older siblings, then, may be viewed as a sacrifice necessary for the achievement of the one-and-a-half and second generation.

Getting to College

As we have gathered from our interviewees, the public school system in Oregon was not particularly helpful in getting these young people to the university. We heard repeated stories of curricular tracking, segregation in ESL classes, and teacher and counselor indifference. Occasionally a caring soul intervened. Carmen, for example, related the following story:

> *I was able to attend college because in my last year of high school a counselor who said that I was too involved with Hispanics—I was queen for the Cinco de Mayo celebration, I did Mexican folklore dancing to keep our traditions alive, I tried to represent Mexican culture—that counselor asked me: "Carmen, what do you want to do with your life?" I told her that I wanted to be a doctor and she told me, but do you realize that for that you need all these classes and lots of math? I told her I didn't know. She got me an application for Oregon State University. When the recruiters came to our school they told me that I lacked three math classes to complete the minimum requirements for admission. I took what I lacked that same year. Had that counselor not spoken to me when I still had a year to go, I would not have been accepted to the university.*

The issue of undocumented immigration status is seen by some of our interviewees as the biggest barrier to a college education. Marta faced this situation: "I didn't put effort in high school because I didn't have [immigration] documents. I didn't do well in school. I wasn't academically prepared to enter college. I just wanted to pass school because I thought that it would be the end. After I graduated from high school I took one year off while waiting for my permanent residency." She became a permanent resident after she graduated from high school and "insisted that my father make us permanent residents so I could go to college and apply for financial aid. I had to wait one year after graduating from high school because my immigration papers were 'in transition.' My father couldn't legalize my older brother because he was twenty-one and *la migra* [immigration officers] took him while he was working in the fields."

We cannot stress enough the issue of civil status (Chávez 1992b). Without documentation, this cohort of informants, who were brought to this country at a young age and who received much of their schooling here, would simply not have had access to college, and their prospects for integration in Oregon communities would have been severely limited. Legal status together with family encouragement and support, even when families lacked the actual means to pay, were crucial to the success of these students. It is interesting that the two youth who came to Oregon with their single mothers both went on to college. José recalled: "My mom always encouraged me to go to college. Right after high school, college was attached, no doubts. Nobody helped me with the application process to Oregon State University." Ricardo sums up in simple but poignant words the role played by his mother in his journey to college: "My mother motivated me to go to the university. She knows it will help me better our lives; that is her legacy."

College Life

The journey to college was a difficult one. Families could contribute very little, but given that all the young men and women in our sample had legal status, they were able to receive financial aid in the form of grants and loans. However, information regarding financial aid was scarce; the youth in this group learned of financial aid from friends rather than college counselors. Alicia was one such case: "My father wanted me to go to college, but there was no information given to Mexicans about coming to college. I didn't know about financial aid. A friend told me to ask for applications and financial aid."

These students found college extremely challenging on a number of fronts. Susana summed up her initial reactions: "It's really difficult for us to be the first in the family to go to college. We have to learn English, learn the American way of how professors expect you to behave and do in school. You have to deal with everyday discrimination and prejudice." The young women in our sample were all single at the time of the interview, and remained so throughout their college experience. Three of the young men started families while in college, so their trajectory was made even more difficult. Another interviewee was forced to drop out after the first quarter, but he returned a year later. He told his counselors, "I am going to return after helping my family because my parents were ejected from their apartment and I had to help them. But I realized that if I continued working as a plumber with my father, I would be a plumber all my life, and I didn't like that."

The college experience changed the lives of all the interviewees. They appreciated the support received from a number of academic support mechanisms such as the Migrant Education Program, the Minority Education Office, and the Education Opportunity Program. In addition, the university's El Centro Cultural César Chávez, served as "a home away from home" for many students. There are also several student groups that provide social networking, events, and activities that keep students tied to the *mexicano* community. Several of these young men and women joined MEChA (Movimiento Estudiantil Chicano de Aztlán)—an organization whose primary mission is to serve the *mexicano* and Chicano communities and to create college access for these students—and report having been transformed by their membership. "I have changed so much in one year at the university," said Marta; "the way I think, the people I know. I'm changing. I have the support of my Mexican friends. I'm involved in MEChA and a dance group."

Danzantes *at* Festival Artístico y Cultural, *Oregon State University, 2008. Photo by Rocío Acosta-González.*

One-and-a-half generation *mexicanos* in college still experience barriers to their success. These students mentioned the following: a) poor language skills and insufficient academics that hadn't prepared them for college work; b) limited self-esteem—they didn't think that they were going to succeed; c) financial pressures; and c) lack of understanding of how the college system works—for example, they didn't know that they could talk to the professors if a subject turned out to be too difficult. However, they were all able to connect with other students like themselves and create strong bonds and a sense of community. Friends thus replaced family in college as the primary support mechanism, and together they were able to form strong identities as members of an ethnic minority within the university setting.

Identity Formation

Most of these youth identified as *mexicanos* before enrolling at OSU, and all continued to identify strongly as Mexican. Many took classes in Chicano history and culture, Spanish for native speakers, and Mexican history. This expanded knowledge base contributed to the process of fine tuning their identities. Those who became politicized through MEChA took on a "Chicano" identity, though they still laid strong claim to their *mexicano* identities. Juan's testimony bears this out: "I'm strong Chicano and also *mexicano*. I learned about Chicanos in college. At home I learned that I'm *mexicano*. Hispanic doesn't say anything about our indigenous past. Latino refers to the European heritage, like Italians."

María talks about the choices she makes with regard to identity labels: "When I arrived here I identified as *mexicana*. I had never heard the word Hispanic; I would write Mexican in the "other" category. Hispanic, Latino, Mexican American are labels I don't use. *Chicana*, I use sometimes, but not when applying for a job." These comments demonstrate that as their knowledge base expanded, the issue of ethnic identity became more nuanced.

Language is an important aspect of their identity. While all are fluent and literate in English, they are also fluent in spoken Spanish, and they are quite comfortable using that language. In fact, Spanish was the predominant language of the interviews, suggesting that when speaking about their personal lives, they prefer their native language. The maintenance of Spanish is crucial to their ability to maintain close ties to their families and kinship networks.

Their one-and-a-half identity also bears visible transnational traces nurtured by frequent visits to family and friends in Mexico. After becoming legal permanent residents, most of the interviewees have returned to Mexico to visit relatives. These visits to the homeland strengthened ties with the extended family, but they also underscore the differences between the country of origin and the host country. For example, Alicia said: "When I went back to my town in Michoacán, I saw it very different from what I remember it. There were more paved streets. I didn't feel like I belonged." Roberto recalled several visits to Tijuana, Chiapas, and Guadalajara. He said: "I visited my grandparents in Guadalajara. It's a beautiful place, but it's deserted by the effects of the migration to the U.S. There are no people there, but you can tell that there were people before."

Their *mexicano* identities notwithstanding, it is clear to these youths that their place is now in Oregon. Roberto makes this clear when he says: "I always say that I'm Mexican, although now I belong more to this country."

María finds life in Mexico more appealing in many ways, yet she prefers life in Oregon:

> *I like life here because there are more luxuries. Money buys more here. You can buy a car, but not be happy. Here, you don't see Mexican traditions. There are no Christmas parties or posadas (Mexican style Christmas carols). Punch just doesn't taste the same! Here, families live apart, very individual. In Mexico, even if you don't have as many luxuries, you live an emotionally happier life because you are with your family and there is always someone there who will help you. Here it is materialistic, and Mexico is more community oriented.*

Enrique's identity might be described as quintessentially transnational, in that he sees himself as belonging to two nation-states: "My alliance is with Mexico because you can't take back what you are. I have more alliance with my country of origin even though I don't live there anymore and I have lost some cultural values. But on the other hand, I do have alliance towards this country because I've grown into it and I've learned the system, and I've learned that this is probably the place where I'm going to spend the rest of my life. So I definitely do have alliance towards this country."

Goals for the Future

Looking ahead to the future, most of the interviewees saw themselves settled in Oregon, married with children, with a good steady job, and in touch with other Mexicans. José said: "I want my main community to be my people so I may pretend that I'm in Mexico." They are looking forward to careers in education, health, or starting up their own business. They are confident that the Latino community will continue to grow in Oregon. As Enrique said: "I know that eventually the Latino population of this place is going to grow and will be more diverse, so I won't have to choose whether I want to live with Mexicans or not." However, regardless of where they choose to live, they all expressed the desire to serve or benefit other immigrants in the state. For example, Marta said: "I look forward to studying something that could help me work with the community."

Commentary on the Experience of the One-and-a-Half Generation

Members of this generation in our sample have several shared characteristics. Most come from stable two-parent families with high levels of labor force participation. The members of our interviewees' families pulled together to achieve collective economic goals, and contributed to the household income in moments of economic distress. For example, the older children helped their parents in agricultural jobs, translated for them, and looked after younger siblings. While in college, they also worked in the fields or in other temporary jobs during the summers. These Mexican youth arrived in Oregon speaking only their native language then progressively became bilingual in English, but Spanish continues to be an important aspect of their identity. Their younger siblings, who arrived in Oregon at less than five years of age, have gradually lost the propensity to speak the native language—linking the experiences of these foreign-born small children with that of the U.S.-born second generation.

Oregon State University students receiving Manuel Pacheco Scholarship Award, 2009. Photo by San Juana Acosta.

The foreign-born parents of these youth entered the country as undocumented farmworkers. Later they were able to obtain permanent residency for them and their families. Most of these adult *mexicanos* have only a few years of schooling and little or no knowledge of English. They are socially defined as nonwhite, though race is for them a source of confusion and ambivalence (Lopez and Stanton-Salazar 2001). They inherit the burden of Mexican "color." Their children recall experiences of perceived structural discrimination—notably in school by peers, teachers, and staff. Rumbaut (1994) points out that coming to grips with discrimination and prejudice is more psychologically damaging for adolescents than for young children. Strong families and community support can shield these youths, but when the available support comes from oppositional peer groups rather than families, the result can be rejection of schooling, church, and parental goals. These youth spoke about older siblings and *mexicano* friends who dropped out of school and adopted disaffected attitudes that are part of dissonant acculturation. Nevertheless, while they acknowledge discrimination, the one-and-a-half generation youth do not attribute all their challenges to racism. Educational aspirations and expectations, as well as the role of significant relations and others in shaping these orientations, are predictors of attainment in adulthood. The immigrant parents of these youth have explicit educational expectations for their children that do not differ by gender. Studies have shown that, relative to the children of U.S.-born parents, the children of foreign-born immigrants have higher educational expectations (Kao and Tienda 1998).

Their college experience undoubtedly contributed to increased options regarding identity formation, as these youths see themselves as both Americans and Mexicans. Their position points directly to the category labeled "selective acculturation" in Portes and Rumbaut's model. The college experience of this group gave them a co-ethnic community of educated Mexican Americans that provided support and enhancement of self-esteem.

The portion of their academic experience that contributed to cultural and historical self-knowledge (i.e., Chicano/a and Latino/a studies) also played an important role in shoring up their identities. Although they were exposed to potentially "adversarial" ways of interpreting U.S. society, the strong and positive *mexicano* identity nurtured by their families protected them. In short, this cohort has been able to choose the best from two cultures to thus enable themselves to claim a role in Oregon communities. This process has also provided these youth with a strong commitment to serving and advocating on behalf of other immigrants. Susana's words sum up this connection to community: "I would like to live here—not in Mexico—because my family is here. I have relatives in Mexico there but I have more security here. I feel that I don't belong anymore. The experiences of my relatives in Mexico have been different from mine. I have more passion to fight against injustice here."

1. A version of this article was published, with the collaboration of Dwaine Plaza, in the *Latino(a) Research Review* 6:1-2 (2006-2007).

2. Although two males were actually born in Los Angeles, California, and taken back to Tijuana, Mexico, shortly after birth, given their life experiences, we have included their stories.

3. All interviews were conducted by José Luis Torres in 2001.

Testimonio

by Edith Quiroz Molina

This testimonio *consists of excerpts taken from an essay commissioned by the authors for a book on 1.5 and second generation immigrants. When she wrote this, Edith was directing a bilingual employment agency she and her husband founded in Portland after their graduation from Oregon State University. The excerpts were selected and arranged by the authors.*

The night was clear and peaceful and it was about one or two o'clock in the morning. My mom, my older brothers, and I had been awake for the last thirty minutes. My mother was very nervous. She had awakened us as we were arriving, saying, "*Ay, Dios mío! Aquí vamos.* Here we go. Evodio, Israel, Edith *levéntensen rápido!* We are about to cross the border. *Qué Dios nos ayude!*" she exclaimed and began to pray. My three other siblings kept on sleeping. We looked out curiously through the small windows of the camper and could see and hear my dad talking to the uniformed immigration officers. They would be the first white people I would see in real life.

My father proceeded to show his green card to the immigration officer. "OK, what do you have in the back of the truck?" the officer asked my father. "Just my wife and my kids, sir," replied my confident father in broken English. "OK, open it up, we have to check it," demanded the officer. "But they are sleeping, sir," responded my father. "It doesn't matter. Wake them up. It will only take a couple of minutes," the officer ordered as he moved quickly to the back of the truck.

My father advanced to open the camper and the officer stood right beside him. It must have been a very impressive scene, because his face looked amazed when the door opened and he saw my nervous, frightened-looking mother. She must have looked like the image of the Virgin Mary, slender with fair skin, carrying a baby in her arms wrapped with a *chal* and surrounded by five other little ones, all of us rubbing our eyes and wondering why this tall person with big blue eyes and blond hair was studying us under the beam of a large flashlight. "Get them out. We need to check the inside," he ordered. My father looked at him, confused and reluctant to follow the order. It was very cold. The officer quickly stated that it would only take a couple of minutes. My mother covered her baby's head with her *chal* and promptly got out with the help of my father, who held her hand, and then one by one he helped all his children out. Immediately after, one of the officers went inside and checked around, then a dog was thrown inside to check as well. The dog sniffed our stuff and I guess he didn't find anything other than our smelly socks, because he got out rapidly. The officer looked at all of us, one by one, as we stood in a straight line, shaking from the cold, still rubbing our eyes trying slowly to wake up.

He must have felt pity and compassion for my parents, because he instantly informed my father that the search was over and to bring us all back inside the truck before we caught a cold. As soon as I lay down close to my mother, I fell sleep and did not wake up until the sun rose again in the mountains of Arizona. My father stopped at a rest area so we could use the bathroom. Our beat-up truck had made it to the other side. We had made it to the United States of America. That was it. That's how I entered this country. This experience is unique and very different from those of most of my friends or of the majority of Mexicans who cross the border daily, exposing their lives to danger and death. I had a positive experience crossing the border, which is why I never felt like an illegal immigrant when I was going through high school.

I was born in Mexico City and was raised there until my eleventh birthday. I have only happy memories of my childhood, but I barely remember the city, its cars, its stores, neighborhood, parks and schools. Now at age eighteen, I was fully developed into a young woman, I had a job, I spoke two languages, learned and practiced new traditions, had friends who did not speak my native language, who did not eat tortillas everyday, played many sports, and who had so much more freedom than me.

My father wanted to instill in me the Mexican and Christian way to be a *señorita*, and all I wanted was to be a regular teenager like my friends in school. Throughout my teen years my father and I could not find a balance, a compromise in this struggle, so we fought. He gave orders, I disobeyed. He imposed rules, I broke them. He constrained, I escaped. He felt angry and hopeless and I felt sad and full of despair, torn between my father's expectations and my own wants.

Then I decided to go to college, and I knew I had to persuade my father to let me go. Either way, I would be going, with or without his permission. I briefly explained to my father the papers in front of him and pleaded for his signature. He ended up signing some papers. Some, I had to signed myself just so that I would get them in on time. When this process was over, it was a done deal. I sat through a long sermon, and a request that I go to the local community college, because I was too young to leave home, and it was not proper for a *señorita* to live alone so far away. But once I read my congratulations and admittance letter to him when it arrived by mail, he conceded.

The day I left for college my father was happy and very proud. He was about to go and leave his older daughter at a U.S. university, not at a job, and not pregnant at a man's house. That has always been his biggest fear, that one of his four daughters would become pregnant out of wedlock at a young age; that would be the biggest disappointment and a disgrace to the family.

Six years later, armed with a liberated mind, solid foundation of activism, great academic knowledge, personal experiences, and family support, I am moving forward to accomplish my dreams and aspirations. It has never been easy and it never will. Oregon is my home, Mexico my birthplace. Spanish is my first language, English my second, but Spanglish my modus operandi. My father is and will always be my hero in spite of his machismo. My mother is and will always be my strength. My spouse and siblings, my motivation. The Creator, my guiding light.

Testimonio

by Ricardo Larios

This testimonio *is the product of an essay commissioned by the authors for a book on 1.5 and second generation immigrants. Ricardo had just recently graduated from Oregon State University when he wrote the piece and was studying for his Masters degree at Willamette University in Salem, where he currently is a public school teacher. The essay appears as written by Ricardo.*

I sit here typing. At last count, my best words per minute was thirty-four. I can even type without looking at the keyboard. I glance at my hands: they are a walnut color on the backside and chalk white on the other. They are soft with no visible blemishes. They tell the story of another generation, the transition my parents have always dreamed of. My father, Cipriano, sometimes known as "Sip" in English-speaking circles, comes from a different place, a different time. His hands have not had the same experience as mine. If you were to shake his hands, you would immediately detect the sandpaper quality of his palms. From a distance, his fists reveal a rock-like appearance with ridges cut long ago into the flesh. On his right hand, the tip of his middle finger resembles an awkward seven. A table saw and my father's middle finger met for a brief and painful moment; bone, cartilage, and skin were no match for the 300 rpm blade. There was no money for doctors, and I imagine his pride prevented from visiting the *médico* as well. "Sip's" inflexible and determined demeanor matches the description of his caramel-colored hands that I imagine were once soft and tender like mine. They starkly contrast with the smoke black remote as he flips through his sixty-five-plus channels of cable on his thirty-two-inch color TV. With the expansion of media, through networks like Univision, Telemundo, and now Telefutura there is no shortage of visual connection to the homeland.

The word homeland conjures a metaphorical womb that engendered, cared for, and colored the existence of Cipriano Larios. However, my existence would not be possible without the literal womb of my mother, Socorro, once mispronounced as Soraco by a secretary calling to remind my mother of a pending dentist appointment. At her *panadería*, she is simply known as Doña Coco. A survey of her hands reveals a honey glaze pigment. Her nails are expertly taken care of by the Korean nail technicians at Nails Now, whenever her busy schedule permits. On special occasions, fancy jewelry adorns her fingers and wrists. My mother's grasp is visionary. Her palms are soft but firm. They weren't always like this, however. When she opened her bakery, the seventeen-hour shifts took a toll on her hands. The skin of her hands looked like wrinkled silk from washing so many dishes. Her nail polish was spotty at best. There was no room for jewelry because there were neither special occasions nor the financial ability to obtain them. Underneath the hardened epidermis stood the strength to steer an entire family, a business, and a king-like husband.

It is this union of hands, in marriage, in faith, that allow me to sit here and type, the comfort to sit here and type. Twelve years ago a computer in the Larios household would only exist in mail-order catalogs. Twenty-five years ago the Larios household consisted of a single-bedroom house. The front door was the only entrance and exit to the humble home. My grandmother, Chuy, tells me with her root-shaped hands that the floor was cement with a light blue hue. The walls were brick, adorned only with calendars from local businesses and religious icons. It only had one bedroom. The living room and the kitchen were separated by a makeshift wall made out of a curtain strung on a wire. In the far edge, as far away as possible, stood an outhouse made of cardboard and scraps of wood. To wash clothes or the dishes, my family, just like everybody else, relied on a *pila*, a rectangular-shaped open water-storage tank. Running water was and is a luxury in this little *pueblo*. Conservation is key as the water arrives every third day. Built right into the cement structure is a washboard. Many hands have gone down this path, washing clothes, washing babies, and washing dishes.

I say twenty-five years because I am twenty-four. I never experienced the reality of my parents or grandparents. Only my three older siblings, Chinto, Susy, and Coco played in the house on the famous *loma* or hill. They were born in Coalcomán, Michoacán, Mexico. You won't find this town in your local travel agency catalog. It is like a neglected stepchild, forgotten in favor of the modern capitals. The nearest town going east or west is at least an hour and half away. The capital city of Morelia is an eight-hour bus ride. Mexico City, for the majority of Coalcomanenses, exists only by word of mouth. For me however, Coalcomán is a mythical place and is just as important as our nation's capital or even Mexico's. I can remember my parents and relatives speaking so highly of it, dreaming of returning, never realizing that they could not return. I could never quite understand why they had to leave it. Why did they have to leave if it was such a great place? Why was I born in Toppenish, Washington, and my older brothers and sisters born more than three thousand miles away, three thousand cultures away, three thousand differences away? Why did they get a green card and I didn't? Why was it I did feel different when I went to Washington Elementary School in Sunnyside, Washington? I could only throw my hands up in frustration.

These questions motivated me to graduate from high school and I took them to college. They fueled my desire to understand and re-search myself and family and how we fit into the larger American society. These questions formed a bulwark as I engaged my *Norte*, my journey to and through college. Although I didn't have to be smuggled in a Volkswagen van like my mom and six-month-old sister Coco or have to cross the Otay Mesa near Tijuana like my father, I did encounter my difficulties in what can be considered an alien environment.

I can still remember the day when Ms. Buckle, the high-school career liaison, asked who was planning on attending college. The hands of my classmates shot up like missiles, hitting their intended targets with chilling precision. Most of the hands were a chalk or pale color. I thought to myself, "College is only for white people." I had no intention of going nor could I even imagine myself a college student. The only reason I attended school was to escape. As a small child I remember waking up before the sun spoke to us in the morning, following my parents on the orchard circuit in Central Washington. Years later, I can still remember the day my dad handed me a half-inch size Craftsman wrench and explained to me that I was going to be his new helper. I was only in the second grade. From that day on, my weekday afternoons and Saturdays (Sunday was our day off) were spent, along with my older brother, in our garage helping my dad repair cars in his makeshift auto-repair shop. I dreaded going home because I knew that the steel half-inch size Craftsman wrench was waiting for me. My other classmates in grade school had no such responsibilities; they went home and played. As I sat through Ms. Buckle's lessons I would stare at her face intently. With all the makeup she wore, she might as well have been a clown. This lecture was a joke. The mathematical equation Ricardo plus college was not equal to success. Besides, no one in my family had even graduated from high school—my older brother dropped out in the tenth grade; my sisters didn't make it past their freshman year.

School was my escape. As the twentieth century came to a close, so did high school. I had made it this far, albeit with poor attendance and even poorer grades. I looked at my hands. There was dirt, sugar, and despair under my fingernails. The Larios family, entrepreneurial at its soul, had opened their very own bakery. It was a family affair, everyone contributed. After school, instead of a half-inch size Craftsman wrench waiting for me, there were some tongs and a cash register. I dreaded going to the *panadería*. My family had worked very hard. My mom especially endured hardships that I will never comprehend. The vows to the family were greater than my distaste as a grocery clerk. A popular bumper sticker that you can see on various cars in Salem reads, "North Salem's Tassel is worth the Hassle." I was excited as I would soon be a proud owner of the coveted symbol conveying the message: High school graduate, non-deviant. A cousin near Modesto, California, and another in Woodburn, Oregon, would also share the same feeling: we did it. Our families' hands applauded in unison. The flight of our tassels was for them as much as it was for us. A crossroad in my yellow brick road was approaching. School or work, at least this was the ultimatum given by my dad. Although honorable, the work of a mechanic or grocery clerk, I could not continue with the day-to-day drudgery. I adopted the latter part of my dad's ultimatum. School would have to do, school was my escape. I decided that college was not only for white people but also for people who looked like me. I had tricked myself; Ms. Buckle wasn't the clown, I was.

So the next phase of my journey had begun. The open door policy of the community college was the only option available and I embraced it. Like many migrants who dream of coming to *el norte*, the idea that I had of college was of a nebulous universe many light years away. I did not know where to begin, only that I had to go north. A compass inside of me born of previous migrant experiences guided me. Everything from parking permits to financing to learning where the bathrooms were was a complete learning experience. Luckily, there would be guiding hands, angel hands. The traveling had made me hungry; the excitement over the journey had muted my growling stomach.

Tenía hambre, I was hungry. My cultural soul lacked adequate nourishment from years of malnutrition. I was given food that did not align with my foreign palette. Shakespeare, Emerson, Melville, Poe were marvelous foods in their own contexts, but I simply wasn't part of that landscape. This hunger persisted until I came across a size ten font description in the course catalog. It read, "Chicano/a Latino/a Studies, Wednesdays 5-9 p.m." The instructor's name read "Rasca." It didn't overwhelmingly sound "Latino" but I matriculated anyway. That first Wednesday there were over sixty students. The desks were arranged in a circular fashion. A few minutes after five, a short man with spectacles and a tweed jacket walked in. He spent the first ten minutes greeting us with a humble, "Hello, how are you? I am Leo Rasca-Hidalgo." We had two texts that quarter, Rodolfo Acuña's *Occupied America* and our life experiences. Like a volcano, my excitement was erupting. It was like walking into a buffet, after years of living on scraps. Every morsel was devoured, the plate licked clean. I lived for every Wednesday; it became the highlight of the week, the highlight of learning. A teacher from the heart, Dr. Leo never gave us the answers, he only asked questions. He took us on a path of introspection, examining our cultural souls. Like a long-lost jigsaw puzzle piece, we begin to see how we fit into the larger American picture. Learning from an alternative perspective ignited the fire that had long been extinguished by material that I could not relate to. Community college would not do; I would have to pursue learning at the next level. For the next seven quarters, I found myself reaching for new educational heights. I stopped clowning around like I did in high school and dedicated my heart and soul to learning. I vowed never to be hungry again.

By this time my hands had grown confident. They were able to maneuver deftly at the junior college level. My mother's hands had regained some of their silky texture. Her days were not as long and on sunny days they would shine intently. My father's hands remained the same. They still reflect a tough and unbreakable façade. Change for some people just doesn't happen, but what didn't was the support and commitment of my family to see me succeed. My mother's hands covered my eyes and ears to limit the distractions. Like a giant sponge she absorbed the *preocupaciones*, the worries, and hid them very well under her motherly mask. She worried for me, for all of us.

The burden that my mother's hands carried allowed me to be successful. They freed up my own walnut-colored hands to pursue the university. In January of 2003, my hands knocked on the office of Dr. Gonzales-Berry, the chair of the Ethnic Studies Department at Oregon State University. Her warm *Hola* and soft-speaking hands made me feel right at home. A quick survey of her office revealed a miniature library. There was even a book with her name on it. My hands began trembling. It was at that moment that I knew I was in the right place... .

We live in a country that prides itself on being able to use our very own hands to lift ourselves up. Yet this very story contradicts this belief, for without other people's hands to lift me up I would not be here.

Conclusion

In the early 2000s the statistical trends that described Oregon's population growth confirmed the clearly visible presence of Mexican workers and their families in workplaces, at the shopping malls, in the public schools, and around the playgrounds in the city parks. Those statistics moved the state to the top fifteen among states that have become "new immigrant destinations." Oregon had been a favored destination for *tejano* and *mexicano* farmworkers for much of the twentieth century—a receiving area for Mexican-origin sojourners and settlers that in some sense resembled a Southwestern state. Current population numbers show that during the 1990s Mexican migration became mainly an urban phenomenon. Portland, Salem-Keizer, and Eugene-Springfield metropolitan areas exerted a pull on immigrants with high human capital and also on workers with less education and training (Hardwick 2008; Singer 2008).

In the first chapters of this book we have underscored the deep roots of *mexicano* settlement in the state, beginning with the pioneers and sojourners in the mid-1800s. These were mule packers who entered Oregon's territory across the Siskiyou Mountains and reached the Rogue Valley, and also *vaqueros* who worked in the ranches of Eastern Oregon's high desert. Many other *mexicanos* have been employed on farms and ranches since then. By the 1930s, more than fifteen hundred farm laborers were sending money orders from Oregon to their families in Mexico. Those laborers were scattered around the state, but most resided in Malheur County, in Hood River, and across the Willamette Valley. The early settlers remained out of sight and out of mind of local reporters and historians—their presence was only occasionally mentioned in newspapers and contemporary accounts. The Bracero Program was to bring a good deal of publicity to migrant workers during World War II. In the post-*bracero* era, agricultural workers continued arriving in Oregon with their well-adjusted system of circular migration to the Pacific Northwest until it was interrupted by IRCA, the Immigration Reform and Control Act of 1986. But even after IRCA, much of the seasonal migration flow remained in place, as recorded in the data of the Mexican Immigration Project analyzed by Fairchild and Simpson (2004). Since the late 1980s, there has been a continuous "spill over" of *mexicano* laborers to jobs in production, construction, and service industries in adjacent urban areas, while other workers and families moved directly to Oregon's cities in search of employment opportunities that were unavailable in already saturated traditional immigrant gateways.

The economic boom that produced Oregon's Silicon Forest created labor shortages in industrial and service occupations. First- and second-generation *mexicanos* moved promptly to fill many of those low-wage entry-level jobs. In applying for and obtaining such positions, these workers benefited from the co-occurrence of two factors: (a) employers in these "new economy" firms that relocated or opened subsidiaries in Oregon were by then accustomed to hiring ethnic workers for low-wage positions, something many employers were doing in traditional inner-city locations such as Los Angeles, Houston, New York, or Chicago; and (b) a number of Mexican Americans were already employed in the secondary sector of Oregon's urban labor markets. These employees provided referrals to both employers and job seekers. The process was also facilitated by the very efficient local networks that agricultural laborers had developed to fulfill the growers' demand for a seasonal workforce. According to network theory,[1] during the 1990s high rent and low wages in traditional immigrant gateways saturated the capacity of social networks to support new arrivals—who typically have low English proficiency and limited formal education—and redirected migrants to places considered new destinations. This theory explains why people originating from one migrant-sending place, such as the Mexican states of Michoacán or Oaxaca, continue to select the same destinations over time, and why migratory streams sometimes carry on after the initial push and pull may have ended; this impulse to migrate from Mexico to the same destinations in the United States is known as cumulative causation.

Thus our discussion in this book emphasizes historicization of the settlement of *mexicanos* in Oregon without neglecting the transnational phenomena and social networks that explain their migration (Waldinger 2008). At the time of widespread economic distress in Mexico—called a "crisis" by Mexican nationals—Oregon's networks supplied information, helped finance trips, provided temporary housing, and assisted newcomers in obtaining jobs not only in agriculture and forestry, but equally important, in light manufacturing, construction, and a variety of services that catered to growing and more affluent urban populations. A wide range of individuals participated in those migration networks, including labor recruiters and contractors, immigration lawyers, auto salesmen, and money-sending agents. Migration networks made possible the arrival of many families from the Mexican states of Michoacán, Oaxaca, Jalisco, Guerrero, and Guanajuato. Other first- and second-generation *mexicanos* moved here from California, Illinois, Texas, and Florida. The majority settled in cities and metropolitan areas in the Willamette Valley, while yet other *mexicanos*, many of indigenous descent, filled out agricultural jobs vacated by those immigrant families who had moved to the cities in search of new jobs, better schools, affordable housing, and urban amenities.

The flux of new immigrants to Portland, Salem, Eugene, and Medford increased to levels that surprised even second- and third-generation Oregonians of Mexican descent who had already developed a sense of belonging and ownership in those places.

Carmen Villegas, a third-generation Mexican American born in Salem, Oregon, in 1976 gave us a vivid account of her memories while she was growing up in a mixed neighborhood of Northeast Portland. Very few Mexican families of working-class backgrounds resided in Portland in the 1980s. Carmen remembered her surprise at seeing for the first time other Mexican laborers in the agricultural fields of suburban Portland in the mid-1980s. She said:

> *After we moved from Salem, our first home in Portland was located on the edge of what people in those parts of town would call the "hood." I guess that is because there was a large African American population there. In school I learned that it used to be against the law to live in Oregon if you were non-white. Blacks, Mexicans, and Asians were not welcomed, and Native Americans were living on the reservations. It was not until World War II that Portland as a major port faced a labor shortage, and the government made provisions for minorities in an area called Vanport—today we call this area Delta Park/ Hayden Meadows. This was a little city within the city, where minorities could reside. Then one day the U.S Army Corps of Engineers was building something along the Columbia River and that project flooded all the people out of Vanport. That is how my neighborhood, located near Vanport, became densely populated with a large ethnic minority population. Now our neighborhood is going through a new change called gentrification. Since all the houses are old and built with old-growth wood that is no longer on the market, our homes ... homes no one wanted before ... are worth sometimes a half million dollars or more. Those of us who grew up there cannot even rent what were once considered slum apartments because those apartments are now condominiums. The reason I tell this part of the story is to let people know the kind of racial and class dynamics I was facing as a young chicana. There were no other Latinos, mexicanos or anybody remotely "Hispanic" in those days, in those parts. What I learned about race and class through the black and white lens is that most other cultures were only referred to as people of the past or*

people from some exotic faraway place. I always thought the only time
we would see other Mexicans was when we would go to California.
But there was this one time, I remember it well, for that was the first
time I had seen mexicanos *in Oregon. When I was still in elementary*
school, my mom decided that we needed some extra cash, so she and
I went to pick strawberries. We drove out by Troutdale. When I was a
child there were many fields out there, growing fruits and vegetables.
Most of those fields are now gone, covered by urban sprawl. Anyways,
when we arrived there what I saw made me curious. Where did those
people come from? I mean, we would always see blacks and whites,
but Mexicans? I thought my dad was the only one. In school, it was
always black and white. In the middle school there were even more
black students than in the elementary school, but I never minded
that. My father felt more comfortable with the black community than
with the whites. As I got older, the Mexican and Latino population
has grown throughout Oregon. The awareness of our peoples' presence
here has also made me more aware of my own cultural background
(interview with Mendoza, 2008).

The foreign-born and native-born alike are often the subjects of unfavorable stereotyping in interactions with other (non-Mexican) Oregonians. Frequently if a person speaks with an accent and "looks Mexican," it is assumed that that person is an undocumented immigrant worker with low skills. In short, possession of one of those characteristics facilitates the stereotyping of first- and second-generation Oregonians. Many Oregonians of Mexican descent are at a loss when they witness such stereotyping and discrimination. For example, a third-generation *mexicana* born in Nyssa told us: "I have friends of different backgrounds, some of my friends do not want Mexicans here; they say that this is not their country, and I don't know how to respond to that."

Racialization and Exclusion

In Oregon, and elsewhere in the country, *mexicanos* are positioned in a uniquely American racialized hierarchy that is generally accepted as natural and contributes to creating and also perpetuating minority status. Second- and even third-generation *mexicanos* may find themselves interpolated in this hierarchy regardless of whether or not they have experienced discrimination. Such discrimination has an effect on the possibilities for economic and social integration of immigrants of Mexican origin. Although the effects of prejudice and stereotyping vary across individual dimensions such as education, occupation, English-language proficiency, residential isolation, legal immigration status, and the strength of a person's ethnic identity, we propose that it continues to affect Mexican Americans in Oregon even in the third generation, particularly those—maybe precisely those—who, because of the pervasive effect of the combination of factors cited above, have not been able to overcome the educational achievement gap.

Clara Galvan shared with us an account of her first encounter with a racialized hierarchy that made her feel disenfranchised in rural Oregon. This foundational event has remained in her memories for more than thirty years. Clara moved from Grants Pass to Springfield and continued her education, graduating with a Masters degree in Sociology from the University of Oregon. She later became an advocate for Latinas who are victims of domestic abuse. Clara told us the following:

> I was born in Mexico in 1941 but grew up in East Los Angeles. I met my first husband in California; he was not Hispanic. He decided to move our family to Grants Pass, Oregon, in 1970. In those days, Grants Pass was a small city; the area was called "rural." There were very few people of Latino, African American, or Asian ancestry. There was much discrimination [towards minorities] at that time. For example, if a black person moved to town, this person would not stay because there was [a group called] "tar and feathers." Do you know what it means? This is when white people do as the KKK group does. They would cover someone's skin with tar—which is sticky and black—and fix white feathers on this person's body. They would take the person from where this person was ... his home, any place and make him feel very bad; they mistreated the person in ways that I don't even want to think about. The day I arrived in Grants Pass, only two hours had passed and I was outside with my son, who was two years old at that time. I saw a white man standing on a slope. I was watching over my child and my husband was talking to the men who were helping us moving our stuff. I saw that this white man was coming directly towards me and I asked myself: "What does he want? Why is he coming towards me?" Because I felt that he had an intense and focused attitude coming directly towards where I was. This man came in front of me and said—it's very difficult for me to reproduce what he said then. He said: "Don't you ever be out by yourself, especially at night." At that moment I had fear, I started to tremble and almost could not breathe. My husband saw the man and came where we were [a little agitated]. "What do you want?" said my husband. "What do you do talking to my wife? What do you want?" Then this man said: "Your wife ... what is she? Is she Indian? Is she

Klamath Falls Indian?" My husband replied: "No, she is not. Why?
What difference does it make what she is?" The white man did not tell
my husband what he had said to me but I could understand enough
English as to realize that I was in danger in that place. I thought
to myself: "¿A dónde llegué? What is this place?" (interview with
Mendoza, 2008).

We argue that Oregon's unwelcoming history with Native Americans and
minority groups paired to the growers' reliance on the labor of seasonal
farmworkers—who often come from impoverished communities and speak
very little English—has prolonged the viability of a social hierarchy in which
mexicanos are considered inferior and perceived as outsiders. In the fall of
2008, Oregon Ballot Measure 58 called for "English immersion" rather than
ESL instruction in public schools. This measure was defeated, but voters
in Columbia County approved Ballot Measure 5-190 that sets penalties for
employers in the county who knowingly or intentionally hire unauthorized
aliens—an initiative measure modeled on Arizona's restrictive Legal Arizona
Workers Act (Wosniacka 2008). With initiatives like these, Oregonians
attempted to control the perceived consequences of an unprecedented
increase in the number of undocumented workers, and also in the number
of children who speak a language other than English at home—according
to statistics produced by the Oregon Department of Education, the large
majority of English language learners in public schools are native speakers
of Spanish.[2]

The current social and political climate in our state has been yet another
incentive to write this book about *mexicanos* in Oregon because we strongly
believe that the ways of the society permeate and inform the work of our
schools, social service agencies, churches, and workplaces—particularly
in a region that has been called "one of the last Caucasian bastions in
the United States." Thus we set out to solicit oral accounts of *tejanos* and
mexicanos, and to study the history and character of Mexican migration
in Oregon with renewed strength. In doing this work, we have identified
several recurring themes intertwined in the stories and lives of *mexicanos*
that serve as windows through which to view their immigrant experience.
Some of the main themes that appear throughout the book are reviewed in
this conclusion.

Social Issues in Oregon's Mexicano Communities

Sustained demand for seasonal agricultural labor by Oregon growers paired
with economic development in metropolitan areas continues to cause the
arrival and settlement of a large number of *mexicanos*. However since many

workers do not have work permits to be employed in the United States, their legal status (or lack thereof) becomes a sign of social exclusion and a stigma. These *mexicanos* find employment in agriculture, and in off seasons they are also employed in a variety of unskilled, entry-level occupations—they are typically young and arrive in Oregon alone or with their families, many start families in our state. After a time, the migrants settle and their children develop a sense of belonging to this beautiful land—almost as deep as their parents' remembrances of Mexico. Other migrant families who have been displaced by economic hardship in traditional gateways such as California, Texas, Florida, or Illinois come to Oregon attracted by the prospect of finding low-skilled jobs in construction and the service industries. Although some have friends and family already settled in communities across our state, many others come to the Pacific Northwest to try their luck.

Uninterrupted migration flows through the twentieth century have lead to the settlement of repeated first generations both in rural and urban areas, which makes the Mexican case quite unlike the experience of Oregonians of European descent who were the majority of immigrants settling in the state during the previous century. The sustained presence of the foreign-born contributes to the viability and endurance of Spanish, leading members of the host culture to believe that *mexicanos* do not wish to learn English, when the opposite is quite true.

The continuing arrival of the foreign-born also contributes to the proliferation of families whose members have mixed immigration status— that is some family members are legal permanent residents, others are American-born, and yet others have an undocumented status; mixed legal status goes hand in hand with mixed generations—some family members are first generation, others are first-and-a-half, others are second- and even third-generation Americans of Mexican descent. To understand the complexities of intergenerational integration of *mexicano* families in Oregon it is important to disentangle the individual legal status of family members (which becomes a stigma and a sign of social exclusion) from their position in the generational order.

The conflation of these workers' low-wage employment and presumed undocumented status produces assumptions and stereotypes that result in what scholars call an "ethnic penalty." These stereotypes may interfere with the treatment and evaluation of *mexicanos*. Assumptions about immigration status, education, and workplace experience are often used to guide people's interactions with the most recent immigrants. Its adverse effects may penalize even the second generation, as if they were not fully American.

A number of Oregonians who self-identify as *mexicanos* now occupy positions in the public sector, as educators and administrators interested in improving the achievement gap in public schools, and as business people (for example, many are members of the Portland's Hispanic Metropolitan Chamber). All contribute to develop a homegrown entrepreneurial middle-class of Mexican origin. These Oregonians are making slow progress as elected and appointed officials (Basson and Conrad 2002). Oregonians of Mexican descent in this educated sector of the middle-class are well aware of the stereotyping and prejudice experienced by the foreign-born workers in low-skilled occupations. Hence they are in a position to advocate for the rights of Latinos regardless of their status as citizens, permanent residents, or "undocumented" individuals.

Oregonians who self-identify as *mexicanos* generally keep strong family ties and enjoy the support of family members.[3] The children of immigrant mothers and fathers often mention the unrestricted support of their parents and siblings as one of the main reasons for their achievements. However the migration of men and women (alone or in families) is a gendered process that inevitably produces changes in gender roles that affect family dynamics, interpersonal relations between husband and wife, and also relations among parents and children. Moreover, men are usually breadwinners but women provide migratory social capital for men (usually husbands), who may access the labor market through their in-laws. In "new urban destinations" where migratory social capital is less commonly available to newcomers, women's networks become ever more important to survive and thrive in

Immigrant rights march, Salem, 2009. Photo by Gwyn Fisher.

the new place.[4] Their children, second-generation Oregonians of Mexican descent raised in mixed-status immigrant families, generally express the interpersonal attachment and bonding created by family ties through social trust and compassionate awareness for the situation of *mexicano* communities throughout the state. Even among supportive immigrant families, unrelenting low socio-economic status may lead to poor educational outcomes and other disadvantages affecting the second- and third-generation Oregonians of Mexican descent—these are social conditions which, if allowed to continue without intervention, may get reproduced across subsequent generations of Mexican Americans.

Compared to their immigrant parents, some one-and-a-half and second-generation *mexicanos* in Oregon seem to integrate at least as rapidly as the second-generation descendants of European immigrants did in the past. A marker pointing to this trend is the considerable reduction in the dropout rate of Latino students in Oregon's public schools during the last ten years. But not all *mexicano* youth are able to succeed. Particularly in the largest urban areas of our state some of these youth appear to be experiencing downward assimilation. Their foreign-born parents expect them to behave as if they were living in Mexico, and they are not taught the skills necessary to thrive in the United States. Likewise, low levels of schooling have kept *mexicanos* in rural areas and small towns concentrated in the working class or in low-level white-collar occupations well into the third generation.

Intergenerational Dynamics among Oregonians of Mexican Descent

The visible presence of newcomers in Oregon's metropolitan areas feeds the distorted perception that *mexicanos* are like other immigrant populations although with unique characteristics such as being younger, less educated, and more linguistically isolated than Oregonians in other population groups. Widespread lack of information on the depth of Mexican settlement in the state creates a blind spot for service providers and policy makers. Such a blind spot may impair their understanding of the intergenerational dynamics among Oregonians of Mexican descent, and may weaken their ability to grasp its consequences for the social integration of the newcomers. Oregonians of Mexican descent include the children of *tejano* and *mexicano* farmworkers who began to settle as early as the 1930s, and also *mexicanos* who arrived just a year ago. In the last fifteen years, some of these Oregonians of Mexican descent (who may be three or more generations removed from migration) intermarried, worked together, interacted, and shared a common ethnic identity with the foreign-born. Yet others dissociated themselves from

Mexican people who brought what they felt was an inferior culture, and adopted patronizing attitudes towards immigrant workers. In our research, we interviewed Mexican Americans like Carmen Villegas, for whom the presence of foreign-born Mexicans strengthened her own ethnic identity. We also encountered seasonal farmworkers who despised Oregonians of Mexican descent, and expressed the same views as the migrants interviewed by Chávez et al. in Idaho: "The ones who are born here [Mexican Americans] feel superior and treat us like dirt" (2006, 1025).

Usually older *mexicanos* who have spent more time in the United States, learned English, completed high school, and intend to remain here permanently would show greater trust in Mexican Americans and in other Americans as well; while recent immigrants situated both at the bottom and at the top of the occupational ladder, the less educated and the professionals— who may encounter isolation, prejudice, and discrimination as most immigrants do— are more prone to express mistrust towards Americans, and dissatisfaction with their life in the United States (Massey and Akresh 2006). Indigenous heritage adds another layer to the intergenerational dynamics among Oregonians of Mexican descent. *Mexicanos* who are members of semi-autonomous indigenous communities and speak their native language are likely to encounter double discrimination, both from their co-nationals and from other Oregonians.

Integrating Oregonians of Mexican Descent

When we asked recent immigrants to name the three most important things that they would request from the American government if they could, our interviewees mentioned instruction in English as a second language, scholarships to earn a GED or an associate degree at a local community college, and the possibility to apply for permanent residency in the United States—accessing a driver's license was often associated and/or included with legal residency. Researchers have documented that *mexicanos* who recently migrated to "new destinations" such as Oregon are generally more educated than those who settled in traditional immigrant gateways (Stamps and Bohon 2006). These new immigrants understand that education is the principal avenue to a middle-class lifestyle. Generally they would encourage their American-born children to pursue a post-secondary education to transition out of the low-wage, low-skill employment held by their parents. However, few of these youth are able to access a college education. While Latinos are the fastest-growing population group in Oregon, they enroll the least in four-year colleges (Kelly 2008). Poor economic and educational opportunities exclude many Oregonians of Mexican descent from successful integration.

Moreover, those who do not have legal resident status must pay out-of-state tuition, even if they graduate from Oregon public schools, and they are not eligible for financial aid.

It is of outmost importance for our state to invest in the upcoming generation of Latino youth, so these youth will be prepared to fully participate in the civic and social life of the places where they live. Children now being born to Mexican parents will begin having children of their own in about twenty years. At that point the largest component of Oregon's Mexican-origin population would be U.S. born. "Growing a new base of middle-class taxpayers is closely related to building a skilled workforce," argued Dowell Myers (2007, 214); "Both hinge on the crucial matter of educational attainment." Analyzing demographic and economic data on California, Myers argued for a new social contract across generations and age groups to help young Latinos be prepared to shoulder the burden of an aging boomer generation. Although the profile of our state's population differs from that of California, we advocate for intergenerational support as well, in particular as it relates to access to public and post-secondary education. This, we believe, is a question not only of equity and social justice but also an important economic consideration in the development and retention of the workforce of our state. Moreover, it is a quality-of-life consideration connected to the willingness of all Oregon residents, those whose parents arrived in last decade or in the past century alike, to become engaged in the civic life of our communities.

---

1. Migration scholars use network theory to explain movement of peoples. This theory can explicate international migration, and also the dispersion of Mexicans outside U.S. locations with high concentrations of immigrants.

2. Oregon school districts enrolled 67,815 students in English language development programs in 2007. In only a few of those districts, however, half of the students reached proficiency and exited the programs; those in the rest of the districts fared worse (Oregon Department of Education 2008).

3. "The Hispanic community still has strong family ties and that's what is getting them through," reported Farquhar and Michael (2004, 446) in research designed to address social capital among Latinos and African Americans in Portland.

4. The role of women in Mexican migration to "new destinations" has been mentioned in passim by Henández-León (2008). We have documented it in the stories of our interviewees.

Works Cited

Newspapers:

El Chavista
El Relámpago
The East Oregonian
Farm Labor News Notes
The Herald
Hood River News
Independence Enterprise
Lincoln City News Guard
Mail Tribune
Monmouth Herald
The Oregon Journal
The Oregon Statesman
The Oregonian
The News Guard
North West Farm News
The Rural Tribune
The Salem Statesman
The Sonoran News

Books and Articles:

Abbot, Carl. 2001. *Greater Portland: Urban Life and Landscapes in the Pacific Northwest.* Philadelphia: University of Pennsylvania Press.

Acevedo, Dolores, and Thomas J. Espenshade. 1992. Implications of the North American Free Trade Agreement for Mexican Migration into the United States. *Population and Development Review* 18 (4):729-44.

Acuña, Rodolfo. 2004. *Occupied America: A History of Chicanos.* Fifth ed. New York: Pearson and Longman.

Aguilera, Michael, Bob Bussel, and Lara Skinner. 2008. Work and Employment of Immigrants in Oregon. In *Understanding the Immigrant Experience in Oregon*, edited by B. Bussel. Eugene: Labor Education and Research Center, University of Oregon.

Akdenizli, Banu, Es. Dionne, Jr., Martin Kaplin, Tom Rosentiel, Roberto Suro. 2008. Democracy in the Age of New Media. Washington:

Brookings Institution and Norman Lear Center. Available from http://www.brookings.edu/~/media/Files/rc/reports/2008/0925_ immigration_dionne/0925_immigration_dionne.pdf.

Alvarez, Kizette, and John Broder. 2006. More and More, Women Risk All to Enter U.S. *The New York Times,* January 10, 2006.

American Federation of Labor and Congress of Industrial Organizations. 2005. *Immigrant Workers at Risk: The Urgent Need for Improved Safety and Health Policies and Programs.* Washington, D.C.: American Federation of Labor and Congress of Industrial Organizations

American G.I. Forum and Texas State Federation of Labor. 1953. *What Price Wetbacks?* Austin: American G.I. Forum and Texas State Federation of Labor.

Andreas, Peter. 1998. The U.S. Immigration Control Offensive: Constructing an Image of Order on the Southwest Border. In *Crossings: Mexican Immigration in Interdisciplinary Perspectives,* edited by M. M. Suárez-Orozco. Cambridge, Massachusetts: Harvard University Press.

Andrews, Tracy J., Vickie D. Ybarra, and Teresa Miramontes. 2002. Negotiating Survival: Undocumented Mexican Immigrant Women in the Pacific Norwest. *The Social Science Journal* 39:431-49.

Audley, John, Demetrios Papademetriou, Sandra Polaski, and Scott Vaughan. 2004. *NAFTA's Promise and Reality: Lessons from Mexico for the Hemisphere.* Carnegie Endowment for International Peace Report. Available from http://www.carnegieendowment.org/publications/ index.cfm?fa=view&id=1390.

Ayre, Art. 2006. Unauthorized Immigrants Working in Oregon. *Employment Department News and Information.* Salem: Oregon Employment Department.

Aysa, María, and Douglas S. Massey. 2004. Wives Left Behind: The Labor Market Behavior of Women in Migrant Communities. In *Crossing the Border: Research from the Mexican Migration Project,* edited by J. Durand and D. S. Massey. New York: Russell Sage Foundation.

Bacon, David. 2008. *Illegal People: How Globalization Creates Migration and Criminalizes Immigrants.* Boston: Beacon Press.

Baksys, Gerry. 2006. Tough Working Trip. *Klamath Falls Herald and News,* October 10.

Balderrama, Francisco E., and Raymond Rodriguez. 1995. *Decade of Betrayal: Mexican Repatriation in the 1930s.* Albuquerque: University of New Mexico Press.

Basson, Bradley, and Rita Conrad. 2002. Elected and Appointed Officials in Oregon: A Report on Race, Ethnicity, and Gender Parity. *Oregon Progress Board.* Available from http://egov.oregon.gov/DAS/OPB/ docs/Parity/Offic02.pdf.

Batalova, Jeanne, and Michael Fix. 2008. *Uneven Progress, the Employment Pathways of Skilled Immigrants in the United States.* Washington D.C.: Migration Policy Institute.

Bates, David, and Katie Wilson. 2005. World Wars Shaped Farmworker Policy. *News Register* (Yamhill Valley, OR), April 23.

Beals, Herbert K. 1995. Spanish Explorers in the Oregon County. In *Nosotros: The Hispanic People of Oregon,* edited by Erasmo Gamboa and Carolyn M. Baun. Portland: Oregon Council for the Humanities.

Bean, Frank D., and Gillian Stevens. 2003. *American's Newcomers and the Dynamics of Diversity.* New York: Russell Sage Foundation.

Boehan, Deborah. 2004. *Gendered Migrations: Shifting Gender Subjectivities in a Transnational Mexican Community.* San Diego: The Center for Comparative Immigration Studies, University of California San Diego.

Boswell, Malcolm G. 2003. A Micro Analysis of Rockwood. *Oregon Labor Market Information System.* Gresham: Oregon Employment Department.

Boswell, Malcolm. 2004. Hispanic-owned Business in Oregon. *Oregon Labor Market Information System.* Salem: Oregon Employment Department.

Boyd, Bob. 1995. Vaqueros on the High Desert Rangeland. In *Nosotros: The Hispanic People of Oregon* edited by Erasmo Gamboa and Carolyn M. Buan. Portland: Oregon Council for the Humanities.

Bracero Archives. n. d. Oregon State University Historical Archives.

Brier, Jonathan, and Ramón Ramírez with Robert Dash. 1998. The State of Immigrants' Rights in Oregon: Backlash Against Latinos from September 1995 to January 1997. Unpublished manuscript prepared by CAUSA. Salem, OR.

Brier, Jonathan, and Alicia Niles. 1998. *Immigrant Labor and Guest Workers in Oregon: Case Study and Policy Context for the H-2A Guestworker Program.* Salem, OR: CAUSA.

Brimelow, Peter. 1995. *Alien Nation. Common Sense About America's Immigration Disaster.* New York: Random House.

Burke, Anita. 2009a. Neo-Nazi Group Based in Phoenix. *Mail Tribune* (Southern Oregon), April 22.

Burke, Anita. 2009b. Taking a Stand against Hate. *Mail Tribune* (Southern Oregon), May 2.

Burr, Chris. 2001. Deaths on the Border, Illegal Immigration and the Impact of Operation Gatekeeper. Working Paper. *JEEPERS* (Fall 2001).

Calavita, Kitty. 1992. *Inside the State: The Bracero Program, Immigration, and the I.N.S .* New York and London: Routledge.

Cardoso, Lawrence, and Arthur F. Corwin. 1979. Labor Emigration to the Southwest, 1916 to 1920: Mexican Attitudes and Policy. In *Mexican*

Workers in the United States: Historical and Political Perspectives, edited by G. C. Kiser and M. W. Kiser. Albuquerque: University of New Mexico Press.

Carroll, Daniel, Ruth M. Samardick, Scott Bernard, Susan Gabbard, and Trish Hernandez. 2005. *Findings from the National Agricultural Workers Survey (NAWS) 2001-2002: A Demographic and Economic Profile of United States Farmworkers*. Burlingame, CA: Aguirre International. Available from http://www.doleta.gov/agworker/report9/naws_rpt9.pdf.

Carter, Stephen. 2007. One in Six Students is Latino. *The Oregonian*, September 1.

Catanzarite, Lisa, and Michael B. Aguilera. 2002. Working with Co-ethnics: Earning Penalties for Latino Immigrants at Latino Jobsites. *Social Problems* 49 (1):101-27.

Cerrutti, Marcela, and Douglas S. Massey. 2004. Trends in Mexican Migration to the United States, 1965 to 1995. In *Crossing The Border: Research from the Mexican Migration Project*, edited by J. Durand and D. S. Massey. New York: Russell Sage Foundation.

Chang, Grace. 2000. *Disposable Domestics: Immigrant Women Workers in the Global Economy*. Cambridge, MA: South End Press.

Chavez, Leo R. 1992a. Paradise at a Cost: The Incorporation of Undocumented Mexican Immigrants into a Local-level Labor Market. In *U.S.-Mexico Relations: Labor Market Interdependence*, edited by J. A. Bustamante, Clark W. Reynolds, and Raul A. Hinojosa Ojeda. Stanford, CA: Stanford University Press.

Chavez, Leo R. 1992b. *Shadowed Lives: Undocumented Immigrants in American Society*. Fort Worth, TX: Harcourt.

Chávez, Maria L., Brian Wampler, and Ross E. Buckhart. 2006. Left Out: Trust and Social Capital Among Seasonal Farmworkers. *Social Science Quarterly* 85 (5):1012-29.

Chicano Literary Group. 2000. *Our Words: Writing by the Chicano Literary Group, A Project of the PEN American Center Readers and Writers Program*. Independence, OR: Milpa Press.

Chirquiar, Daniel. 2005. *Globalization, Regional Wage Differentials and the Stolper-Samuelson Theorem: Evidence from Mexico*. Dallas, TX: Federal Reserve Bank of Dallas.

Clifford, Elizabeth, Susan C. Pearce, and Reena Tandon. 2005. Two Steps Forward? Reinventing US Immigration Policy for Women. Paper presented at Eighth International Women's Policy Research Conference, June 2005. Available from http://www.iwpr.org/PDF/05_Proceedings/Clifford_Elizabeth.pdf.

Compean, Mario. 2008. Mexican Americans in the Columbian River Basin: Historical Overview. Columbia River Basin Ethnic History Archive. Oregon Historical Research Library, http://www.vancouver.wsu.edu/crbeha/ma/index.htm.

Cornelius, Wayne A. 1978. *Mexican Migration to the United States: Causes, Consequences, and the U.S. Responses.* Cambridge, MA: Center for International Studies, Massachusetts Institute for Technology.

Cornelius, Wayne A. 1990. Impacts of the 1986 U.S. Immigration Law on Emigration from Rural Mexican Sending Communities. In *Undocumented Migration to the United States: IRCA and the Experiences of the 1980's,* edited by F. D. Bean, B. Edmonston, and J. S. Passel. Santa Monica, CA: Rand Corp. and Washington D.C.: Urban Institute Press.

Cornelius, Wayne A. 1992. From Sojourners to Settlers: The Changing Profile of Mexican Immigration to the United States. In *U.S.-Mexico Relations: Labor Market Interdependence,* edited by J. A. Bustamante, Clark W. Reynolds, and Raul A. Hinojosa Ojeda. Stanford, CA: Stanford University Press.

Cornelius, Wayne, Scott Borger, Adam Sawyer, David Keyes, Clare Appleby, Kristen Parks, Gabriel Lozada, and Jonathan Hicken. 2008. *Controlling Unauthorized Immigration from Mexico: The Failure of "Prevention through Deterrence" and the Need for Comprehensive Reform.* Washington, D.C.: Immigration Policy Center Available from http://www.immigrationforum.org/images/uploads/CCISbriefing061008.pdf.

Council for the Humanities Hispanic Oral History Project, 1992-1993. Oregon Historical Society Library. Portland.

Craig, Richard B. 1971. *The Bracero Program: Interest Groups and Foreign Policy.* Austin: University of Texas Press.

Crummett, María de los Angeles. 1993 Gender, Class, and Households: Migration Patterns in Aguascalientes, Mexico. In *Building with our Hands, Directions in Chicana Studies* edited by Adela De La Torre and Beatriz Pesquera. Berkeley: University of California Press.

Current, Tom, and Mark Martínez Infante. 1959. Final Report of the 1958-59 Migrant Farm Labor Studies in Oregon Including Material From the Preliminary Report of the Bureau of Labor Entitled "We Talked To the Migrants...and Migrant Problems Demand Attention." Salem: Oregon Bureau of Labor.

Cuthbert, Richard W., and Joe B. Stevens. 1980. Economic Incentives Facing Mexican Workers at Hood River, Oregon. In *Special Report*

567. Corvallis, Oregon: Agricultural Experiment Station, Oregon State University.

Dash, Robert. 1996. Mexican Labor and Oregon Agriculture: The Changing Terrain of Conflict. *Agriculture and Human Values* 13 (4):10-20.

Dash, Robert, and Robert E. Hawkinson. 2001. Mexicans and "Business as Usual": Small Town Politics in Oregon. *Aztlan: A Journal of Chicano Studies* 26 (2):87-121.

Diaz McConnell, Eileen. 2004. Latinos in the Rural Midwest: The Twentieth-Century Historical Context Leading to Contemporary Challenges. In *Apple Pie & Enchiladas: Latino Newcomers in the Rural Midwest*, edited by Ann V. Millard and Jorge Chapa. Austin: University of Texas Press.

Dodge-Vera, Tina, and Megan M. Patton-Lopez. 2008. *Las Comidas Latinas. Community Needs Assessment for Nutrition Education Programming*. Corvallis: Oregon State University Extension Services.

Donato, Katherine M., and Evelyn Patterson. 2004. Women and Men on the Move: Undocumented Border Crossing. In *Crossing the Border: Research from the Mexican Migration Project*, edited by Jorge Durand aand Douglas Massey. New York: Russell Sage Foundation.

Driscoll, Barbara. 1999. *The Tracks North: The Railroad Bracero Program of World War II*. Austin: University of Texas Press.

Duke, Lauren. 2008. Rule Could Impact Migrant Farm Workers. *The Bulletin* (Bend, OR), July 29.

Durán, Pilar. 2003. Children as Mediators for the Second Language Learning of their Migrant Parents. *Language and Education* 17 (5):311-31.

Durand, Jorge, and Douglas S. Massey, eds. 2004. *Crossing the Border: Research from the Mexican Migration Project*. New York: Russell Sage Foundation.

Durand, Jorge, Douglas S. Massey, and Chiara Capoferro. 2005. The New Geography of Mexican Immigration. In *New Destinations: Mexican Immigration in the United States*, edited by V. Zuniga and R. Hernández-Leon. New York: Russell Sage Foundations.

Elguezabal, Mary Ann Dority. n.d. Unpublished paper: Nyssa Public Library.

Fairchild, Stephen L., and Nicole B. Simpson. 2004. Mexican Migration to the United States. Pacific Northwest. *Population Research and Policy Review* 24 (3):219-34.

Farquahar, Stephanie A., and Yvonne L. Michael. 2004. *Poder es Salud/* Power for Health: An Application of the Community Health Worker

Model in Portland, Oregon. *Journal of Interprofessional Care* 18:445-47.

Farquhar, Stephanie, Nargess Shadbeth, Julie Samples, Santiago Ventura, and Nancy Goff. 2008a. Occupational Conditions and Well-Being of Indigenous Farmworkers. *American Journal of Public Health* 98 (11):1956-59.

Farquhar, Stephanie, Julie Samples, Santiago Ventura, Shelley Davis, Michelle Abernathy, Linda McCauley, Nancy Cuilwik, and Nargess Shadbeh. 2008b. Promoting the Occupational Health of Indigenous Farmworkers. *Journal of Immigrant and Minority Health* 10:269-80.

Farr, Marcia. 2006. *Rancheros in Chocagoacan: Language and Identity in a Transnational Community.* Austin: University of Texas Press.

Fernández, Roberto M., and Isabel Fernández Mateo. 2006. Networks, Race, and Hiring. *American Sociological Review* 71:42-71.

Ferrara, Pamela. 2006. Hard Work, Education Help Hispanics Advance in Oregon's Workforce. In *Oregon Labor Market Information System.* Salem: Oregon Employment Department.

Filsinger, Cara. 2004. Farmworker Labor. *Background Brief State of Oregon* 2 (1).

Flores, Elizabeth. 2004. Festejando Community: Celebrating Fiesta Mexicana in Woodburn, Oregon. In *Chicanas and Chicanos in Contemporary Society,* edited by R. M. De Anda. New York: Rowman & Littlefield Publishers, Inc.

Foerster, Robert F. 1925. *The Racial Problems Involved in Immigration from Latin America and the West Indies to the United States*: A Report Submitted to the Secretary of Labor. Washington, D.C.: G.P.O. Available from http://pds.lib.harvard.edu/pds/view/4905592?op=n&n=1&treeaction=expand.

Foley, Neil. 1997. Becoming Hispanic: Mexican Americans and the Faustian Pact with Whiteness. In *Reflexiones: New Directions in Mexican Americans Studies,* edited by N. Foley. Austin: University of Texas Press.

Frazier, Joseph B. 2006. Mexican Immigrants Who Speak Little English or Spanish Face Challenges. *El Hispanic News* (Portland, OR), September 21, pp. 4, 6.

Fry, Richard. 2006. *Gender and Migration.* Washington, D.C.: Pew Hispanic Center.

Fuller, Varden. 1953. No Work Today! In *Public Affairs Pamphlet* No. 190. New York: Public Affairs Committee, Inc.

Galarza, Ernesto. 1965. *Merchants of Labor: The Mexican Bracero Story.* Charlotte, California: McNally and Loftin Publishers.

Gamboa, Erasmo. 1990. *Mexican Labor and World War II: Braceros in the Pacific Northwest, 1942-1947*. Austin: University of Texas Press.

Gamboa, Erasmo. 1991. Mexican Mule Packers and Oregon's Second Regiment Mounted Volunteers, 1885-1856. *Oregon Historical Quarterly* 92 (Spring):41-59.

Gamboa, Erasmo. 1993. Oregon's Hispanic Heritage. In *Varieties of Hope: An Anthology of Oregon Prose*, edited by G. B. Dodds. Corvallis: Oregon State University Press.

Gamboa, Erasmo. 1995a. The Bracero Program. In *Nosotros: The Hispanic People of Oregon*, edited by Erasmo Gamboa and Carolyn M. Baun. Portland: Oregon Council for the Humanities.

Gamboa, Erasmo. 1995b. El Movimiento: Oregon's Mexican-American Civil Rights Movement. In *Nosotros: The Hispanic People of Oregon*, edited by Erasmo Gamboa and Carolyn M, Baun. Portland: Oregon Council for the Humanities.

Gamboa, Erasmo, and Carolyn M. Baun, eds. 1995. *Nosotros: The Hispanic People of Oregon: Essays and Recollections*. Portland: Oregon Council for the Humanities.

Gamio, Manuel. 1930. *Mexican Immigration to the United States*. Chicago: University of Chicago Press.

Garcia, Jerry. 2005a. Mexican and Japanese Labor in the Pacific Northwest, 1900-1945. In *Memory, Community and Activism: Mexican Migration and Labor in the Pacific Northwest*, edited by Jerry Garcia and Gilberto Garcia. East Lansing, Michigan: Julian Samora Research Institute.

Garcia, Jerry. 2005b. Beyond the Spanish Moment: Mexicans in the Pacific Northwest. In *Memory, Community, and Activism: Mexican Migration and Labor in the Pacific Northwest*, edited by Jerry Garcia and Gilberto Garcia. East Lansing, Michigan: Julian Samora Research Institute.

Garcia, Jerry, and Gilberto Garcia, eds. 2005. *Memory, Community, and Activism: Mexican Migration and Labor in the Pacific Northwest*. East Lansing, Michigan: Julian Samora Research Institute.

Garcia, Juan Rámon. 1980. *Operation Wetback: The Mass Deportation of Mexican Undocumented Workers in 1954*. Westport, CT: Greenwood Press.

Geoghegan, Michael, and Kari Koch. 2006. *Faces of Free Trade and Job Loss Confronting Oregon's Shifting Economy*. Portland: The Oregon Fair Trade Campaign's Oregon Stories Project. Available from http://www.citizenstrade.org/pdf2/Faces_of_Free_Trade.pdf.

Goldring, Luin. 1996. Gendered Memory: Construction of Rurality Among Mexican Transnational Migrants. In *Creating the Countryside: The*

Politics of Rural and Environmental Discourse, edited by E. Melanie Dupuis and Peter Vandergeest. Philadelphia, PA: Temple University Press.

Gómez-Quiñones, Juan. 1981. The Historical Context of Undocumented Mexican Immigration to the United States. In *Mexican Immigrant Workers in the U.S.*, edited by A. Rios-Bustamante. Los Angeles: UCLA Chicano Studies Research Center Publications.

Gonzalez, Juan. 2001. *Harvest of Empire: A History of Latinos in America.* New York: Penguin Group.

Gonzales-Berry, Erlinda, and David Maciel, eds. 2000. *The Contested Homeland: A Chicano History of New Mexico.* Albuquerque: University of New Mexico Press.

Gonzales-Berry, Erlinda, Marcela Mendoza, and Dwaine Plaza. 2006-2007. Segmented Assimilation and the One-and-a-Half Generation Mexican Youth in Oregon. *Latino(a) Research Review* 6 (1-2):94-118.

Gordon, M. M. 1964. *Assimilation in American Life: The Role of Race, Religion and National Origin.* New York: Oxford University Press.

Gouveia, Lourdes, Miguel A. Carranza, and Jasney Cogua. 2005. The Great Plains Migration: Mexicanos and Latinos in Nebraska. In *New Destinations: Mexican Immigration in the United States*, edited by V. Zuniga and R. Hernandez-Leon. New York: Russell Sage Foundation.

Griffin, Anna. 2008. Day Labor Center Opens. *The Oregonian* June 13. Available from http://blog.oregonlive.com/portlandcityhall/2008/06/day_laborer_center_opens.html.

Grussing, Jay D. 2007. *Predicting County-Level Food Security and Hunger in Oregon.* MA Thesis, Oregon State University, Corvallis.

Guerin-Gonzales, Camille. 1994. *Mexican Workers and American Dream: Immigration, Repatriation and California Farm Labor 1900-1939.* New Brunswick, NJ: Rutgers University Press.

Hancock, Tina. 2007. Sin Papeles: Undocumented Mexicanas in the Rural United States. *Affilia: Journal of Women and Social Work* 22 (2):175-84.

Hardwick, Susan. 2008. Toward a Suburban Immigrant Nation. In *Twenty-First Century Gateways, Immigrant Incorporation in Suburban America*, edited by S. H. Audrey Singer and Caroline B. Brettell. Washington, D.C: Brookings Institution Press.

Hardwick, Susan W., and Justyna Goworoska. 2008. Urban Immigration in Oregon: The City as Context. In *Understanding the Immigrant Experience in Oregon*, edited by R. Bussel. Eugene, OR: Labor Education and Research Center, University of Oregon.

Harvey, Thomas. 1998. The Changing Face of the Pacific Northwest. *Journal of the West* 37 (3):22-32.

Hernández-Coss, Raúl. 2004. *Lessons from the U.S.-Mexico Remittances Corridor on Shifting from Informal to Formal Transfer Systems.* Washington, D.C.: The World Bank.

Hernández-León, Rubén. 2008. *Metropolitan Migrants, the Migration of Urban Mexicans to the United States.* Berkeley: University of California Press.

Hinojosa-Ojeda, Raul, and Sherwin Robinson. 1992. Labor Issues in a North American Free Trade Area. In *North American Free Trade: Assessing the Impact,* edited by Barry P. Bosworth, Nora Lustig, and Robert Z. Lawrence. Washington, D.C.: The Brookings Institution Press.

Hirsch, Jennifer. 2003. *A Courtship after Marriage: Sexuality and Love in Mexican Transnational Families.* Berkeley, Los Angeles, London: University of California Press.

Hitchman, James H. 1990. *A Maritime History of the Pacific Coast, 1540-1980.* Lanham, MD: University Press of America.

Hondagneu-Sotelo, Pierrette. 1994. *Gendered Transitions: Mexican Experiences of Immigration.* Berkeley: University of California Press.

Hondagneu-Sotelo, Pierrette. 2002. Families on the Frontier: From Braceros in the Fields to Braceras in the Home. In *Latinos: Remaking America,* edited by M. Suárez-Orozco and Mariela Páez. Berkeley, Los Angeles and London: University of California Press and David Rockefeller Center for Latin American Studies, Harvard University.

Hondagneu-Sotelo, Pierrette. 2004. Gender and the Latino Experience in Late-Twentieth-Century America. In *The Colombia History of Latinos in the United States Since 1960,* edited by D. Gutiérrez. New York: Columbia University Press.

Hondagneu-Sotelo, Pierrette, and Ernestine Alvez. 1999. "I'm Here, but I'm There": The Meaning of Latina Transnational Motherhood. In *Gender and U.S. Immigration: Contemporary Trends,* edited by Pierrette Hondagneu-Sotelo. Berkeley: University California Press.

Ibarra, María de la Luz. 2003. Buscando la vida: Mexican Immigrant Women's Memories of Home, Yearning and Border Crossings. *Frontiers* 24 (2-3):261-81.

Jaeger, William K. 2008. *Potential Economic Impacts in Oregon of Implementing Proposed Department of Homeland Security "No Match" Immigration Rules.* Portland: Coalition for a Working Oregon. Available from http://www.nilc.org/immsemplymnt/SSA_Related_Info/Oregon-study.pdf.

Johnson, Ed. 2008. Nursery Owners: Rules No Match for East County. *The Gresham Outlook,* July 30.

Kandel, William A. 2004. A Profile of Mexican Workers in U.S. Agriculture. In *Crossing the Border: Research from the Mexican Migration Project,* edited by Jorge Durand and Douglas Massey. New York: Russell Sage Foundation.

Kandel, William, and Douglas S. Massey. 2002. The Culture of Mexican Migration: A Theoretical and Empirical Analysis. *Social Forces* 80 (3):981-1004.

Kao, Grace, and Marta Tienda 1998. Educational Aspirations of Minority Youth. *Journal of Education* 106 (3):349-84.

Kelly, Patrick J. 2008. *Beyond Social Justice, the Threat of Inequality to Workforce Development in the Western United States.* Boulder, CO: Western Interstate Commission for Higher Education.

Kiser, George C., and Martha Woody Kiser, eds. 1979. *Mexican Workers in the United States: Historical and Political Perspectives.* Albuquerque: University of New Mexico Press.

Kiser, George, and David Silverman. 1979. Mexican Repatriation during the Great Depression. In *Mexican Workers in the United States: Historical and Political Perspectives,* edited by George C. Kiser and Martha Woody Kiser. Albuquerque: University of New Mexico Press.

Kissam, Ed. 2008. *Migration and the Global Economy in Woodburn, Oregon: 2008.* Paper presented at the Conference on Immigration Reform: Implications for Farmers, Farmworkers, and Communities, University of California Davis.

Kretsedemas, Philip. 2008. Redefining "Race" in North America. *Current Sociology* 56(6):826-44.

Krissman, Fred. 2000. Immigrant Labor Recruitment: U.S. Agribusiness and Undocumented Migration from Mexico. In *Immigration Research for a New Century: Multidisciplinary Perspectives,* edited by Nancy Foner, Ruben G. Rumbaut, and Steven J. Gold. New York: Russell Sage Foundation.

Larson, Alice C. 2002. *Migrant and Seasonal Farmworker Enumeration Profiles Study.* Vashon Island, WA: Larson Assistance Services.

Latino Oral History Project. n.d. Independence Historical Museum, Independence, OR.

Latinos in Oregon Oral History Project. n.d. Oregon Historical Society Library, Portland.

Leonhardt, David. 2007. "Truth, Fiction and Lou Dobbs." *The New York Times,* May 30.

Libby, Tucker. 2007. Hispanic Fill Most New Construction Jobs in Oregon in '06. *Daily Journal of Commerce,* March 13.

Library Index. n.d. *Immigration Laws and Policies Since the 1980s: The Immigration Reform and Control Act of 1986*: Library Index.

Llana, Sara Miller. 2008. Mexicans in the United States Sending Fewer Dollars Home. *The Christian Science Monitor*, June 19.

López, David E., and Ricardo D. Stanton-Salazar 2001. Mexican Americans, a Second Generation at Risk. In *Ethnicities, Children of Immigrant America*, edited by Ruben G. Rumbaut and Alejandro Portes. Berkeley: University of California Press.

Loprinzi, Colleen Marie. 1991. *Hispanic Migrant Labor in Oregon, 1940-1990*. MA Thesis. Portland State University, Portland, OR.

Maldonado, Carlos. 2000. *Colegio Cesar Chavez, 1973-1982: A Chicano Struggle for Educational Self-determination*. New York: Garland Publishing Inc.

Maldonado, Carlos. 2005. Testimonio de un Tejano en Oregón: Contratista Julián Ruiz. In *Memory, Community, and Activism: Mexican Migration and Labor in the Pacific Northwest*, edited by Jerry Garcia and Gilberto Garcia. East Lansing, Michigan: Julian Samora Research Institute.

Maldonado, Marta Maria. 2009. "It Is Their Nature to Do Menial Labor": the Racialization of "Latino/a Workers" by Agricultural Employers. *Ethnic and Racial Studies* 32(6):1017-36.

Martin, Philip. 1993. *Trade and Migration: NAFTA and Agriculture*. Washington D.C.: Institute for International Economics.

Martínez, Charles R., Heather H. McClure, and J. Mark Eddy. 2008. Latino Immigrant Children and Families: Demographics, Challenges, and Promise. In *The Immigrant Experience in Oregon*, edited by R. Bussel. Eugene, OR: University of Oregon.

Martínez, Rubén. 2001. *Crossing Over: A Mexican Family on the Migrant Trail*. New York: Metropolitan Books.

Mason, Robert, Timothy Cross, and Carole Nuckton. 1993. *Agricultural Industries in Oregon: Nursery Crops, Christmas Trees, and Strawberries in the Willamette Valley and Pears in the Hood River Valley*. Corvallis: Oregon State University Agricultural Experiment Station.

Massey, Douglas. 1990. Social Structure, Household Strategies, and the Cumulative Causation of Migration. *Population Index*. Washington, D.C.: The World Bank.

Massey, Douglas S., Rafael Alarcón, Jorge Durand, and Humberto González. 1987. *Return to Aztlan: The Social Process of International Migration from Western Mexico*. Berkeley: University of California Press.

Massey, Douglas S., Jorge Durand, and Nolan J. Malone. 2002. *Beyond Smoke and Mirrors: Mexican Immigration in an Era of Economic Integration*. New York: Russell Sage Foundation.

Massey, Douglas S., and Ilana Redstone Akresh. 2006. Immigrant Intentions and Mobility in a Global Economy: The Attitudes and

Behavior of Recently Arrived U.S. Immigrants. *Social Science Quarterly* 87 (5):954-71.

Mathers, Hanna M. 2004. How do Oregon and Ohio Hispanic Nursery Workforces Differ? *Ornamental Plants Annual Reports and Research Reviews* 2003. Special Circular 193. Ohio State University. Available from http://ohioline.osu.edu/sc193/sc193_18.pdf.

Mattoo, Aaditya, Ileana Christina Neagu, and Çaglar Özden. 2005. Brain Waste? Educated Immigrants in the U.S. Labor Market. *World Bank Policy Research Working Paper* 3581. Washington, D.C.: The World Bank.

McCauley, Linda A., Marco Beltran, Jacki Phillips, Michael Lasarev, and Diana Sticker. 2001. The Oregon Migrant Farmworkers Community: An Evolving Model for Participatory Research. *Environmental Health Perspectives* (Supplement 3):449-55.

McCoy, Adam, Mudziviri Nziramasanga, and Jonathan Yoder. 2007. An Empirical Examination of the Factors Affecting Remittance by Mexican Migrants in the United States. Paper read at Annual Meeting of the American Agricultural Economics Association, Portland, OR, July 29-August 1, 2007.

McGlade, Michael S. 2002. Mexican Farm Labor Networks and Population Increase in the Pacific Northwest. *Yearbook of the Association of Pacific Coast Geographers* 64:28-54.

McGlade, Michael S., and Marie Dahlstrom. 2001. *Salir Adelante, A Needs and Assets Assessment of the Hispanic Community of Multnomah County*. Portland, OR: Multnomah County Department of Community and Family Services. Available from http://www2.co.multnomah.or.us/cfm/ourcommission/pdf/schoolpart/saliradelanted.pdf.

Mendoza, Marcela. 2009. Parenthood in a Foreign Land: Latino Mothers and Fathers Raising American Children in Bicultural and Bilingual Families. Paper presented at the Conference on Philosophical Inquiry into Pregnancy, Childbirth, and Mothering, Eugene, OR, May 14-16, 2009.

Michael, Yvonne L., Stephanie A. Farquhar, Noelle Wiggins, and Mandy K. Green. 2008. Finding from a Community-based Participatory Prevention Research Intervention Designed to Increase Social Capital in Latino and African American Communities. *Journal of Immigrant and Minority Health* 10:281-89.

Millard, Ann V., and Jorge Chapa. 2004. *Apple Pie and Enchiladas: Latino Newcomers in the Rural Midwest*. Austin: University of Texas Press.

Mines, Richard, Susan Gabbard, and Ruth Sanardiek. 1993. *U.S. Farmworkers in the Post-IRCA Period: Based on Data From the*

National Agricultural Workers Survey (NAWS). Office of Program Economics Research Report 4. Washington, D.C.: U.S. Department of Labor.

Montejano, David. 1987. *Anglos and Mexicans in the Making of Texas, 1836-1986*. Austin: University of Texas Press.

Morales, M. 1925. *Illustrated Catalog No.5 Hand Forged Bits, One-Piece Spurs*. Portland OR. [Reprint by Jeri J. Pitman Publisher, San Gabriel, CA, 1987].

Moreno-Brid, Juan Carlos, Jesus Santamaria, and Juan Carlos Rivas Valdivia. 2005. Industrialization and Economic Growth in Mexico after NAFTA: The Road Travelled. *Development and Change* 36 (6):1095-1119.

Moseley, Cassandra. 2006a. Ethnic Differences in Job Quality among Contract Forest Workers on Six National Forests. *Policy Sciences* 39:113-33.

Moseley, Cassandra. 2006b. Working Conditions in Labor-Intensive Forestry Jobs in Oregon. *EWP Working Paper* Number 14, Fall. Eugene: Ecosystem Workforce Program, University of Oregon.

Mulcahy, Joanne B. 2005. The Root and the Flower. *Journal of American Folklore* 118(486):45-53.

Myers, Dowell. 2007. *Immigrants and Boomers Forging a New Social Contract for the Future of America*. New York: Russell Sage Foundation.

Navas, Melissa. 2008. Undocumented Worker Ruling Could Rattle Oregon's Economy. *The Oregonian*, July 22.

Nelson, Leonard S. 1974. *Social Action as Social Change through a Process of Insulation*. MS Thesis, Portland State University, Portland, OR.

Nelson, Lise. 2007. Farmworker Housing and Spaces of Belonging in Woodburn. *Geographical Review* 97 (4):520-41.

Nelson, Lise, and Nancy Hiemstra. 2008. Latino Immigrants and the Renegotiation of Place and Belonging in Small Town America. *Social and Cultural Geography* 9(3):319-42.

Nevins, Joseph. 2002. *Operation Gatekeeper: The Rise of the "Illegal Alien" and the Making of the U.S.-Mexico Boundary*. New York: Routledge.

Nishihara, Janet 2007. Japanese Americans in Eastern Oregon: The Wartime Roots of an Unexpected Community. In *Seeing Color: Indigenous Peoples and Racialized Ethnic Minorities in Oregon*, edited by J. Xing, Erlinda Gonzales-Berry, Patti Sakurai, Robert Thompson, and Kurt Peters. Lanham, MD: University Press of America.

Nusz, Nancy, and Gabriella Ricciardi. 2003. *Our Ways: History and Culture*. Available from http://www.historycooperative.org/journals/ohq/104.1/nusz.html.

O'Connor, Pat. 2006. Occupations by Race in Oregon. *Oregon Labor Trends* June pp. 6-9. Available from http://www.olmis.org/pubs/olt/06/olt-0606.pdf.

O'Connor, Pat. 2008. Salem Metro Area's Construction Sector Paves Way for Job Growth. *Oregon Labor Market Information System.* Salem: Oregon Employment Department.

Ogden, Johanna. 2005. Race, Labor and Getting out the Harvest: The Bracero Program in World War II Hood River, Oregon. In *Memory, Community, and Activism: Mexican Migration and Labor in the Pacific Northwest,* edited by Jerry Garcia and Gilberto Garcia. East Lansing: Julian Samora Research Press.

Ong Hing, Bill. 2004. *Defining America through Immigration Policy.* Philadelphia, PA: Temple University Press.

Opinion Research Northwest. 2008. *Oregon Population Survey.* Seattle, WA. Available from www.oregon.gov/DAS/OPB/docs/PopSurv/2008ofs/OPS_2008_Presentation.pdf.

Oregon Bureau of Labor. 1958. *"Vámonos pa'l Norte" (Let's Go North): A Social Profile of the Spanish Speaking Migratory Farm Laborer.* Salem: Oregon Bureau of Labor.

Oregon Council of Churches. 1960. *Annual Report.* Portland: Department of Research and Survey, Oregon Council of Churches.

Oregon Council for the Humanities. 1992-1993. *Hispanics in Oregon Oral History Project.* Portland: Oregon Historical Society Library.

Oregon Department of Education. 2008. *State Issues Progress Report on English Language Proficiency in Oregon Schools News Release.* Available from http://www.ode.state.or.us/news/releases/?yr=0000&kw=&rid=674 .

Oregon Department of Education. 2008-2009. *Student Ethnicity Report.* Available from http://www.ode.state.or.us/sfda/reports/r0067Select2.asp.

Oregon Department of Human Services. 2007. *Vital Statistics Report,* Volume 1, Section 2, Table 2-8: Oregon Residents' Births by Ethnicity and Residence of the Mother. Salem: Center for Health Statistics.

Oregon Department of Human Services. 2008. *Demographic Characteristics by Mother's County, Race and Ethnicity, Oregon Residents 2005-2007.* Salem: Center for Health Statistics.

Oregon Interagency Committee on Migratory Labor. 1958. *Report of the Interagency Committee on Migratory Labor in Oregon.* Salem: Governor's Office, Oregon Interagency Committee on Migratory Labor.

Oregon Interagency Committee on Migratory Labor. 1966. *Report of the Interagency Committee on Migratory Labor for 1959-1961* (includes reports through 1966). Salem: Governor's Office, Oregon Interagency Committee on Migratory Labor.

Oregon Legislative Assembly Interim Committee on Migratory Labor. 1958 *Migratory Labor in Oregon*. Portland: Oregon Legislative Assembly Interim Committee on Migratory Labor.

Oregon Progress Board. 2009. *Oregon Population Survey 2008*. Salem: Department of Administrative Services. Available from http://www.oregon.gov/DAS/OPB/docs/PopSurv/2008OPS/OPS_2008_Presentation.pdf.

Oregon State Board of Health. 1971. *Annual Report Oregon Migrant Health Project 1964-65, 1968, 1961, 1970, 1971*. Portland: Oregon State Board of Health, Occupational Health Section.

Oregon University System Brief. 2009. *Educational Attainment in Oregon.* Available from http://www.ous.edu/about/legnote09/files/Sec7a7.pdf.

Orloff, Leslye. 2003. Women Immigrants and Domestic Violence. In *Women Immigrants in the United States*, edited by Philippa Strum and Danielle Tarantolo. Washington, D.C.: Woodrow International Center for Scholars.

Palmer, Susan. 2006. Immigrant Issues Key for Industry. *The Register-Guard*, March 31.

Parra-Cardona, José Rubén, Laurie A. Bulock, David R. Imig, Francisco A. Villaruel, and Steven J. Gold. 2006. *Trabajando Duro Todos Los Días*: Learning From the Life Experiences of Mexican-Origin Immigrant Families. *Family Relations* 55 (3):361-75.

Partida, Jorge. 1996. The Effects of Immigration on Children in the Mexican-American Community. *Child and Adolescent Social Work Journal* 15 (3):241-54.

Passell, Jeffrey S. 2005. *Estimates of the Size and Characteristics of the Undocumented Population*. Washington, D.C.: Pew Hispanic Center.

Peón, Máximo. 1966. *Como Viven los Mexicanos en los Estados Unidos.* Mexico D.F.: Costa-Amic.

Pérez, Ramón "Tianguis." 1991. *Diary of an Undocumented Immigrant.* Translated by T. D. J. Reavis. Houston: Arte Público Press.

Perilla, Julia L. 1999. Domestic Violence as a Human Rights Issue: The Case of Immigrant Latinos. *Hispanic Journal of Behavioral Sciences* 22 (2):107-33.

Perlmann, Joel. 2002. Second-generation Transnationalism. In *The Changing Face of Home: The Transnational Lives of the Second Generation*, edited by Peggy Levitt and Mary C. Waters. New York: Russell Sage Foundation.

Perreira, Krista M., Mimi V. Chapman, and Gabriela L. Stein. 2006. Becoming an American: Overcoming Challenges and Finding Strength in a New Immigrant Latino Community. *Journal of Family Issues* 27 (10):1383-1414.

Perspectives on Migrant Labor in Oregon: Proceedings of a Statewide Conference. 1968. Corvallis: Oregon State University.

Peters, Elizabeth. 2007. *Nursery Association Leader Invites Talk Show Host to "Walk a Day in the Shoes" of Oregon Farmers.* Oregon Association of Nurseries. Available from http://oan.org/displaycommon. cfm?an=1&subarticlenbr=594.

Peterson del Mar, David. 2003. *Oregon's Promise: An Interpretive History.* Corvallis: Oregon State University Press.

Pierpont, Claudia Roth. 2004. The Measure of America. *The New Yorker. 80:3 (March 8, 2004)*

Podobnik, Bruce. 2003. New Urbanism and the Generation of Social Capital: Evidence from Orenco Station. *National Civic Review* 91 (3):245-55.

Portes, Alejandro, and Rubén Rumbaut. 1996. *Immigrant America: A Portrait.* Berkeley: University of California Press.

Portes, Alejandro, and Rubén Rumbaut. 2001. *Legacies: The Story of the Immigrant Second Generation.* Berkeley: University of California Press.

Portes, Alejandro and Min Zhou. 1993. The New Second Generation: Segmented Assimilation and Its Variants Among Post-1965 Immigrant Youth. *Annals of the American Academy of Political and Social Science* 530:74-96.

Pransky, Glenn, Daniel Moshenberg, Katy Benjamin, Silvia Portillo, Jeffrey Lee Thackrey, and Carolyn Hill-Fotouhi. 2002. Occupational Risks and Injuries in Non-agricultural Immigrant Latino Workers. *American Journal of Industrial Medicine* 42 (2):117-23.

Quiñones-Mayo, Yolanda, and Patricia Dempsey. 2005. Finding the Bicultural Balance: Immigrant Latino Mothers Raising "American" Adolescents. *Child Welfare* LXXXIV (5):649-67.

Rasmussen, Wayne David. 1951. *A History of the Emergency Farm Labor Supply Program, 1943-47.* Washington, D.C.: U.S. Department of Agriculture, Bureau of Agricultural Economics.

Ray, Brian, Demetrious Papademetriou, and Maia Jachinowicz. 2004. *Immigrants and Homeownership in Urban America: An Examination of Nativity, Socio-Economic Status and Place.* Washington, D.C.: Migration Policy Institute.

Reisler, Mark. 1976. *By the Sweat of their Brow: Mexican Immigrant Labor in the United States, 1900-1940.* Westport, CT: Greenwood Press.

Reisler, Mark. 1997. Always the Laborer, Never the Citizen: Anglo Perceptions of the Mexican Immigrant in the 1920s. In *Between Two Worlds: Mexican Immigrants in the United States*, edited by D. Gutiérrez. Wilmington, DE: Scholarly Resources Inc.

Ricciardi, Gabriella. 2006. Telling Stories, Building Altars: Mexican American Women's Altars in Oregon. *Oregon Historical Quarterly* 107 (4):536-53.

Richter, Susan M., J. Edward Taylor, and Antonio Naude. 2005. Impacts of Policy Reforms on Labor Migration from Rural Mexico to the United States. National Bureau of Economic Research *Working Paper* 11428. Available from http://www.nber.org/papers/w11428.

Rivera, Tomás. 1991. *Y no se lo tragó la tierra/ and the Earth Did not Devour Him*. Houston, TX: Arte Público Press.

Rouse, Roger. 1996. Mexican Migration and the Social Space of Postmodernism. In *Between Two Worlds: Mexican Immigrants in the United States*, edited by D. G. Gutiérrez. Wilmington, Delaware: A Scholarly Resources Inc.

Rumbaut, Rubén G. 1991. Agony of Exile: A Study of the Migration and Adaptation of Indochinese Refugees in the United States. In *Refugee Policy: Canada and the United States*, edited by Frederick L. Ahearn, Jr., and Jean Athey. Toronto, Canada: York Lanes Press.

Rumbaut, Rubén G. 1994. The Crucible Within: Ethnic Identity, Self-Esteem, and Segmented Assimilation among Children of Immigrants. *The International Migration Review* 28 (4):748-94.

Saenz, Rogelio. 1991. Interregional Migration Patterns of Chicanos: The Core, Periphery, and Frontier. *Social Science Quarterly* 72 (1):135-48.

Saenz, Rogelio. 2008. A Demographic Profile of U.S. Workers Around the Clock. *Population Reference Bureau*, September. Available from http://www.prb.org/Articles/2008/workingaroundtheclock.aspx.

Salas, Elizabeth. 2006. Latinas in the Pacific Northwest. In *Latinas in the United States*, edited by V. Ruiz and V. S. Korrol. Bloomington: Indiana University Press.

Salinas, Jose P. 2007. *Educational Experiences of Children in the Migrant Stream: Ecological Factors Necessary for Academic Success*. Bowling Green, OH: Bowling Green State University.

Samora, Julian. 1971. *Los Mojados: The Wetback Story*. Notre Dame, IN: University of Notre Dame Press.

Sarathy, Brinda. 2006. Latinization of Forest Management Work in Southern Oregon: A Case from the Rogue Valley. *Journal of Forestry*: 359-65.

Sarathy, Brinda. 2008. The Marginalization of Pineros in the Pacific Northwest. *Society and Natural Resources* 21(8):671-86.

Sassen, Saskia. 1997. U.S. Immigration Policy toward Mexico in a Global Economy. In *Between Two Worlds: Mexican Immigrants in the United States*, edited by D. G. Gutiérrez. Wilmington, DE: Scholarly Resources Inc.

Scruggs, Otey M. 1988. *Braceros, "Wetbacks," and the Farm Labor Problems: Mexican Agricultural Labor in the United States 1942-1954*. New York: Garland Publishing, Inc.

Searle, Brent. 2007. Farm Employment, Worker Availability, and Cost. *The State of Oregon Agriculture*. Salem: Oregon Department of Agriculture.

Silverstein, Paul A. 2005. Immigrant Racialization and the New Savage Slot: Race, Migration, and Immigration in the New Europe. *Annual Review of Anthropology* 34:363-84.

Singer, Audrey. 2008. Twenty-First Century Gateways, an Introduction. In *Twenty-First Century Gateways, Immigrant Incorporation in Suburban America*, edited by S. H. Audrey Singer, Susan Hardwick, and Caroline B. Brettell. Washington, D.C: Brookings Institution Press.

Slatta, Richard W. 1975. Chicanos in the Pacific Northwest: An Historical Overview of Oregon's Chicanos. *Aztlan* 6 (3):327-36.

Smokowski, Paul, Roderick Rose, and Martica L. Bacallao. 2008. Acculturation and Latino Family Processes: How Cultural Involvement, Biculturalism, and Acculturation Influence Family Dynamics. *Family Relations* 57:295-308.

Specht, Sanne. 2009. Two Sides of the Street. *Mail Tribune* (Southern Oregon), April 27.

Speck, Gordon. 1954. *Northwest Explorations*. Portland, OR: Binfords and Mort.

Stamps, Katherine, and Stephanie A. Bohon. 2006. Educational Attainment in New and Established Latino Metropolitan Destinations. *Social Science Quarterly* 87 (5):1225-40.

Stephen, Lynn. 2001. Globalization, the State, and the Creation of Flexible Indigenous Workers: Mextec Farmworkers in Oregon. *Urban Anthropology and Studies of Cultural Systems and World Economic Development* 30 (2-3).

Stephen, Lynn. 2007. *Transborder Lives: Indigenous Oaxacans in Mexico, California, and Oregon*. Durham, NC, and London: Duke University Press.

Stephen, Lynn, Marcela Mendoza, and Mauricio Magaña. 2008. Latin American Immigration in Rural Oregon. *Understanding the Immigrant Experience in Oregon*, edited by R. Bussel. Eugene: University of Oregon Labor Education and Research Center.

Stephen, Lynn, and PCUN. 2001. *The Story of PCUN and the Farmworker Movement in Oregon.* Eugene: University of Oregon Department of Anthropology.

Sweet, Stephen, and Peter Meiksins. 2008. *Changing Contours of Work, Job and Opportunities in the New Economy.* Thousand Oaks, CA: Pine Forge Press.

Taylor, Paul S. 1937. Migratory Farm Labor in the United States. *Monthly Labor Review* 44 (3):537-49.

Turner, Brenda, and Mary Wood. 1998. *Hispanics in Oregon's Workforce.* RS PUB 124. Salem: State of Oregon, Employment Department.

Valdes, Guadalupe. 1996. *Con Respeto: Bridging the Distance between Culturally Diverse Families and Schools: An Ethnographic Portrait.* New York: Teachers College Press.

Velez-Ibañez, Carlos G., Anna Sampaio, and Manono Gonzáles-Estay. 2002. *Transnational Latina/o Communities: Politics, Processes, and Cultures.* Lanham, Maryland: Rowan and Littlefield Publishers, Inc.

Viruell-Fuentes, Edna. 2006. "My Heart is Always There": The Transnational Practices of First-Generation Mexican Immigrant and Second-Generation Mexican American Women. *Identities: Global Studies in Culture and Power* 13:335-362.

Waldinger, Roger. 1997. Black Immigrant Competition Re=Assessed: Nee Evidence from Los Angeles. *Sociological Perspectives* 40 (2).

Waldinger, Roger. 2008. Immigrant "Transnationalism" and the Presence of the Past. In *From Arrival to Incorporation, Migrants to the U.S. in a Global Era*, edited by Elliot Barkan, Hasia R. Diner, and Alan M. Kraut. New York: New York University Press.

Waldinger, Roger, and M. Lichter. 2003. *How the Other Half Works: Immigration and the Social Organization of Labor.* Berkeley: University of California Press.

Waldinger, Roger, Nelson Lim, and David Cort. 2007. Bad Jobs, Good Jobs, No Jobs? The Employment Experience of the Mexican American Second Generation. *Journal of Ethnic and Migration Studies* 33 (1):1-35.

Weber, Bruce, Maria Addessi, Ann Schauber, and Mike Knutz. 2007. *Strengthening Oregon's Communities, Latino Community Leadership.* Oregon State University Extension Service. Available from http://extension.oregonstate.edu/internal/sites/default/files/documents/LatinoCommunityLeadershipProgram.pdf.

Weber, David. 1998. The Spanish Moment in the Pacific Northwest. *Pacifica: People and Place in the Northwest States and Western Canada*, edited by Paul W. Hirt. Pullman: Washington State University Press.

Wells, Miriam J. 1976. Emigrants from the Migrant Stream: Environment and Incentives in Relocation. *Aztlán: A Journal of Chicano Studies* 7 (2):267-89.

Williams, Anne. 2008. More Students Line Up for School Breakfast, Lunch. *The Register Guard* November 30. Available from http://www.thefreelibrary.com/More+students+line+up+for+school+breakfast,+lunch.-a0190721003.

Wozniacka, Gosia. 2008. Voters Go After Businesses that Hire Illegal Workers. *The Oregonian* November 2. Available from http://www.oregonlive.com/news/index.ssf/2008/11/voters_go_after_businesses_tha.html.

Wright, Phil. 2008. Group Eyes Eastern Oregon as 51st State. *The East Oregonian* April 24.

Xing, Jun, Erlinda Gonzales-Berry, Patti Sakurai, Robert Thompson, and Kurt Peters, eds. 2007. *Seeing Color: Indigenous Peoples and Racialized Ethnic Minorities in Oregon.* Lanham, MD: University Press of America.

Zhou, Min. 1997. Segmented Assimilation: Issues, Controversies, and Recent Research on the New Second Generation. *International Migration* 31 (4):975-1008.

Zhou, Min. 2003. Contemporary Female Migration to the United States: A Demographic Profile. In *Women Immigrants in the United States*, edited by Philippa Strum and Danielle Tarantolo. Washington, D.C.: Woodrow Wilson International Center for Scholars.

Zuniga, Victor, and Ruben Hernandez-Leon, eds. 2005. *New Destinations: Mexican Immigration in the United States.* New York: Russell Sage Foundation.

Index

Figures in **bold**; Tables in *italics*